# PHARMACY LAW

## TEXTBOOK AND REVIEW

**Debra B. Feinberg, RPh, BS Pharm, JD**

Executive Director
New York State Council of Health-system Pharmacists
Associate Adjunct Professor, Jurisprudence
Albany College of Pharmacy
Albany, New York

New York   Chicago   San Francisco   Lisbon   London   Madrid   Mexico City   Milan
New Delhi   San Juan   Seoul   Singapore   Sydney   Toronto

**Pharmacy Law: Textbook and Review**

1 2 3 4 5 6 7 8 9 0  DOC/DOC  0 9 8 7

ISBN 978-0-07-148635-4; MHID 0-07-148635-6
Book ISBN 978-0-07-154880-9; Book MHID 0-07-154880-7
CD ISBN 978-07-154881-6; CD MHID 0-07-154881-5

This book was set in Melior by International Typesetting and Composition.
The editors were Catherine Johnson and Kim J. Davis.
The production supervisor was Catherine Saggese.
The cover designer was Aimee Davis.
The index was prepared by Robert Swanson.
Project management was provided by International Typesetting and Composition.
RR Donnelley was the printer and binder.

This book is printed on acid-free paper.

### NOTICE

Medicine is an ever-changing science. As new research and clinical experience broaden our knowledge, changes in treatment and drug therapy are required. The authors and the publisher of this work have checked with sources believed to be reliable in their efforts to provide information that is complete and generally in accord with the standards accepted at the time of publication. However, in view of the possibility of human error or changes in medical sciences, neither the authors nor the publisher nor any other party who has been involved in the preparation or publication of this work warrants that the information contained herein is in every respect accurate or complete, and they are not responsible for any errors or omissions or for the results obtained from use of such information. Readers are encouraged to confirm the information contained herein with other sources. For example and in particular, readers are advised to check the product information sheet included in the package of each drug they plan to administer to be certain that the information contained in this book is accurate and that changes have not been made in the recommended dose or in the contraindications for administration. This recommendation is of particular importance in connection with new or infrequently used drugs.

**Library of Congress Cataloging-in-Publication Data**

Feinberg, Debra B.
    Pharmacy law : textbook and review / Debra B. Feinberg.
      p. ; cm.
    Includes index.
    ISBN-13: 978-0-07-148635-4 (pbk. : alk. paper)
    ISBN-10: 0-07-148635-6 (pbk. : alk. paper)
    1. Pharmacy—Law and legislation—United States.  2. Drugs—Law and legislation—
United States.  I. Title.
    [DNLM: 1. Legislation, Drug—United States.  2. Legislation, Pharmacy—United States.
3. Drug Industry—legislation & jurisprudence—United States.  4. Pharmaceutical
Preparations—standards—United States.  5. Pharmaceutical Services—legislation &
jurisprudence—United States. QV 33 AA1 F299p 2008]
    KF1.9.Z9F45 2008
    344.04′16—dc22

To Edward, Samantha, and Ross

# Contents

# Contents

# Preface

This is the first edition of *Pharmacy Law: Textbook and Review.* As an Assistant Adjunct Professor at Albany College of Pharmacy in Albany, New York for the past seven years, I have taught Jurisprudence to the fifth year PharmD class. My primary goal in teaching Jurisprudence is to prepare students for the Pharmacy Boards. The goal of this book is to prepare you to be successful in your endeavor to pass the federal portion of the Pharmacy Boards. For those of you who have been successful in passing the Pharmacy Boards, this book will serve as a reference tool as you advance the practice of pharmacy.

The book is divided into topics including a description of the federal entities that guide and regulate the practice of pharmacy; a history of pharmacy law; a demonstration of the drug approval process; a review of drug product substitution; a comprehensive review of the controlled substances act; a review of opioid treatment; an overview of medical devices, dietary supplements, herbals, homeophathics, and cosmetics; drug product packaging and labeling; and other regulations such as HIPPA, USP 797, bar coding, and the methamphetamine act. Where possible each chapter provides web sites helpful in further discussion of the topic.

The final section of the book contains more than 400 questions in the format utilized by the MPJE. These questions are also included on the bind-in CD-ROM at the back of this book to give you experience answering questions in a board-simulating interface. Most states have their laws available online. It is important for you to know the laws of your state and be able to distinguish your state law from federal law when necessary for both the Pharmacy Boards and in your practice.

I wish you success as you prepare to take the Pharmacy Boards and continued success as you embark on your career as a pharmacist.

*Debra B. Feinberg, RPh, BS Pharm, JD*

# 1 Drug Regulation and Standards

## Food and Drug Administration

The United States Food and Drug Administration (FDA) is located in Rockville, Maryland, 1-888-INFO-FDA (1-888-463-6332). It is available electronically at <<www.fda.gov>>. The FDA is the public health agency charged with protecting the American consumer from products that are not safe, not pure, and ineffective. The FDA is an Agency of the Department of Health and Human Services. The FDA enforces laws enacted by the U.S. Congress and enforces regulations established by the agency covering the following products: food (excluding red meat and poultry), drugs, medical devices, blood, biologicals, and cosmetics. The laws enforced by the FDA assure that:

1. Food
   a. For human consumption is pure, wholesome, and safe
   b. Is packaged with truthful labeling
   c. Is produced under sanitary conditions
2. Drugs and medical devices
   a. Are safe and effective for the use for which they were intended
   b. Are manufactured under sanitary conditions and quality controls that assure the standards and quality of the product
   c. Are labeled with truthful, informative, and accurate information
3. Cosmetics
   a. Are safe and effective for the use for which they are intended
   b. Are packaged containing accurate information

4. Blood products
   a. Are safe
   b. Are in adequate supply
5. Transplanted tissues:
   a. Are safe and effective
6. Equipment utilizing radiant energy (i.e., x-ray machines and microwave ovens)
   a. Is compliant with radiation safety performance standards

The FDA implements regulations that will inform and guide the industry and the public in the application of the regulations. FDA regulations are enforceable in court. These regulations must be reasonable and not arbitrary and capricious.

## Official Compendia

Federal law recognizes several Official Compendia: *United States Pharmacopeia/National Formulary (USP/NF)* and *Homeopathic Pharmacopeia (HPUS)*. The *USP* helps to ensure that consumers receive quality medicines by establishing state-of-the-art standards that pharmaceutical manufacturers must meet. The *USP* is the world's most highly recognized and technologically advanced pharmacopeia, providing standards for more than 3800 medicines, dietary supplements, and other health care products; and over 11,000 generic drugs. *USP/NF* is a product of the United States Pharmacopeial Convention, Inc, not the FDA. The FDA does provide input in the development of standards. It is published every 5 years. The current version is *USP25/NF20*: official from 1-1-05 through 12-31-10. Proposals for revisions are published bimonthly in the *Pharmacopeial Forum (PF)*.

The *USP/NF* standards are officially recognized in the Pure Food and Drug Act of 1906 and the Food, Drug and Cosmetic Act (FDCA) of 1938 and are enforceable by the FDA. The *USP/NF* monographs establish legally recognized standards for drugs and excipients, specifications for packaging, labeling, and storage, tests and assays for strength, quality, purity, and identification standards for medical devices, diagnostics, and botanicals. It also contains abstracts of the Controlled Substance Act; the Poison Prevention Packaging Act; the FDCA; and Good Manufacturing Practices.

*USP/NF Supplements* are published twice a year containing all approved changes. The *USP* contains monographs for active substances and dosage forms while the *NF* contains monographs for inactive ingredient. The *USP* and *NF* were combined into one book in 1980 but are still considered separate entities.

The Federal FDCA mandates that a drug must bear an established name. An established name is defined by the FDCA as "*the official name; the name of an official compendium; or the common or usual name.*"

If a *USP* monograph exists for a drug product, the product is subject to *USP* standards whether the product bears the *USP* symbols after the name or not. If a product differs from existing *USP* standards (strength, quality, purity) the label must state "Not *USP*." If it is not stated as "Not *USP*" then the product would be deemed misbranded or adulterated.

If a drug is official in the *USP*, it must meet the standards established in the *USP* monograph unless it is distinctly marketed and labeled as a homeopathic drug.

The *USP DI* provides dispensing information in three volumes used by prescribers, dispensers, and consumers of medication which it publishes once a year:

- *Volume I: Drug Information for the Health Care Professional*
- *Volume II: Advice for the Patient-Drug Information in Lay Language*
- *Volume III: Approved Drug Products and Legal Requirements*

These are not officially recognized in the FDCA.

The *HPUS* is the official publication of homeopathic drugs monographs. Homeopathic drugs are recognized as drugs under the FDCA. The initials *HPUS* on the label of a drug product assures that legal standards of strength, quality, purity, and packaging exist for the drug product. The active ingredients are official and are found in the current *HPUS*. The standards that must be met in order to append *HPUS* to a product are established by the Homeopathic Pharmacopeia Convention of the United States. The Convention works closely with the FDA and homeopathic organizations such as the American Institute of Homeopathy and the American Association of Homeopathic Pharmacists. Guidelines are published for prescriptions or over-the-counter homeopathic drug products.

The rules that the FDA enforces are codified in the Code of Federal Regulations (CFR). The CFR is a codification of general and permanent rules published in the *Federal Register* by the executive departments and agencies of the Federal Government. It is divided into 50 titles that represent broad areas subject to Federal regulation. Each volume of the CFR is updated once each calendar year and is issued on a quarterly basis. The FDA's portion of the CFR interprets the FDCA and related statutes. Section 21 of the CFR contains most regulations pertaining to food and drugs and documents all actions of all drug sponsors that are required under Federal law.

The *Federal Register* is the official daily publication for rules, proposed rules, and notices of Federal agencies and organizations, as well as executive orders and other presidential documents. It is published by the Office of the Federal Register, National Archives and Records Administration. The CFR and the *Federal Register* documents are available through the U.S. Government Printing Office (GPO) electronically at <<http://www.access.gpo.gov/nara/cfr/index.html>>.

# Drug Enforcement Administration

The Drug Enforcement Administration (DEA) is located at 2401 Jefferson Davis Highway, Alexandria, VA 22301, 1-800-882-9539. It is available electronically at <<www.dea.gov>>.

The DEA is responsible for enforcing the controlled substance laws (Controlled Substances Act 21 U.S.C. §§ 801-970) and regulations of the United States. The DEA works in conjunction with state agencies to prevent the diversion of controlled substances for illicit use. The DEA works closely with foreign as well as domestic state and local governments, private industry, and other organizations concerned with drug abuse and diversion, as well as working under the aegis of international treaties. Because controlled substances are drugs, not only are they regulated by the DEA but they are also regulated by the FDCA through the FDA thereby requiring that the FDA and DEA work together in their regulation.

**SUGGESTED READINGS**

U.S. Drug Enforcement Administration Web site. www.dea.gov. Accessed December 15, 2006.

U.S. Food and Drug Administration Web site. www.fda.gov. Accessed December 15, 2006.

U.S. Pharmacopeia Web site. www.usp.org. Accessed December 15, 2006.

# 2

# The History of Federal Pharmacy Drug Laws: A Timeline of Drug Law

## Rationale Supporting the Drug Laws in the United States

The main reason for all pharmacy drug laws in the United States is protection of the public. Before regulation, drug products routinely contained narcotics such as opium, morphine, heroin, and cocaine. Information provided in the labeling was limited. The labeling frequently omitted any listing of active and inactive ingredients; warnings about habit-forming drug products; information about misuse or improper use of the drug product; directions for use and dosage recommendations. Statements that products would "cure disease" were routinely contained in the labeling information. Many products were contaminated. As unacceptable results became evident, public safety became a major concern.

## Timeline

**1820: U.S. PHARMACOPEIA**

Eleven physicians met to establish the first compendial standard of drug products.

**1848: Drug Importation Act**

U.S. Customs were given the authority to inspect drug products imported into the United States as an attempt to prevent the importation of adulterated drugs.

**1862: Bureau of Chemistry**

President Lincoln appointed a chemist to serve the Department of Agriculture in the Bureau of Chemistry. The Bureau of Chemistry was a predecessor to the Food and Drug Administration (FDA).

**1868: Pharmacy Act of 1868**

Testing and registration of dispensed drug products containing morphine, cocaine, and barbiturates was required.

**1906: Federal Pure Food and Drugs Act (P.L. 59-384) (Repealed in 1938 by 21 U.S.C. Sec 329 (a))**

The U.S. Congress passed the Federal Food and Drugs Act in 1906. This act prevented the manufacture, sale, or transportation of adulterated, misbranded, poisonous, or deleterious foods, drugs, medicines, and liquors in interstate commerce. Any person engaged in this activity was guilty of a misdemeanor. This act was very limited in its application. It did not require the listing of ingredients or directions for use on the manufacturer's labeling or packaging. Nor did it regulate cosmetics or medical devices. Administration of the new law was assigned to the Bureau of Chemistry. However, the act did recognize the *United States Pharmacopeia (USP)* and *National Formulary (NF)* as the official compendia for drug standards for misbranding and adulteration purposes, thereby establishing a mechanism to measure the purity and quality of drug products. After the act was implemented, the deficiencies of the act became more apparent.

**1914: Harrison Narcotic Act (P.L. 223)**

This act established a record keeping requirement for the receipt and dispensing of opium or coca leaf products. A tax was assessed, also, for the dispensing of these products. Physicians were allowed to prescribe these products in the course of legitimate treatment to patients other than drug addicts. The possession of narcotics without a prescription became illegal.

**1915: Bureau of Internal Revenue**

This agency was responsible for the regulation of controlled substances.

**1922: Narcotic Drug Import and Export Act**

Increased restrictions were imposed on the import and export of opium and coca.

| | |
|---|---|
| **1924: HEROIN ACT** | The manufacture and possession of heroin became illegal. |
| **1927: BUREAU OF PROHIBITION** | This bureau was responsible for the enforcement of drug and alcohol laws. |
| **1927: FOOD, DRUG AND INSECTICIDE ADMINISTRATION** | The Bureau of Chemistry became the Food, Drug and Insecticide Administration and the Bureau of Chemistry and Soils. |
| **1930: FOOD AND DRUG ADMINISTRATION** | The Food, Drug and Insecticide Administration was renamed the Food and Drug Administration. |
| **1930: BUREAU OF NARCOTICS** | The Bureau of Prohibition was replaced by the Bureau of Narcotics, moving enforcement of drug laws to the Department of Justice. The Bureau of Narcotics was responsible for the control of marijuana and narcotics containing opium and coca. |
| **1932: UNIFORM STATE NARCOTIC ACT** | States were encouraged to enact laws similar to the Narcotic Drug Import and Export Act, which restricted the import and export of opium and coca. The act also encouraged the states to enact legislation prohibiting cannabis use. |
| **1937: MARIHUANA TAX ACT** | The purchase or sale of cannabis became illegal without the payment of a transfer tax. This act became unconstitutional in 1969. |
| **1938: FOOD, DRUG AND COSMETIC ACT (21 U.S.C. § 301 ET SEQ 52 STAT. 1040)** | The Food, Drug and Cosmetic Act (FDCA) of 1938 was enacted as a result of a tragedy in Europe in 1937. In 1937, there were 107 deaths caused by the use of diethylene glycol in a sulfanilamide elixir. Sulfanilamide was an anti-infective sulfa drug. The manufacturer developed an elixir using diethylene glycol as the solvent. No toxicity tests were performed on the diethylene glycol. Today, diethylene glycol is used as an industrial solvent. The deaths resulted from the solvent in the elixir. In 1937, the FDA had no authority to ban the use of any unsafe drug products. In order to remove the drug product from the market, the FDA claimed that the drug was misbranded because it was labeled as an elixir. By definition, an elixir had to contain alcohol and this drug product did not contain alcohol. |

The FDCA was targeted at drug safety. New drugs had to be proven safe when used according to the directions for use prior to their marketing approval.

FDCA addressed the following:

1. All new drugs had to be proven safe when used according to the directions for use prior to marketing.
2. All cosmetics and medical devices were regulated, including color additives.
3. Proof of fraud intent was no longer required to stop false claims or misbranding for drug products.
4. Warnings of habit-forming drugs were required on all package labeling.
5. Adequate directions for use were required on all drug product labeling.
6. Predistribution clearance was required for safety of new drugs (approved New Drug Application) prior to the manufacturers commercial distribution.
7. Authority was granted for factory inspections.
8. The FDA was given the authority to obtain injunctions against violations in addition to the previous remedies of product seizure and criminal prosecutions.
9. A fast track approval process was established for certain drug products. The drugs that were fast tracked were those that were intended for the treatment of a serious or life-threatening condition and those drugs that demonstrated the potential to address unmet medical needs for such a condition (Investigational new drugs). The FDCA also recognized the need for research and investigation into drugs for the treatment of rare diseases and conditions. A rare disease or condition refers to any disease or condition that affects less than 200,000 persons in the United States, or affects more than 200,000 in the United States with no reasonable expectation that the cost of developing the drug will be recovered from sales of such drug.
10. Drugs marketed prior to 1938 were exempt from the safety requirement. Pre-1938 drugs were called "grandfathered drugs." Examples of these drugs include digoxin, nitroglycerine, and phenobarbital.

**FOOD, DRUG AND COSMETIC ACT DEFINITIONS (21 U.S.C. § 321)**

***DRUG*** The term "drug" means (A) articles recognized in the official *USP*, official *Homeopathic Pharmacopeia of the United States (HPUS)*, or official *NF*, or any supplement to any of them; (B) articles intended for use in the diagnosis, cure, mitigation, treatment, or prevention of disease in man or other animals; (C) articles (other than food) intended to affect the structure or any function of the body of man or other animals; and (D) articles intended for use as a component of any articles specified in clause (A), (B), or (C).

***COUNTERFEIT DRUG*** The term "counterfeit drug" means a drug which, or the container or labeling of which, without authorization, bears the trademark, trade name, or other identifying mark, imprint, or device, or any likeness thereof, of a drug manufacturer, processor, packer, or distributor other than the person or persons who in fact manufactured, processed, packed, or distributed such drug and which thereby falsely purports or is represented to be the product of, or to have been packed or distributed by, such other drug manufacturer, processor, packer, or distributor.

***FOOD*** The term "food" means (1) articles used for food or drink for man or other animals, (2) chewing gum, and (3) articles used for components of any such article.

***COSMETIC*** The term "cosmetic" means (1) articles intended to be rubbed, poured, sprinkled, or sprayed on, introduced into, or otherwise applied to the human body or any part thereof for cleansing, beautifying, promoting attractiveness, or altering the appearance, and (2) articles intended for use as a component of any such articles; except that such term shall not include soap.

***DEVICE*** The term "device" means an instrument, apparatus, implement, machine, contrivance, implant, in vitro reagent, or other similar or related article, including any component, part, or accessory, which is:

1. Recognized in the official *NF*, or the *USP*, or any supplement to them, or
2. Intended for use in the diagnosis of disease or other conditions, or in the cure, mitigation, treatment, or prevention of disease, in man or other animals, or

3. Intended to affect the structure or any function of the body of man or other animals, and which does not achieve its primary intended purposes through chemical action within or on the body of man or other animals and which is not dependent upon being metabolized for the achievement of its primary intended purposes.

**OFFICIAL COMPENDIUM** The term "official compendium" means the official *USP*, official *HPUS*, official *NF*, or any supplement to any of them.

**NEW DRUG** The term "new drug" means:

1. Any drug (except a new animal drug or an animal feed bearing or containing a new animal drug) the composition of which is such that such drug is not generally recognized, among experts qualified by scientific training and experience to evaluate the safety and effectiveness of drugs, as safe and effective for use under the conditions prescribed, recommended, or suggested in the labeling thereof, except that such a drug not so recognized shall not be deemed to be a "new drug" if at any time prior to the enactment of this act it was subject to the Food and Drugs Act of June 30, 1906, as amended, and if at such time its labeling contained the same representations concerning the conditions of its use; or
2. Any drug (except a new animal drug or an animal feed bearing or containing a new animal drug) the composition of which is such that such drug, as a result of investigations to determine its safety and effectiveness for use under such conditions, has become so recognized, but which has not, otherwise than in such investigations, been used to a material extent or for a material time under such conditions.

**COLOR ADDITIVE** The term "color additive" means a material which:

A. Is a dye, pigment, or other substance made by a process of synthesis or similar artifice, or extracted, isolated, or otherwise derived, with or without intermediate or final change of identity, from a vegetable, animal, mineral, or other source, and

B. When added or applied to a food, drug, or cosmetic, or to the human body or any part thereof, is capable (alone or through reaction with other substance) of imparting color thereto; except that such term does not include any material which the Secretary, by regulation, determines is used (or intended to be used) solely for a purpose or purposes other than coloring.

Penalties for violations of FDCA include injunction or restraining order and seizure of the adulterated or misbranded product. Injunction or restraining order halts the action that the party was engaging in. Seizure takes possession of the product.

**ADULTERATION**   Refers to:

1. A product that contains filthy, putrid, or decomposed substances
2. A product packed under unsanitary conditions
3. A drug product manufacturing process that does not conform to good manufacturing practices
4. A product that is represented as a drug that is recognized in an official compendium, and its characteristics differ from the standards set forth in the compendium
5. A product that is not represented as a drug in an official compendium and the product differs from the product representation
6. A product that is combined with an ingredient that reduces the quality or strength of the product
7. A product contains an unapproved color additive

**MISBRANDING**   Refers to:

1. Labeling that is false or misleading
2. Packaging that contains incorrect information regarding the name and place of business of the manufacturer, packer, or distributor; and/or incorrect statements of the quantity of the contents in terms of weight, measure, or numerical count
3. Failing to place required information prominently and conspicuously so as to be read and understood by an ordinary person
4. Failing to use the established name
5. Failing to provide adequate directions for use and warnings

**1941: INSULIN AMENDMENT**

The FDA was responsible for testing and certifying the purity and potency of insulin. Nearly 300 people died from the distribution of sulfathiazole tablets containing phenobarbital.

**1945: PENICILLIN AMENDMENT**

The FDA was responsible for testing and certifying the safety and effectiveness of penicillin products. (Repealed in 1983, no longer required.)

**1951: DURHAM-HUMPHREY AMENDMENT (21 U.S.C. § 353)**

The FDCA required that all drug products be labeled with adequate directions for use. Labeling did not take into consideration that many drug products are not safe for administration without medical supervision. This amendment addressed this issue by establishing two classes of drugs: over-the-counter or nonprescription drugs and prescription or legend drugs. Legend refers to the use of the phrase: "Caution: Federal law prohibits dispensing without a prescription." The legend is required on the manufacturer's label for all prescription drug products. Prescription drugs are those that are unsafe for use except under the supervision of a practitioner or those subject to the new drug application process. The use of the legend obviates the need for the drug product to contain adequate directions for use. This amendment also legalized the use of transmitting prescriptions orally, legalized the pharmacists recognition of refills of prescriptions as indicated by the prescriber, and established minimal label information requirements on the prescription.

Minimal labeling requirements include the following:

1. The label must not be false or misleading.
2. The drug must not be an imitation drug.
3. The drug must not be sold under the name of another drug.
4. The packaging and labeling must conform to official compendium standards.
5. The product must be labeled appropriately for storage requirements.
6. The product must be packaged in childproof containers unless waived.

**1953: DEPARTMENT OF HEALTH, EDUCATION, AND WELFARE**

Federal Security Agency became the Department of Health, Education, and Welfare from 1939 until 1979.

**1960: COLOR ADDITIVE LAW (21 U.S.C. § 376)**

The FDA established additional conditions for the safe use of color additives in foods, drugs, and cosmetics. Manufacturers were required to perform scientific investigations to establish safety for intended use. Any color shown to cause cancer was prohibited.

**1962: KEFAUVER-HARRIS AMENDMENT (DRUG EFFICACY AMENDMENT)**

The drug thalidomide was used widely in Europe as a tranquilizer. This drug was not approved for use in the United States. Thalidomide was associated with many birth defects. As a result of the thalidomide tragedy in Europe, this amendment was passed, requiring that all new drugs marketed in the United States had to be not only safe but also effective for the use for which they were intended. This amendment applied to products marketed between 1938 and 1962 unlike the FDCA which did not apply to those drugs manufactured prior to 1938 (grandfathered drugs).

The Drug Efficacy Amendment established the following:

1. All new drugs marketed had to be safe and effective.
2. Jurisdiction over drug advertising was transferred from the Federal Trade Commission to the FDA.
3. Individuals participating in clinical investigations were required to complete informed consent forms and report adverse drug reactions.
4. Good Manufacturing Practices were established for drugs manufactured in the United States.

**1965: DRUG ABUSE CONTROL AMENDMENTS (P.L. 89-74)**

This amendment established strict control of abused drugs such as stimulants, depressants, and hallucinogens.

**1966: FAIR PACKAGING AND LABELING ACT (P.L. 89-755)**

Consumer products in interstate commerce had to be honestly and fairly labeled.

**1966: FDA BUREAU OF DRUG ABUSE CONTROL**

The Department of Health, Education, and Welfare's Bureau of Drug Abuse Control was responsible for the control of dangerous drugs, including depressants, stimulants, and hallucinogens, such as lysergic acid diethylamide (LSD).

**1968: BUREAU OF NARCOTICS AND DANGEROUS DRUGS**

The Bureau of Narcotics and the Bureau of Drug Abuse Control was transferred to the Department of Justice and renamed the Bureau of Narcotics and Dangerous Drugs (BNDD). BNDD was responsible for the policing of illegal drug traffic. International and interstate activities were the targeted activities that BNDD was responsible for drug law enforcement.

**1968: DRUG EFFICACY STUDY IMPLEMENTATION**

The FDA formed the Drug Efficacy Study Implementation (DESI) to review recommendations of the National Academy of Sciences' investigation of the effectiveness of drugs marketed between 1938 and 1962.

**1970: CONTROL SUBSTANCE ACT: COMPREHENSIVE DRUG ABUSE PREVENTION AND CONTROL ACT (P.L. 91-513)**

The Drug Abuse Control Amendments were repealed and five schedules of controlled substances were established. The five schedules categorized drugs based on their accepted medical use and abuse potential. BNDD became the Drug Enforcement Administration (DEA).

**1970: POISON PREVENTION PACKAGING ACT (U.S.C. §§ 1471-1474)**

Special packaging requirements were implemented to protect small children from poisoning. This applied to household substances, over-the-counter products, and prescription drug products.

**1972: OVER-THE-COUNTER DRUG REVIEW**

Over-the-counter drug product review was implemented to improve safety and effectiveness. The review process included labeling of over-the-counter drugs products.

**1973: DRUG ENFORCEMENT ADMINISTRATION**

Several law enforcement agencies and the BNDD were combined under the purview of the Department of Justice.

**1976: MEDICAL DEVICE AMENDMENTS (P.L. 94-294)**

The FDA was concerned with useless and dangerous devices. This amendment required safety and efficacy studies on medical devices including diagnostics and laboratory products prior to marketing of the device. Regulation over devices included better classification with a grading function based on the performance of the device; registration; device listing; premarket approval;

investigational device exemptions; conformance with Good Manufacturing Practices; adherence with recording and reporting requirements; and performance standards.

**1982: Tamper-Resistant Packaging (U.S.C. § 1365)**

Tylenol products were tampered with when cyanide was placed inside Tylenol capsules. The regulation required visible product tampering methods that would alert the consumer to the fact that the product may have been tampered with. This regulation made it a crime for an individual to tamper or threaten to tamper with consumer products.

**1983: Orphan Drug Act (P.L. 97-414)**

This act provided tax and licensing incentives for the research and marketing of drugs for rare diseases. A rare disease is defined as a disease that affects less than 200,000 people in the United States.

**1984: Drug Price Competition and Patent Term Restoration Act (P.L. 98-417)**

The FDA was granted the authority to accept Abbreviated New Drug Applications for generic versions of drug products approved after 1962. Manufacturers of generic drug products were no longer required to repeat the costly, lengthy new drug application process for generic versions of already approved brand name drugs. This was a huge benefit to generic manufacturers with the cost savings eventually passed onto the consumer. Brand manufacturers could apply for a patent extension of up to 5 years of additional patent protection to compensate for time lost in the preapproval evaluation process for new drugs.

**1984: Medical Device Reporting Rule**

Manufacturers and importers were required to report within 5 days information that their medical device caused or contributed to a death or serious injury or that their device had malfunctioned and was likely to cause injury.

**1984: Diversion Control Amendments (P.L. 98-473); 1984: Controlled Substance Registrant Protection Act (18 U.S.C. § 2118)**

This act established penalties for burglaries and robberies of controlled substance.

**1984: NARCOTIC ADDICT TREATMENT ACT (P.L. 89-793)**

This act established treatment for narcotic addiction as an alternative to incarceration.

**1986: ANTIDRUG ABUSE ACT (P.L. 99-570)**

This act established mandatory minimum sentences for violations (5- and 10-year mandatory minimums) for drug distribution or importation, depending on the quantity of the substance which contained a detectable amount of the prohibited drug.

**1986: FEDERAL ANALOGUE ACT**

The act allowed any chemical "substantially similar" to an illegal drug (in Schedule I or II) to be treated as if it were also in Schedule I, but only if it is intended for human consumption.

**1988: FOOD AND DRUG ADMINISTRATION ACT (P.L. 100-607)**

The FDA was officially established as an agency of the Department of Health and Human Services.

**1988: PRESCRIPTION DRUG MARKETING ACT (P.L. 100-293)**

The act was a further attempt to reduce public health risks from adulterated, misbranded, and counterfeit drug products that enter the marketplace. This act:

1. Banned the sale, purchase, or trade of drug samples and drug coupons.
2. Restricted reimportation of prescription drugs to the manufacturer of the drug product or for emergency medical care.
3. Established requirements for drug sample distribution, storage, and handling.
4. Required state licensure of wholesale distributors of prescription drugs.
5. Established requirements for wholesale distribution of prescription drugs by unauthorized distributors. Retail pharmacies may not possess prescription drug samples regardless of the source of the product.
6. Prohibited the sale, purchase, or trade of prescription drugs that were purchased by hospitals or other health care entities, or donated or supplied at a reduced price to charities.
7. Required sales representatives to keep records or all samples received, stored, destroyed, stolen, and distributed with annual inventories.
8. Established criminal and civil penalties for violations.

| | |
|---|---|
| **1988: ANTIDRUG ABUSE ACT (21 U.S.C. § 862)** | A definition of abuse was established and the government's authority to confiscate property was strengthened with the death penalty added for drug traffickers. |
| **1988: OFFICE OF NATIONAL DRUG CONTROL POLICY** | This office was established by the Antidrug Abuse Act. The principal purpose was to establish policies, priorities, and objectives for the Nation's drug control program. The goals of the program were to reduce illicit drug use, manufacturing and trafficking, drug-related crime and violence, and drug-related health consequences. |
| **1988: CHEMICAL DIVERSION AND TRAFFICKING ACT (SEC. 6051 21 U.S.C. 801 NOTE)** | This act amended the Controlled Substance Act and imposed record keeping and import/export reporting requirements on transactions involving precursor chemicals, essential chemicals, tableting machines, and encapsulating machines. |
| **1990: SAFE MEDICAL DEVICE ACT (P.L. 101-629)** | Nursing homes, hospitals, and other facilities that utilize medical devices were required to report to the FDA information arising out of medical devices that contributed to the death or serious injury of a patient. The FDA acquired the authority to order device recalls. Manufacturers of devices were required to conduct post-market surveillance on all permanently implanted devices whose failure might cause serious harm or death. |
| **1990: NUTRITION LABELING AND EDUCATION ACT (P.L. 101-535)** | As consumers became more interested in health and nutrition, this act required nutrition labeling on food products. Health claims were authorized provided they were in compliance with FDA guidelines and regulations. |
| **1990: SAFE MEDICAL DEVICE ACT (P.L. 101-629)** | Manufacturers were required to report to the Department of Health and Human Services any device that caused or contributed to the death, illness, or serious injury of a patient. User device problem reporting systems were required, in addition to a tracking mechanism for devices. |
| **1991: FDA USER FEES REGULATIONS** | Regulations were passed to speed up the review process of drugs for the treatment of life-threatening diseases. |
| **1992: GENERIC DRUG ENFORCEMENT ACT (P.L. 102-282)** | Penalties were established for illegal acts involving abbreviated drug applications. |

**1992: PRESCRIPTION DRUG USER FEE ACT (P.L. 102-571)**

Due to an increase in the number for new drug products requiring review, drug and biologics manufacturers were required to pay fees for product applications and supplement reviews. The fees were used to subsidize the review process at the FDA, thereby shortening the review time. User fees allowed the FDA to hire additional staff. This act was an extension of the 1991 FDA User Fee regulations for life-threatening conditions.

The User Fee Act exempted small emerging companies, those companies with less than 500 employees from the full fee charged, by reducing their fee by 50%. Fees for manufacturers of orphan drugs were exempted also. Certain products were exempt from the user fees: generic antibiotics, allergenic extracts, whole blood or blood components, intravenous drugs, and medical devices. The act was revised in 1997 and 2002.

**1993: DOMESTIC CHEMICAL DIVERSION CONTROL ACT (P.L. 103-200)**

This act amended the Comprehensive Drug Abuse Prevention and Control Act of 1970 in an effort to control the diversion of certain chemicals used in the illicit production of controlled substances such as metheathinane and methamphetamine.

**1994: DIETARY SUPPLEMENT HEALTH AND EDUCATION ACT (P.L. 103-417)**

The FDA established Good Manufacturing Practices for dietary supplements. Dietary supplements and dietary ingredients were defined as food. A Commission was established for the regulation of claims with regard to dietary supplements. This act established labeling requirements also.

**1996: COMPREHENSIVE METHAMPHETAMINE CONTROL ACT (21 CFR PARTS 1300, 1309, 1310)**

This act removed the exemption for drug products that contain pseudoephedrine, phenylpropanolamine, or ephedrine and established a 24-g threshold for the sale of pseudoephedrine or phenylpropanolamine products by a retail distributor. The definition was also amended to provide that the sale of ordinary over-the-counter pseudoephedrine or phenylpropanolamine products by retail distributors shall not be a regulated transaction.

**1997: FOOD AND DRUG ADMINISTRATION MODERNIZATION ACT (P.L. 105-115)**

The FDA Modernization Act took the Prescription Drug User Fee Act and expanded it to improve and speed up the approval process for new drugs and devices. A fast track approval process was implemented for serious or life-threatening disease products that demonstrated the potential to address unmet medical needs. Inactive ingredient labeling requirements were implemented for over-the-counter drug products. New prescription drug labeling requirements were established also, eliminating the requirement for the Legend statement, provided the labeling contained the words "Rx only."

| | |
|---|---|
| **2005: COMBAT METHAMPHETAMINE EPIDEMIC ACT (P.L. 109-177)** | Pseudoephedrine, phenylpropronolamine, and ephedrine were reclassified as Schedule Listed Chemicals. The act established a Federal per-transaction sales limit which was reduced to 3.6 g. All regulated drug products must be stored behind the counter or in a locked cabinet. A written log of purchases must be maintained. Monthly sales are restricted to no more than 9 g to a single purchaser, including Internet purchases, with submission of certification of compliance by retailers. |

## SUGGESTED READING

U.S.s Food and Drug Administration Web site. www.fda.gov. Accessed December 15, 2006.

# 3

# The Drug Approval Process

## Investigational New Drugs (21 CFR Part 312)

The Food, Drug, and Cosmetic Act (FDCA) requires that all new drugs be approved for marketing prior to distribution or transportation of the new drug products across state lines. A new drug sponsor must seek an exemption from the Food and Drug Administration (FDA), in order to distribute these new drug products across state lines. The Investigational New Drug (IND) application is the exemption that affords the drug company the right to place a new drug into interstate commerce. The IND application is also referred to as the Notice of Claimed Investigational Exemption for a New Drug.

The drug sponsor conducts preliminary investigations to determine the safety and efficacy of the product. These preliminary investigations include tests to determine the pharmacologic action and acute toxicity of the product in animal subjects. The clinical investigation phase involves experiments where the drug is administered to human subjects with informed consent. Each IND application lists an investigator who is responsible for conducting the clinical investigation. The application has a sponsor who initiates and oversees responsibility for the clinical investigation. The sponsor is responsible for hiring the clinical investigator if they are not one and the same. If the sponsor and the investigator are the same they are referred to as sponsor-investigator. The sponsor may be an individual, a partnership, a corporation, a pharmaceutical company, a governmental entity, an educational/scientific institution, or a private organization.

INDs are classified into three different categories:

1. Investigator IND applications are usually submitted by a physician who has discovered an off-label use for an already approved drug product. By submitting an Investigator IND application, the physician is responsible for initiating and conducting the clinical investigation.
2. Emergency Use IND applications are usually granted for those situations where time does not allow for submission of the IND through the normal channels. Patients usually do not meet the criteria of an existing protocol.
3. Treatment IND applications are usually used for drug products with a potential for treating a serious or immediately life-threatening disease or condition that has not been through the entire FDA review process.

## Investigational New Drug Application

The FDA is very specific as to the contents of the IND application.

1. The application must contain information on animal pharmacology and toxicology studies, including preclinical data, manufacturing information, clinical protocols, and sponsor/investigator information. Is the product safe for initial testing in humans? Was the drug approved and used in foreign countries? What data have been collected from use in other countries?
2. The manufacturing information includes drug-specific information: drug composition; manufacturer; drug stability and controls utilized in the manufacturing process. Can the manufacturer produce and supply the drug adequately to meet the demand? should the drug be approved?
3. The clinical protocol determines whether the protocol will expose subjects to unnecessary risks. The protocol contains the qualifications and credentials of the investigator(s). The protocols are very detailed including the qualifications of all professionals administering the nonapproved drug product. Protocols for each phase of clinical study are required. All human research subjects must be informed of all the risks and benefits of the drug product. Informed consent must be obtained from all subjects prior to enrollment in the clinical trial.

4. An Institutional Review Board (IRB) must be solicited for review of the clinical study. All IND regulations must be followed.

The sponsor submits the IND application and waits 30 days before beginning the clinical trial phase of the drug process. The FDA reviews the IND application to assure safety and no untoward risk to the subjects. Figure 3-1 illustrates the process that a new drug goes through prior to approval for mass marketing.

CDER is the Center for Drug Evaluation and Research, a department of the FDA. CDER determines if the drug product is suitable for use in clinical trials. Section 21 of the Code of Federal Regulations documents all actions of all drug sponsors that are required under Federal law.

## Clinical Investigations: Phases

Phase 1 determines the drug product's human pharmacologic actions: absorption, metabolism and elimination, dosage, and acute side effects. Phase 1 of the clinical trial is conducted on a small number, usually 20–80, of healthy human subjects for a short period of time of usually less than 2 weeks. The protocols for Phase 1 are very general. Protocols include an estimate of the number of subjects, a description of the safety exclusions, a description of the dosing plan including duration, and the method to be used in determining dosage. The only items in the protocol that are specific are those items critical to the safety of the human subject.

Phase 2 determines the usefulness of the drug treating or preventing the disease for which the drug product is intended. The number of human subjects is greater, usually 100–300 participants. Phase 2 collects data on the different doses of the drug product, safety, adverse effects, toxicity, drug interactions, pharmacologic effects, and pharmacokinetics. The main purpose of Phase 2 is to obtain information on the drug's safety and efficacy. If the drug is effective and the risks are within acceptable limits then the drug moves to Phase 3.

Phase 3 further tests the drug for safety and effectiveness in a much larger group of people, usually 1000–3000 subjects, in varied geographic areas. The test group has the disease for which the drug product is indicated. If there is a standard treatment for the disease the investigational drug is tested against the standard.

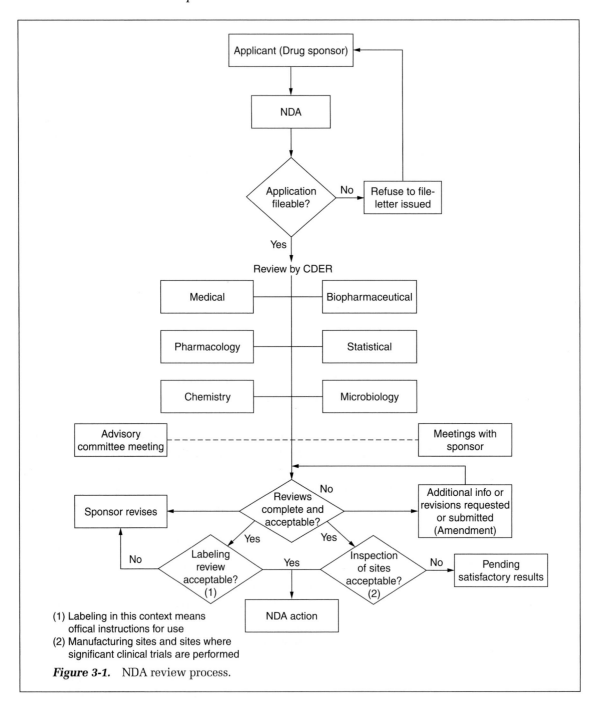

**Figure 3-1.** NDA review process.

## Clinical Trials

Clinical trials frequently utilize "control" standards in Phase 2 and Phase 3. One group will receive the investigational drug and the second group will receive the standard treatment drug product if one exists or a placebo. Determination of which group a participant is placed in is usually done by randomization. A randomized clinical trial is a scientific procedure used in the testing of the efficacy of medicines. It is considered very reliable because it is designed to eliminate biases. "Blinding" is also utilized to eliminate bias. Single-blind and double-blind trials are used. In a single-blind trial, the researcher knows the details of the treatment but the patient does not. The placebo effect should be eliminated because the patient does not know which treatment he or she is receiving. Due to the fact that the researcher has knowledge of the treatment the patient is receiving, this could create bias in the study. In a double-blind trial, one researcher allocates a series of numbers to "new treatment" or "old treatment." The second researcher is told the numbers, but not what he or she has been allocated to. Due to the fact that the researchers do not know which patient is receiving "new treatment" or "old treatment," bias is eliminated. Since double-blind trials are better at distributing the trial amongst sexes and ages of the patients and bias is eliminated, double-blind randomized trials are preferred.

An investigator is responsible for ensuring that an investigation is conducted according to the signed Investigator statement, the investigational plan, and applicable regulations; for protecting the rights, safety, and welfare of subjects under the investigator's care; and for the control of drugs under investigation. The investigator furnishes all progress reports to the sponsor of the drug who is responsible for collecting and evaluating the results obtained. The investigator promptly reports to the sponsor any adverse effect that may reasonably be regarded as caused by, or probably caused by, the drug. The investigator provides the sponsor with an adequate report shortly after completion of the investigator's participation in the investigation. The Investigator is also responsible for providing the sponsor with accurate financial information. The Investigator assures that an IRB will be responsible for the initial and continuing review and approval of the proposed clinical study.

An IRB has the authority to approve, to require modifications, or to disapprove research. The purpose of the IRB is to assure that the rights and welfare of the subjects is protected in clinical trials.

## New Drug Application

The next step in getting a new drug product to market is the New Drug Application (NDA) process. The data collected during the animal studies and clinical trials of the IND process are incorporated into the NDA. The purpose of the NDA process is to determine the safety and effectiveness of the drug product for the intended use; to determine if the benefits of the drug product outweigh the risks associated with the drug product; to determine if the proposed labeling is appropriate; and to determine if the manufacturing methods are sufficient to insure the drug's identity, strength, quality, and purity.

If the NDA is approved then the drug product may be marketed to the public. Postmarketing surveillance or Phase 4 trials involve safety monitoring and ongoing technical support of a drug. Postmarketing safety monitoring is designed to detect any rare or long-term adverse effects over a much larger patient population and greater period of time than was possible during the initial clinical trials. Such adverse effects detected by Phase 4 trials may result in the withdrawal or restriction of a drug—recent examples include cerivastatin (Baycol and Lipobay), troglitazone (Rezulin), and rofecoxib (Vioxx).

## Supplemental New Drug Application

The Supplemental New Drug Application (SNDA) is an abbreviated application process for drug products that have been approved, that request a change to the formulation of the product or the written material about the product.

## Abbreviated New Drug Application

The Abbreviated New Drug Application (ANDA) process is a shortened process for those drug products that are "me too" drugs or generic drugs. Once the patent on an approved drug product expires, generic manufacturers may submit applications for approval of their similar product. The manufacturer is required to submit data demonstrating pharmacokinetic properties, bioavailability, and clinical activity similar to the original drug product.

## Patent Protection for New Drugs

A patent is the grant of a property right to the inventor issued by the Patent and Trademark Office of the United States. The patent excludes others from making, using, offering for sale, selling the invention in the United States, or importing the invention into the United States. The life of the patent is 20 years from the date of first filing of the patent application. Because manufacturers usually file for patent protection prior to product marketing, the effective term of the patent is less than 20 years. The Drug Price Competition and Patent Term Restoration Act of 1984 (P.L. 98-417) provides manufacturers with an opportunity to extend the life of the patent for an additional 5 years. With the 5-year extension, the total patent life of the drug product cannot exceed 14 years from the approval date of the drug product.

### SUGGESTED READINGS

Center for Drug Evaluation and Research (CDER). U.S. Food and Drug Administration Web site. www.fda.gov/cder. Accessed December 15, 2006.

Center for Biologics Evaluation and Research (CBER). U.S. Food and Drug Administration Web site. www.fda.gov/cber. Accessed December 15, 2006.

# 4 *Federal Reporting Programs*

## MEDWATCH

MEDWATCH began in 1993 as a program for adverse drug event reporting. In 1998, MEDWATCH became the Food and Drug Administration (FDA) Medical Products Reporting and Safety Information Program. MEDWATCH is currently the FDA Safety and Information and Adverse Event Reporting Program. MEDWATCH is involved in risk identification through gathering information about marketed drug products and communication of the gathered information to the public and health care providers. The MEDWATCH web site, <<http://www.fda.gov/medwatch/>>, is essential to e-mailing product notification in a timely manner. The web site contains safety alerts for drugs, biologicals, devices, dietary supplements, herbal products, and safety-related drug labeling changes. Letters to health care professionals address safety labeling changes, Class I recalls, and withdrawals. Public Health Advisories are also initiated through MEDWATCH. Not all safety-related labeling changes warrant a letter to the health care provider. These changes address dosing and administration, interactions, high-risk populations, and new adverse reactions. There is an e-mail alert list that is available to the public and health care providers alike. The web site contains reporting forms for voluntary reporting of safety-related issues. The types of problems reported can be serious, resulting in death, life-threatening situations, hospitalization, disability, and intervention by health care providers. Some examples of problems reported through MEDWATCH are defective devices, label mix-up, and product contamination. Vaccine-related problems are

29

reported to the Vaccine Adverse Event Reporting System (VAERS), <<http://vaers.hhs.gov/>>.

# MEDMARX

The United States Pharmacopeia (USP) collects medication error and adverse event data from hospitals and health systems through MEDMARX, <<https://www.medmarx.com/>>. Hospitals and health systems participate on a voluntary basis, with anonymous submissions. Subscribers have the ability to share data amongst hospitals and health systems.

## Safety Programs Implemented by the FDA

**iPLEDGE**

The **iPLEDGE** program, <<www.ipledgeprogram.com>>, is a computer-based risk management program to control the distribution and use of isotretinoin. Isotretinoin is used to treat severe recalcitrant nodular acne. It has a high risk of birth defects when used in pregnant women. Because of the risk, use of isotretinoin in women is very restrictive. The previous SMART program was not as effective as the FDA wanted. This new program requires registration of all wholesalers distributing isotretinoin, all prescribers prescribing isotretinoin, all pharmacies dispensing isotretinoin, and all male and female patients prescribed isotretinoin. Patients after registering with iPLEDGE must complete an informed consent form, receive counseling about the risks and requirements for safe use of the drug, and women must comply with the pregnancy requirement. Women of childbearing age must select and commit to using two forms of effective birth control simultaneously 1 month prior to, during, and 1 month after isotretinoin therapy. Women must have two negative pregnancy tests before receiving the prescription and must have a pregnancy test done every month. The first test may be conducted in a physician's office. All subsequent tests must be conducted in a CLIA (Clinical Laboratory Improvement Amendments)-certified laboratory. Prescriptions will not be issued unless a negative pregnancy result is confirmed. The process requires that each month, the prescriber enters the female patient's pregnancy results and the two forms of contraception she has been using in the iPLEDGE system. The iPLEDGE system verifies that all criteria have been met by the prescriber, patient, and pharmacy prior to granting the pharmacy authorization to fill and dispense isotretinoin. The pharmacist must obtain authorization from the iPLEDGE system via the program web site or phone system prior to dispensing each isotretinoin prescription for both male and female patients. All pregnancies associated with the use of isotretinoin must be reported to FDA's MEDWATCH and to the iPLEDGE pregnancy registry at 1-866-495-0654 or <<www.ipledgeprogram.com>>. Use of isotretinoin has also been associated with risks of psychiatric symptoms and depression. These risks have been added to the list of warnings associated with the drug product. The following companies are registered with iPLEDGE: Roche Laboratories, Inc. (Accutane); Mylan Pharmaceuticals, Inc. (Amnesteem); Barr Laboratories, Inc. (Claravis); and Ranbaxy Laboratories, Inc. (Sotret).

**STEPS—SYSTEM FOR THALIDOMIDE EDUCATION AND PRESCRIBING SAFETY**

Celgene's restricted distribution program was implemented because the use of thalidomide (Thalomid) is associated with severe life-threatening birth defects. Thalidomide has legitimate medical uses in the United States. The indications for thalidomide include cutaneous manifestations for moderate to severe erythema nodosum leprosum and multiple myeloma when used in combination with dexamethasone. STEPS was implemented to minimize the risk of birth defects. Prescribers must be registered with STEPS prior to prescribing thalidomide. Women of childbearing age must select and commit to using two forms of effective birth control simultaneously 1 month prior to, during, and 1 month after thalidomide therapy. Women must have a pregnancy test done weekly for the first 4 weeks of thalidomide use. After the first 4 weeks, pregnancy tests should be conducted every 2–4 weeks depending on the regularity of the patient's menstrual cycle. Male patients must use a condom. All patients will receive informed consent. Patients must acknowledge both oral and written receipt of warnings associated with the use of thalidomide. Any suspected fetal exposure to thalidomide must be reported to MEDWATCH and the Celgene Corporation.

### SUGGESTED READINGS

iPLEDGE Web site. www.ipledgeprogram.com. Accessed December 15, 2006.

S.T.E.P.S.® 3.0 Celgene's Innovative Restricted Distribution Program. Thalomid® Web site. www.thalomid.com/steps_program.aspx. Accessed December 15, 2006.

U.S. Pharmacopeia, MEDMARX, Patient Safety Solutions Web site. www.medmarx.com. United States Department of Health and Human Services, Vaccine Adverse Event Reporting Program Web site. www.vaers.hhs.gov. Accessed December 15, 2006.

The FDA Safety Information and Adverse Event Reporting Program. U.S. Food and Drug Administration, MedWatch Web site. www.fda.gov/medwatch. Accessed December 15, 2006.

# 5 Prescription to Over-the-Counter Switch

## Over-the-Counter Review

The over-the-counter (OTC) review process was initiated in 1972. The Food and Drug Administration (FDA) appointed qualified experts to advisory review panels. These experts reviewed drug products based on their product therapeutic classification, that is, laxative, emetic, analgesics, to determine if they are safe and effective for OTC administration. It took over 10 years to review over 700 ingredients and over 400,000 products. In the initial evaluation of OTC drug products, the OTC drug advisory panels classified the ingredients by the following:

- *Category I*: conditions under which OTC ingredients are generally recognized as safe and effective and are not misbranded.
- *Category II*: conditions under which OTC ingredients are not generally recognized as safe and effective or are misbranded.
- *Category III*: conditions under which the available data are insufficient to permit final classification at this time as Category I or II.

For those drug products classified in Categories II and III, the ingredients are designated as "S" for safety or "E" for effectiveness. The review process resulted in the withdrawal of drug products from the market due mostly to the inability to demonstrate product effectiveness for the use for which the product was intended.

Manufacturers had plenty of time to reformulate their product to meet the review requirements. Those that did not reformulate their products had their products removed.

## Prescription to Over-the-Counter Drug Classification

There are three ways a prescription drug product can obtain OTC drug status.

1. The manufacturer can submit a supplemental New Drug Application. The FDA reviews the safety of the drug product and looks at the data on adverse effects.
2. Any interested party may petition the FDA for reclassification of drug product status. Claritin was switched due to a request by a managed care company.
3. The OTC review process may initiate review through the Nonprescription Drug Review Committee.

The most common mechanism for the switch is the OTC review process. An advisory review panel makes a recommendation to the FDA. If the FDA agrees with the recommendation, it publishes a final OTC drug monograph about the switch. The switch process can also result in a product being switched from OTC status to prescription. In 1977, hexachlorophene was switched from OTC status to prescription status because of overdoses in infants in France.

## Generally Recognized Safe and Effective Over-the-Counter Drugs

Over-the-counter human drugs that are generally recognized as safe and effective and therefore not misbranded must meet the following conditions:

1. The product must be manufactured in accordance with good manufacturing practices.
2. The manufacturer must be registered.
3. The product must be labeled in accordance with the Food, Drug and Cosmetic Act with adequate directions for use.
4. The product label must contain approved, established uses.
5. Advertising must be in compliance with the approved indication or use.
6. Inactive ingredients must be suitable and must not interfere with the effectiveness of the product.

7.  The labeling must contain appropriate warnings about unsafe use, side effects, and adverse reactions.
8.  The dosage limitation, even if a maximum daily dose, must be established.
9.  Must contain information about pregnancy and nursing.

## SUGGESTED READINGS

Center for Drug Evaluation and Research (CDER). U.S. Food and Drug Administration Web site. www.fda.gov/cder/about/smallbiz/OTC.htm. Accessed December 15, 2006.

Center for Drug Evaluation and Research (CDER). U.S. Food and Drug Administration Web site. www.fda.gov/cder/handbook/otc.htm. Accessed December 15, 2006.

Center for Drug Evaluation and Research (CDER). U.S. Food and Drug Administration Web site. www.fda.gov/cder/Offices/OTC/default.htm. Accessed December 15, 2006.

Center for Drug Evaluation and Research (CDER). U.S. Food and Drug Administration Web site. www.fda.gov/cder/about/smallbiz/OTC_FAQ.htm. Accessed December 15, 2006.

# 6 Substitution of Drug Products

## Drug Product Substitution

The Drug, Price and Competition Act (P.L. 98-417) of 1984 requires that the Food and Drug Administration (FDA) publish a list of all drugs approved for safety and effectiveness. The FDA publishes a guide to drug product substitution, *Approved Drug Products with Therapeutic Equivalence and Evaluations* known as the Orange Book. This book identifies drug products approved by the FDA. The Orange Book does not contain drug products that were marketed prior to 1938, that is, "grandfathered drugs." However, if a manufacturer initiated a drug product review for safety and efficacy for a product marketed prior to 1938, the product may be contained in the Orange Book. Products marketed between 1938 (safety requirement) and 1962 (safety and efficacy requirement) that are subject to the Drug Efficacy Study Implementation (DESI) review, are also not included in the Orange Book unless their review met the FDA requirements for efficacy. This book provides formulary guidance only, it is not law. Drug product substitution is a necessary component to the reduction of escalating health care costs in the United States. Most states regulate drug product substitution through laws, rules, or regulations, in an effort to provide consumers with necessary medication in a cost-efficient manner.

## Using the Orange Book

The Orange Book is used as a guide by consumers and health care professionals in drug product selection. In utilizing the Orange Book as a resource, it is important to understand the terminology used.

37

**Single source products** are drug products that are the only product approved by the FDA for that active ingredient, dosage form, route of administration, and strength.

**Multisource drug products** are drug products that are manufactured by several manufacturers.

**Pharmaceutical equivalence** refers to drug products with the same active ingredients, same dosage form, same route of administration, and identical in strength or concentration. These products must meet the same compendial standards for purity, quality, strength, and labeling.

**Therapeutic equivalents** are those products that are pharmaceutical equivalents and bioequivalent. The FDA utilizes the following criteria to determine if a drug product is a therapeutic equivalent:

1. Approved for safety and effectiveness
2. Pharmaceutical equivalent
3. Bioequivalent
4. Adequate labeling
5. Manufactured in compliance with Good Manufacturing Practices

**Bioavailability** is the rate that the active ingredient of the drug product is absorbed from the product and made available to the site of action.

**Bioequivalent drug products** are products that are pharmaceutically equivalent that provide the same results of drug delivery with the same pharmacokinetic properties.

**Reference listed drug (RLD)** is the standard against which all generic drug products are compared. The RLD has filed a New Drug Application that has been approved by the FDA. Upon expiration of the RLD patent, generic manufacturers can file an Abbreviated New Drug Application for approval of their generic product. All bioavailability is measured against the information for the RLD product. The generic drug product must demonstrate that the drug product provides the same results as the RLD product through bioavailability studies.

**Pharmaceutical alternatives** are drug products that contain the same therapeutic moiety, but are different salts, esters, or complexes of that moiety, or are different dosage forms or strengths.

The Orange Book utilizes a letter designation for the public to use in determining whether a product is equivalent or not. The FDA includes multisource drug product information as well as single source product information. Multisource drug products receive an equivalence code. No therapeutic equivalence code is included for the single source drug products.

- **A**—products are considered to be therapeutically equivalent to other pharmaceutically equivalent products. These products utilize the designation of:
  - **AA**—products in conventional dosage forms not presenting bioequivalence problems
  - **AN**—solutions and powders for aerosolization
  - **AO**—injectible oil solutions
  - **AP**—injectible aqueous solutions and some IV nonaqueous solutions
  - **AT**—topical products depending on the dosage form
  - **AB**—products with actual or potential bioequivalence problems that have been resolved in vivo or in vitro
- **B**—products are not therapeutically equivalent. The problem usually is with dosage forms not the active ingredients in the drug products.

Therapeutic substitution refers to the right to substitute a different drug for the one written on the prescription without consulting with the prescriber. When RLDs are not single source, those drugs are listed with a number because the RLDs have the same active ingredients, however, they are not bioequivalent to each other. Generic products will be given the same code including the number when listed in the Orange Book.

The Orange Book is available electronically at <<http://www.fda.gov/cder/ob/default.htm>>. The Electronic Orange Book can be searched by active ingredient, proprietary name, applicant holder name, applicant number, or patent. The drug lists are arranged by active ingredient in alphabetical order. Discontinued products are published also.

When utilizing the Orange Book, you need to identify the active ingredient of the drug product and determine if the drug is a single source drug or a multisource drug. If the drug is single source then there will be no generic alternative to that drug product. If the drug is multisourced then the Orange Book can be utilized to determine what manufacturer may provide a cheaper equivalent drug product. Caution needs to be exercised to make sure that the same formulations of drug products are being compared.

## Pharmacists Use of the Orange Book

The Orange Book is very easy to use. There are a few basics that you need to know to use it. Please refer to Tables 6-1, 6-2, and 6-3.

1. Search for drug product (Table 6-1 and 6-3). The search can be done by both active ingredient and/or proprietary name (Table 6-2). The active ingredient search is the one that will show you if there are multisourced drug products. The proprietary search is limited to only that brand name product.
2. Review the headings at the top of the page. Each page is set up with the drug product application number (Appl. No.), the therapeutic code (TE Code), RLD, active ingredient, dosage form/route, strength, proprietary name, and applicant.

*Table 6-1.* **ELECTRONIC ORANGE BOOK ACTIVE INGREDIENT SEARCH FOR PREGABALIN**[*]

| Appl. No. | TE Code | RLD | Active Ingredient | Dosage Form; Route | Strength | Proprietary Name | Applicant |
|---|---|---|---|---|---|---|---|
| 021446 | No | | Pregabalin | Capsule; oral | 100 mg | Lyrica | CP Pharms |
| 021446 | No | | Pregabalin | Capsule; oral | 150 mg | Lyrica | CP Pharms |
| 021446 | No | | Pregabalin | Capsule; oral | 200 mg | Lyrica | CP Pharms |
| 021446 | No | | Pregabalin | Capsule; oral | 225 mg | Lyrica | CP Pharms |
| 021446 | No | | Pregabalin | Capsule; oral | 25 mg | Lyrica | CP Pharms |
| 021446 | Yes | | Pregabalin | Capsule; oral | 300 mg | Lyrica | CP Pharms |
| 021446 | No | | Pregabalin | Capsule; oral | 50 mg | Lyrica | CP Pharms |
| 021446 | No | | Pregabalin | Capsule; oral | 75 mg | Lyrica | CP Pharms |

FDA/Center for Drug Evaluation and Research
Office of Generic Drugs
Division of Labeling and Program Support
Update frequency:
  Orange Book Data—**Monthly**
  Generic Drug Product Information & Patent Information—**Daily**
  Orange Book Data Updated Through July 2006
  Patent and Generic Drug Product Data Last Updated: August 21, 2006

[*]Active ingredient search results from "OB_Rx" table for query on "Pregabalin."

*Table 6-2.* **ELECTRONIC ORANGE BOOK ACTIVE INGREDIENT SEARCH FOR LYRICA**[*]

| APPL. NO. | TE CODE | RLD | ACTIVE INGREDIENT | DOSAGE FORM; ROUTE | STRENGTH | PROPRIETARY NAME | APPLICANT |
|---|---|---|---|---|---|---|---|
| 021446 | No | | Pregabalin | Capsule; oral | 100 mg | Lyrica | CP Pharms |
| 021446 | No | | Pregabalin | Capsule; oral | 150 mg | Lyrica | CP Pharms |
| 021446 | No | | Pregabalin | Capsule; oral | 200 mg | Lyrica | CP Pharms |
| 021446 | No | | Pregabalin | Capsule; oral | 225 mg | Lyrica | CP Pharms |
| 021446 | No | | Pregabalin | Capsule; oral | 25 mg | Lyrica | CP Pharms |
| 021446 | Yes | | Pregabalin | Capsule; oral | 300 mg | Lyrica | CP Pharms |
| 021446 | No | | Pregabalin | Capsule; oral | 50 mg | Lyrica | CP Pharms |
| 021446 | No | | Pregabalin | Capsule; oral | 75 mg | Lyrica | CP Pharms |

FDA/Center for Drug Evaluation and Research
Office of Generic Drugs
Division of Labeling and Program Support
Update frequency:
  Orange Book Data—**Monthly**
  Generic Drug Product Information & Patent Information—**Daily**
  Orange Book Data Updated Through July 2006
  Patent and Generic Drug Product Data Last Updated: August 21, 2006

[*]Proprietary name search results from "OB_Rx" table for query on "Lyrica."

3. Determine which drug is the RLD. This will be indicated by the word "Yes" in the RLD column.
4. Match up the strength and dosage form and route of administration so that the same products are being compared (pharmaceutical equivalent).
5. In the TE Code column look for a letter designation. Letter "A" means that the product is substitutable. Letter "B" means that it is not.
6. If "A" is the letter designation, then review the listed applicants to determine which company to use for the drug product.

# Narrow Therapeutic Index Drugs

Narrow therapeutic index is a term that is used to refer to drug products that may require close patient monitoring to achieve the maximum effectiveness of the medication. The narrow therapeutic ratio refers to the ratio of the median lethal dose to the median effective dose or the median toxic concentration to the median

***Table 6-3.*** **ELECTRONIC ORANGE BOOK ACTIVE INGREDIENT SEARCH FOR SIMVASTATIN***

| APPL. NO. | TE CODE | RLD | ACTIVE INGREDIENT | DOSAGE FORM; ROUTE | STRENGTH | PROPRIETARY NAME | APPLICANT |
|---|---|---|---|---|---|---|---|
| 021687 | No | | Ezetimibe; simvastatin | Tablet; oral | 10 mg; 10 mg | Vytorin | MSP Singapore |
| 021687 | No | | Ezetimibe; simvastatin | Tablet; oral | 10 mg; 20 mg | Vytorin | MSP Singapore |
| 021687 | No | | Ezetimibe; simvastatin | Tablet; oral | 10 mg; 40 mg | Vytorin | MSP Singapore |
| 021687 | Yes | | Ezetimibe; simvastatin | Tablet; oral | 10 mg; 80 mg | Vytorin | MSP Singapore |
| 076052 AB | No | | Simvastatin | Tablet; oral | 10 mg | Simvastatin | IVAX Pharms |
| 076052 AB | No | | Simvastatin | Tablet; oral | 20 mg | Simvastatin | IVAX Pharms |
| 076052 AB | No | | Simvastatin | Tablet; oral | 40 mg | Simvastatin | IVAX Pharms |
| 076052 AB | No | | Simvastatin | Tablet; oral | 5 mg | Simvastatin | IVAX Pharms |
| 019766 AB | No | | Simvastatin | Tablet; oral | 10 mg | Zocor | Merck |
| 019766 AB | No | | Simvastatin | Tablet; oral | 20 mg | Zocor | Merck |
| 019766 AB | No | | Simvastatin | Tablet; oral | 40 mg | Zocor | Merck |
| 019766 AB | No | | Simvastatin | Tablet; oral | 5 mg | Zocor | Merck |
| 019766 AB | Yes | | Simvastatin | Tablet; oral | 80 mg | Zocor | Merck |
| 076285 AB | No | | Simvastatin | Tablet; oral | 80 mg | Simvastatin | Ranbaxy |

FDA/Center for Drug Evaluation and Research
Office of Generic Drugs
Division of Labeling and Program Support
Update frequency:
  Orange Book Data—**Monthly**
  Generic Drug Product Information & Patent Information—**Daily**
  Orange Book Data Updated Through July 2006
  Patent and Generic Drug Product Data Last Updated: August 21, 2006

*Active ingredient search results from "OB_Rx" table for query on "simvastatin."

effective concentration. (21 CFR § 320.33(c)). Drugs that are considered to have a narrow therapeutic index have a ratio less than or equal to 2. The FDA does not formally recognize narrow therapeutic index drugs as a category for drug classification when evaluating drugs for bioequivalence. Examples of drugs that require close patient monitoring are theophylline, levothyroxine, digoxin, lithium, phenytoin, and warfarin.

## SUGGESTED READING

Center for Drug Evaluation and Research Electronic Orange Book. U.S. Food and Drug Administration Web site. www.fda.gov/cder/ob. Accessed December 15, 2006.

# 7 Medical Devices, Cosmetics, Homeopathic, and Dietary Supplements

Medical devices are regulated by the Food, Drug, and Cosmetic Act, the Center for Devices and Radiological Health, and the Office of Device Regulation. Device classification: <<http://www.fda.gov/cdrh/devadvice/313.html>>.

## Classification of Medical Devices

**CLASS I, GENERAL CONTROLS**

The General Controls requirements apply to all devices regardless of their classification. All devices must meet the requirements of General Controls and possibly additional requirements depending on the function of the device. Requirements are (21 CFR § 807, 1010):

1. Truthful labeling
2. Establishment registration: Any entity involved in the production and distribution of medical devices must register with the Food and Drug Administration (FDA). This includes manufacturers, distributors, repackagers, importers, relabelers, and exporters. There is no fee for registration

3. Product listing requires that an establishment register with the FDA all devices for commercial distribution
4. Premarket notification unless exempt
5. Record keeping
6. Adherence to Good Manufacturing Practices (GMP) unless exempt

Devices classified as Class I *only* are very simple by design and have a very low potential to cause harm. Examples include toothbrushes, tongue depressors, elastic bandages, examination gloves, eye pads, ice bags, nasal rubber bulb syringes, hand-held surgical instruments.

## CLASS II, PERFORMANCE STANDARDS

Performance Standards assure safety and effectiveness for those products which are not generally safe and effective through the General Controls Standards. All devices that must meet Class II standards must also meet Class I standards. Requirements are:

1. Specific construction requirements, components, ingredients, and properties of the device
2. These standards usually require special labeling
3. Mandatory performance standards
4. Postmarket surveillance

Examples include insulin syringes, blood pressure gauges, most diagnostic reagents, adult incontinent products, electric heating pads, clinical electronic thermometers, powered wheel chairs, infusion pumps, and surgical drapes.

## CLASS III, PREMARKET APPROVAL

Premarket Approval applies to life-supporting or life-sustaining devices. Class III devices are those that support or sustain human life, are of substantial importance in preventing impairment of human health, or which present a potential, unreasonable risk of illness or injury. Those devices that if used improperly may cause unreasonable risk or illness or injury to a person. These devices must meet the standards set forth in Class I and Class II in addition to premarket approval of Class III. Examples include heart pacemakers, replacement heart valves, implanted spinal cord stimulators, silicone gel-filled breast implants.

# Restricted Devices

The FDA has the authority to restrict the sale, distribution, or use of a device to prescription only if there is potential for harm if the device is not used properly. Examples of restricted devices include diaphragms, antiembolism stockings, and TENS (**T**ranscutaneous **E**lectrical **N**erve **S**timulation) units. Hearing aids require hearing loss evaluation by a physician at least 6 months prior to the sale of the hearing aid to the patient.

The same laws that apply to adulterated and misbranded drugs apply to medical devices.

# Cosmetics

The Food, Drug, and Cosmetic Act defines cosmetics as articles intended for cleansing, beautifying, promoting attractiveness, or altering the appearance without affecting the body's structure or function. Examples of cosmetics include skin creams, lotions, perfumes, lipsticks, fingernail polishes, eye and facial makeup preparations, shampoos, permanent waves, hair colors, toothpastes, deodorants, and any material intended for use as a component of a cosmetic product. Soaps are not considered cosmetics provided they consist primarily of an alkali salt of fatty acid and they make no label claim other than cleansing of the human body. If the product is intended for cleansing, moisturizing, and beautifying then the product is a cosmetic. If the product is intended for cleansing and the treatment or prevention of disease then the product is a drug. If the label claims that the product is antibacterial, antiperspirant, or antiacne, the product is considered a drug and the label must list the active ingredients as required for all drug products.

# Cosmetics That are Drug Products

Cosmetics that are intended to treat or prevent disease or alter a body function are considered drug products. Examples include toothpastes with fluoride (prevent cavities), suntanning lotions/creams (prevent exposure to UV light), antiperspirants that are also deodorants (prevent perspiration), and antidandruff shampoos (prevent or treat dandruff). The key in determining whether a product is a cosmetic or a drug-cosmetic product is the product's claim? Does the label claim that the product will treat or prevent disease?

48        *Chapter 7*

## Cosmetic Labeling Requirements

The Food, Drug, and Cosmetic Act and the Fair Packaging and Labeling Act have established different labeling requirements for cosmetics. Requirements are:

1. All labeling must be conspicuous.
2. Ingredients must be listed in descending order of predominance.
3. Color additives and ingredients in quantities of 1% or less may be listed without regard to order of predominance.
4. If the cosmetic contains a drug product, the active ingredient of the drug product must be listed first before listing the cosmetic ingredients.
5. All label statements must appear in English on the outside packaging as well as on the inside packaging of the cosmetic.
6. The labeling must be prominent to the consumer and must state the name of the product, the description or demonstration of the use of the product, and an accurate statement of the net quantity of contents in terms of weight, measure, numerical count, or a combination thereof.
7. All labels must contain adequate directions for use and any warnings of hazardous use to the consumer.

## Cosmetic Manufacturers

The FDA does not require cosmetic safety testing prior to marketing. However, cosmetic manufacturers are strongly encouraged by the FDA to engage in safety testing so that the product will not be deemed to be misbranded and subject to regulatory action. If the manufacturer has not established that the product is safe prior to marketing, the manufacturer must include a statement that the product is not deemed safe. "Warning—The safety of this product has not been determined." If the product does not contain this warning label the product may be deemed misbranded.

Cosmetic manufacturers are not required to register their establishments, file data on ingredients, or report cosmetic-related injuries to FDA. However, companies are encouraged to register their establishments and file Cosmetic Product Ingredient Statements with the FDA's Voluntary Cosmetic Registration

Program. The Cosmetic Ingredient Review was established in 1976 by the Cosmetic, Toiletry, & Fragrance Association with support of the FDA and the Consumer Federation of America. The Cosmetic Ingredient Review reviews and assesses the safety of ingredients used in cosmetics and publishes the results.

Cosmetics are not subject to the FDA's premarket approval, except for color additives. Adulterated cosmetics are those products that may be injurious to the consumer because it contains a harmful substance; it contains filth; it contains a noncertified color additive; or it is manufactured under unsanitary conditions. Misbranded cosmetics are those products with false or misleading labeling; with misleading container presentation or fill or those products whose labeling is not conspicuous or does not contain the required information on the label. The FDA does inspect cosmetic manufacturers. GMP does not apply to cosmetic manufactures. The FDA does not have the authority to initiate a cosmetic recall. However, if they deem that a cosmetic is adulterated or misbranded, the FDA can initiate a restraining order or seizure through the Department of Justice.

Tamper-resistant packaging is required on all liquid oral hygiene products and all cosmetic vaginal products if sold over the counter. Tamper-resistant packaging refers to a barrier or product that alerts the consumer to the fact that the product may have been tampered with. Must products have a breakable seal on the package and a statement on the product that advises the consumer that if the seal is broken the product may have been tampered with and that the consumer should not purchase the product.

## Homeopathic Drug Products and Herbal Products

**HOMEOPATHY**

Homeopathy is the practice of treating the syndromes and conditions which constitute disease with remedies that have produced similar syndromes and conditions in healthy subjects. Homeopathic medicine stimulates the person's natural defense system, helps heal illness, and raises the general level of health.

**HOMEOPATHIC PHARMACOPEIA OF THE UNITED STATES**

Official homeopathic drugs are those that have been monographed and accepted for inclusion in the *Homeopathic Pharmacopeia of the United States (HPUS)*. The potencies of homeopathic drugs are specified in terms of dilution, that is, $1 \times (1/10$ dilution),

$2 \times (1/100$ dilution), and so on. All ingredients in homeopathic products must be official homeopathic products. If a homeopathic product is combined with a nonhomeopathic product, the product is not considered a homeopathic product.

**HOMEOPATHIC DRUGS**    Homeopathic drugs are recognized as drugs under the Food, Drug, and Cosmetic Act. The initials *HPUS* on the label of a drug product assures that the legal standards of strength, quality, purity, and packaging have been met for that homeopathic drug product. The active ingredients are official and are found in the current *HPUS*. The standards that afford the initials *HPUS* after a recognized homeopathic product are established by the Homeopathic Pharmacopeia Convention of the United States. The convention works closely with the FDA and homeopathic organizations such as the American Institute of Homeopathy and the American Association of Homeopathic Pharmacists. Guidelines are published for the prescriptions or over-the-counter status of homeopathic drug products.

**HOMEOPATHIC PRODUCT LABELING**    Homeopathic product labeling must include:

1. The name and place of business of the manufacturer, packer, or distributor
2. Adequate directions for use
3. Quantity and amount of ingredient(s)
4. Established name of the product in English or Latin if available
5. Homeopathic drug products must comply with GMP. However, homeopathic products are exempt from expiration dating and laboratory determination of identity and strength of each active ingredient prior to release for distribution
6. Prescription Homeopathic Drugs must contain the legend, Caution: Federal law prohibits dispensing without a prescription
7. Tamper-resistant packaging is required for all products
8. The labeling of homeopathic products for over-the-counter use must include an ingredient list, instructions for safe self-administration, at least one indicated use of the product and the dilution.

# Dietary Supplements

**DIETARY SUPPLEMENT REGULATION**

For years, dietary supplements were regulated as food products. In 1990, the Nutritional Labeling and Education Act prohibited the use of disease-preventing claims in food labeling unless the claim conformed with FDA regulation. In order to be compliant, dietary supplement suppliers had to submit a petition containing considerable information supporting the supplement claim. This requirement was not very popular with suppliers and consumers. The Dietary Supplement Health and Education Act of 1994 was implemented to ensure safety and appropriate labeling of dietary supplements.

**DIETARY SUPPLEMENT DEFINITION**

The act defined a dietary supplement as:

- A product containing one or more of the following dietary ingredients: a vitamin, a mineral, an herb or other botanical, an amino acid, a dietary substance for use by man to supplement the diet by increasing the total daily intake, or a concentrate, metabolite, constituent, extract, or combinations of these ingredients.
- A product intended for ingestion in pill, capsule, tablet, or liquid form.
- A product not represented for use as a conventional food or as the sole item of a meal or diet.
- A product labeled as a "dietary supplement."
- Products such as an approved new drug, certified antibiotic, or licensed biologic that was marketed as a dietary supplement or food before approval, certification, or license.

# Permissible Labeling Claims

The following structure/function claims are permissible for use with dietary supplements:

- Description of the role of the dietary supplement in affecting the structure or function of the body. That is, "calcium supplement with vitamin D for strong bones; helps maintain a healthy heart."
- Identification of the mechanism utilized by the dietary supplement to maintain structure and function. That is, "fiber maintains bowel regularity."

- Description of the benefit from consumption of the supplement. That is, "helps body adapt and promote physical performance."
- Description of a benefit of a classic nutrient deficiency disease as long as the prevalence of the disease in the United States is stated in the claim.

The manufacturer is responsible for ensuring the accuracy and truthfulness of these claims. Dietary supplements are not preapproved by FDA. The labeling of dietary supplements must be truthful and not misleading. If a dietary supplement label contains one of the permissible claims, the label must include the following statement, "This statement has not been evaluated by the Food and Drug Administration. This product is not intended to diagnose, treat, cure, or prevent any disease."

### SUGGESTED READINGS

**MEDICAL DEVICES**

Device Labeling Guidance #G91-1 Web site. http://www.fda.gov/cdrh/g91-1.html. Accessed December 15, 2006.

Guidance to Medical Device Patient Labeling: Final Guidance for Industry and FDA Reviewers Web site. http://www.fda.gov.cdhr.ohoip/guidance/1128.html. Accessed December 15, 2006.

**COSMETICS**

U. S. Food and Drug Administration, Center for Device and Radiological Health (CDRH) Web site. www.fda.gov/cdrh/devadvice/313.html. Accessed December 15, 2006.

U. S. Food and Drug Administration, Center for Food Safety and Applied Nutrition, Cosmetics Web site. www.cfsan.fda.gov/~dms/cos-prd.html. Accessed December 15, 2006.

U. S. Food and Drug Administration, Center for Food Safety and Applied Nutrition, Cosmetics Web site. www.cfsan.fda.gov/~dms/cos-lbl.html. Accessed December 15, 2006.

**HOMEOPATHIC DRUG PRODUCTS AND HERBAL PRODUCTS**

The Homeopathic Pharmacopeia of the United State Web site. www.hpus.com. Accessed December 15, 2006.

**DIETARY SUPPLEMENTS**

Center for Food Safety and Applied Nutrition (CFSAN). U.S. Food and Drug Administration Web site. www.cfsan.fda.gov/~dms/supplmnt. Accessed December 15, 2006.

# 8 Product Recall

## Drug Recall

The Food and Drug Administration (FDA) does not have the authority to initiate a recall. In most circumstances, a manufacturer initiates the recall and then notifies the FDA of the recall. If a manufacturer does not initiate a recall upon the recommendation of the FDA, the FDA has the authority to seek legal action under the Food, Drug and Cosmetic Act (FDCA) in the form of seizure or injunction. In a seizure, the FDA takes control of the product, condemns the product, and destroys the product. An injunction prevents further manufacture or distribution of the product.

## Levels of Recall

There are three levels of recalls. The *consumer or user level* can affect the patient or the physician depending on the extent of the distribution of the product. The *retail level* affects the pharmacy, dispensing physicians, clinics, hospitals, and long-term care facilities. At this level the product has not reached the patient or consumer. The *wholesale level* is limited to manufacturers and retailers. There are three types of recalls.

1. *Class I* recalls have a reasonable probability that the use of the product or exposure to the product will cause serious, adverse health consequences or death. An example of a Class I recall is a label mix-up of two potent drugs or a defective replacement heart valve. The recall should include all stocks of the

53

two drugs in pharmacies with notification of all patients who received the product. If the recall involves heart valves, all hospitals and all heart valve recepients would receive notification.

2. *Class II* recalls involve products that the use of the product or exposure to the product may cause temporary or medically reversible health consequences or where probability of serious harm is remote. An example of a Class II recall is a subpotent drug product. The recall usually includes the stocks of drugs in pharmacies.

3. *Class III* recalls involve the use of or exposure to product that is not likely to cause adverse health consequences. An example of a Class III recall is inclusion of material not intended for inclusion in the product such as dirt, plastic, animal parts.

It is the responsibility of a pharmacist to know what products have been recalled. All recalls are published in the FDA Enforcement Report Index as soon as information about the recall is available. This report is available online at <<http://www.fda.gov/opacom/Enforce.html>>.

### SUGGESTED READINGS

FDA Enforcement Reports Index. U.S. Food and Drug Administration Web site. www.fda.gov/opacom/Enforce.html. Accessed December 15, 2006.

MedWatch. U.S. Food and Drug Administration Web site. www.fda.gov/medwatch. Accessed December 15, 2006.

# 9

# Drug Product Labeling

## Drug Use in Pregnancy

In 1975, the Food and Drug Administration (FDA) required pregnancy warnings in drug product labeling advising of the potential of birth defects and the effect that the drug may have on reproduction and pregnancy. Five categories have been identified for the pregnancy warning classification.

- **A**  Adequate, well-controlled studies in pregnant women have not shown an increased risk of fetal abnormalities.
- **B**  Animal studies have revealed no evidence of harm to the fetus; however, there are no adequate and well-controlled studies in pregnant women; or animal studies have shown an adverse effect, but adequate and well-controlled studies in pregnant women have failed to demonstrate a risk to the fetus.
- **C**  Animal studies have shown an adverse effect to the fetus and there are no adequate and well-controlled studies in pregnant women; or no animal studies have been conducted and there are no adequate and well-controlled studies in pregnant women.
- **D**  Studies, adequate well-controlled or observational, in pregnant women have demonstrated a risk to the fetus. However, the benefits of therapy may outweigh the potential risk.
- **X**  Studies, adequate well-controlled or observational, in animals or pregnant women have demonstrated positive evidence of fetal abnormalities. The use of the product is contraindicated in women who are or may become pregnant.

Drugs that are clearly contraindicated in pregnant women are isotretinoin and thalidomide as indicated by the use of these products with distribution programs such as iPLEDGE (a computer-based risk management program) and STEPS (System for Thalidomide Education and Prescribing Safety).

## Package Insert

Package inserts for prescription medication are intended to provide additional prescribing information to the health care professional. This information is not always appropriate for dissemination to the patient. It is written for the professional not the layperson. The package insert usually contains more information than the patient needs to be successful on the medication prescribed. The package insert typically contains the following information (different manufactures may use different headings for the sections):

- **Drug name**—contains the brand name and the generic name of the product.
- **Description**—chemical name of the drug, formulation of the drug, route of administration, inactive ingredients, and food allergies.
- **Clinical pharmacology**—absorption, distribution, metabolism, and elimination and results of clinical trials.
- **Indications and usage**—the use for which the product has been approved.
- **Contraindications**—those incidences when the medication should not be used.
- **Warnings**—side effects that may be hazardous to the patient's health, such as driving or operation of heavy machinery while on the medication.
- **Precautions**—how to use the medication safely with other medications, food, over-the-counter products, substances such as alcohol and information about the effects that the drug may have on the person's ability to function.
- **Adverse reaction**—side effects of the medication.
- **Drug abuse and dependence**—information about prolonged use of the medication.
- **Overdosage**—information on what to do in the case of an overdose.
- **Dosage and administration**—recommended daily dosage for various ages and limitations.

- **How supplied**—physical characteristics of the medication along with storage requirements.
- **References**—additional information sources.

## Patient Package Inserts

Patient package inserts provide patients with additional information necessary for the appropriate use of the medication. The FDA required the first patient package insert in 1968 for isoproterenol inhalation. The major concern with isoproterenol inhalation was that excessive use might cause increased breathing difficulties. The next patient package insert required by the FDA was for oral contraceptives. Oral contraceptive patient package inserts contain information about the risks and benefits of the medication. The format for patient package inserts is regulated by the FDA.

In 2006, the FDA developed a new format for patient package inserts to more effectively manage the risks of medication use and to reduce medication errors. The new format is easier to read and it highlights those pieces of information that are the most critical to both the patient and the prescriber. The new format will contain a section entitled *Highlights* and a *Table of Contents*. *Highlights* will include the date of approval of the original drug product; a section entitled, *Recent Major Changes*, that will list all substantive changes to the prescribing information made during that year which will be contained in the *Boxed Warning, Indications and Usage, Dosage and Administration, Contraindications and Warning and Precautions*; and *Adverse Drug Reporting Information*. The *Highlights* section will contain concise information that is crucial to the safe and effective use of the drug product with cross-references. This information will highlight the changes to the drug product and make it easier for the patient and prescriber to determine what changes are important to the appropriate use of the medication. The *Table of Contents* will reference other sections of the full prescribing information.

## Electronic Prescription Labeling

In November 2005, the FDA required that manufacturers submit prescription labeling information to the FDA in an electronic format. The new electronic format utilizes embedded computer tags and standardized medical terminology that affords the prescriber easy, quick access to prescribing information, thereby reducing medication errors. The new electronic product labels will be the sources of information for "DailyMed," an online health information clearinghouse created by the FDA and the National Library of Medicine for the benefit of patient and health care professionals. DailyMed is available electronically at <<http://dailymed.nlm.nih.gov>>.

## Appendix: DailyMed

ALBUTEROL
TABLETS, USP
2 mg and 4 mg
Rx only

**DESCRIPTION**

Albuterol tablets contain albuterol sulfate, USP, the racemic form of albuterol and a relatively selective beta$_2$-adrenergic bronchodilator. Albuterol sulfate has the chemical name $\alpha_1$-[(*tert*-butylamino)methyl]-4-hydroxy-*m*-xylene-$\alpha,\alpha'$-diol sulfate (2:1) (salt) and the following structural formula:

Albuterol sulfate has a molecular weight of 576.71, and the molecular formula is $(C_{13}H_{21}NO_3)_2 \cdot H_2SO_4$. Albuterol sulfate is a white or practically white powder, freely soluble in water and slightly soluble in ethanol.

The World Health Organization recommended name for albuterol base is salbutamol.

Each albuterol tablet for oral administration contains 2 or 4 mg of albuterol as 2.4 or 4.8 mg of albuterol sulfate, respectively. Each tablet also contains the following inactive ingredients: lactose (hydrous), magnesium stearate, pregelatinized (corn) starch, and sodium lauryl sulfate.

**CLINICAL
PHARMACOLOGY**

In vitro studies and in vivo pharmacologic studies have demonstrated that albuterol has a preferential effect on beta$_2$-adrenergic receptors compared with isoproterenol. While it is recognized that beta$_2$-adrenergic receptors are the predominant receptors in bronchial smooth muscle, data indicate that there is a population of beta$_2$-receptors in the human heart existing in a concentration between 10 and 50%. The precise function of these receptors has not been established (see "Warnings," below).

The pharmacologic effects of beta-adrenergic agonist drugs, including albuterol, are at least in part attributable to stimulation through beta-adrenergic receptors of intracellular adenyl cyclase, the enzyme that catalyzes the conversion of adenosine triphosphate (ATP) to cyclic-3′,5′-adenosine monophosphate (cyclic AMP). Increased cyclic AMP levels are associated with relaxation of bronchial smooth muscle and inhibition of release of mediators of immediate hypersensitivity from cells, especially from mast cells.

Albuterol has been shown in most controlled clinical trials to have more effect on the respiratory tract, in the form of bronchial smooth muscle relaxation, than isoproterenol at comparable doses while producing fewer cardiovascular effects.

Albuterol is longer acting than isoproterenol in most patients by any route of administration because it is not a substrate for the cellular uptake processes for catecholamines nor for catechol-*O*-methyl transferase.

*PRECLINICAL*  Intravenous studies in rats with albuterol sulfate have demonstrated that albuterol crosses the blood-brain barrier and reaches brain concentrations amounting to approximately 5% of the plasma concentrations. In structures outside the brain barrier (pineal and pituitary glands), albuterol concentrations were found to be 100 times those in the whole brain.

Studies in laboratory animals (minipigs, rodents, and dogs) have demonstrated the occurrence of cardiac arrhythmias and sudden death (with histologic evidence of myocardial necrosis) when beta-agonists and methylxanthines are administered concurrently. The clinical significance of these findings is unknown.

*PHARMAC OKINETICS*  Albuterol is rapidly absorbed after oral administration of one 4 mg albuterol tablet in normal volunteers.

Maximum plasma concentrations of about 18 ng/mL of albuterol are achieved within 2 hours, and the drug is eliminated with a half-life of about 5 hours.

In other studies, the analysis of urine samples of patients given 8 mg of tritiated albuterol orally showed that 76% of the dose was excreted over 3 days, with the majority of the dose being excreted within the first 24 hours. Sixty percent of this radioactivity was shown to be the metabolite. Feces collected over this period contained 4% of the administered dose.

**CLINICAL TRIALS**   In controlled clinical trials in patients with asthma, the onset of improvement in pulmonary function, as measured by maximum midexpiratory flow rate (MMEF), was within 30 minutes after a dose of albuterol tablets, with peak improvement occurring between 2 and 3 hours. In controlled clinical trials in which measurements were conducted for 6 hours, clinically significant improvement (defined as maintaining a 15% or more increase in forced expiratory volume in 1 second [$FEV_1$] and a 20% or more increase in MMEF over baseline values) was observed in 60% of patients at 4 hours and in 40% at 6 hours. In other single-dose, controlled clinical trials, clinically significant improvement was observed in at least 40% of the patients at 8 hours. No decrease in the effectiveness of albuterol tablets was reported in patients who received long-term treatment with the drug in uncontrolled studies for periods up to 6 months.

**INDICATIONS AND USAGE**

Albuterol tablets are indicated for the relief of bronchospasm in adults and children 6 years of age and older with reversible obstructive airway disease.

**CONTRAINDICATIONS**

Albuterol tablets are contraindicated in patients with a history of hypersensitivity to albuterol, or any of its components.

**WARNINGS**

**PARADOXICAL BRONCHOSPASM**   Albuterol tablets can produce paradoxical bronchospasm, which may be life threatening. If paradoxical bronchospasm occurs, albuterol tablets should be discontinued immediately and alternative therapy instituted.

**CARDIOVASCULAR EFFECTS**   Albuterol tablets, like all other beta-adrenergic agonists, can produce a clinically significant cardiovascular effect in some patients as measured by pulse rate, blood pressure, and/or symptoms. Although such effects are uncommon after administration of albuterol tablets at recommended doses, if they occur, the drug may need to be discontinued. In addition, beta-agonists have been reported to produce electrocardiogram (ECG) changes, such as flattening of the T wave, prolongation of the QTc interval, and ST-segment depression. The clinical significance of these findings is unknown. Therefore, albuterol tablets, like all sympathomimetic amines, should be used with caution in patients with cardiovascular disorders, especially coronary insufficiency, cardiac arrhythmias, and hypertension.

***DETERIORATION OF ASTHMA*** Asthma may deteriorate acutely over a period of hours or chronically over several days or longer. If the patient needs more doses of albuterol tablets than usual, this may be a marker of destabilization of asthma and requires re-evaluation of the patient and treatment regimen, giving special consideration to the possible need for anti-inflammatory treatment, for example, corticosteroids.

***USE OF ANTI-INFLAMMATORY AGENTS*** The use of beta-adrenergic agonist bronchodilators alone may not be adequate to control asthma in many patients. Early consideration should be given to adding anti-inflammatory agents, for example, corticosteroids.

***IMMEDIATE HYPERSENSITIVITY REACTIONS*** Immediate hypersensitivity reactions may occur after administration of albuterol, as demonstrated by rare cases of urticaria, angioedema, rash, bronchospasm, and oropharyngeal edema. Albuterol, like other beta-adrenergic agonists, can produce a significant cardiovascular effect in some patients, as measured by pulse rate, blood pressure, symptoms, and/or electrocardiographic changes.

Rarely, erythema multiforme and Stevens-Johnson syndrome have been associated with the administration of oral albuterol sulfate in children.

**PRECAUTIONS**          ***GENERAL*** Albuterol, as with all sympathomimetic amines, should be used with caution in patients with cardiovascular disorders, especially coronary insufficiency, cardiac arrhythmias, and hypertension; in patients with convulsive disorders, hyperthyroidism, or diabetes mellitus; and in patients who are unusually responsive to sympathomimetic amines. Clinically significant changes in systolic and diastolic blood pressure have been seen in individual patients and could be expected to occur in some patients after use of any beta-adrenergic bronchodilator.

Large doses of intravenous albuterol have been reported to aggravate preexisting diabetes mellitus and ketoacidosis. As with other beta-agonists, albuterol may produce significant hypokalemia in some patients, possibly through intracellular shunting, which has the potential to produce adverse cardiovascular effects. The decrease is usually transient, not requiring supplementation.

***INFORMATION FOR PATIENTS***    The action of albuterol tablets may last up to 8 hours or longer. Albuterol tablets should not be taken more frequently than recommended. Do not increase the dose or frequency of albuterol tablets without consulting your physician. If you find that treatment with albuterol tablets becomes less effective for symptomatic relief, your symptoms get worse, and/or you need to take the product more frequently than usual, you should seek medical attention immediately. While you are taking albuterol tablets, other asthma medications and inhaled drugs should be taken only as directed by your physician. Common adverse effects include palpitations, chest pain, rapid heart rate, and tremor or nervousness. If you are pregnant or nursing, contact your physician about use of albuterol tablets. Effective and safe use of albuterol tablets includes an understanding of the way that it should be administered.

***DRUG INTERACTIONS***    The concomitant use of albuterol tablets and other oral sympathomimetic agents is not recommended since such combined use may lead to deleterious cardiovascular effects. This recommendation does not preclude the judicious use of an aerosol bronchodilator of the adrenergic stimulant type in patients receiving albuterol tablets. Such concomitant use, however, should be individualized and not given on a routine basis. If regular coadministration is required, then alternative therapy should be considered.

***MONAMINE OXIDASE INHIBITORS OR TRICYCLIC ANTIDEPRESSANTS*** Albuterol should be administered with extreme caution to patients being treated with monoamine oxidase inhibitors or tricyclic antidepressants, or within 2 weeks of discontinuation of such agents, because the action of albuterol on the vascular system may be potentiated.

**BETA-BLOCKERS** Beta-adrenergic receptor blocking agents not only block the pulmonary effect of beta-agonists, such as albuterol tablets, but may produce severe bronchospasm in asthmatic patients. Therefore, patients with asthma should not normally be treated with beta-blockers. However, under certain circumstances, for example, as prophylaxis after myocardial infarction, there may be no acceptable alternatives to the use of beta-adrenergic blocking agents in patients with asthma. In this setting, cardioselective beta-blockers could be considered, although they should be administered with caution.

**DIURETICS** The ECG changes and/or hypokalemia that may result from the administration of non-potassium-sparing diuretics (such as loop or thiazide diuretics) can be acutely worsened by beta-agonists, especially when the recommended dose of the beta-agonist is exceeded. Although the clinical significance of these effects is not known, caution is advised in the coadministration of beta-agonists with non-potassium-sparing diuretics.

**DIGOXIN** Mean decreases of 16–22% in serum digoxin levels were demonstrated after single-dose intravenous and oral administration of albuterol, respectively, to normal volunteers who had received digoxin for 10 days. The clinical significance of these findings for patients with obstructive airway disease who are receiving albuterol and digoxin on a chronic basis is unclear. Nevertheless, it would be prudent to carefully evaluate the serum digoxin levels in patients who are currently receiving digoxin and albuterol.

**CARCINOGENESIS, MUTAGENESIS, IMPAIRMENT OF FERTILITY** In a 2-year study in Sprague-Dawley rats, albuterol sulfate caused a significant dose-related increase in the incidence of benign leiomyomas of the mesovarium at dietary doses of 2, 10, and 50 mg/kg (approximately 1/2, 3, and 15 times, respectively, the maximum recommended daily oral dose for adults on a mg/m$^2$ basis, or, 2/5, 2, and 10 times, respectively, the maximum recommended daily oral dose for children on a mg/m$^2$ basis). In another study, this effect was blocked by the coadministration of propranolol, a non-selective beta-adrenergic antagonist.

In an 18-month study in CD-1 mice, albuterol sulfate showed no evidence of tumorigenicity at dietary doses of up to 500 mg/kg (approximately 65 times the maximum recommended daily oral dose for adults on a mg/m$^2$ basis, or, approximately 50 times the maximum recommended daily oral dose for children on a mg/m$^2$ basis). In a 22-month study in the Golden hamster, albuterol sulfate showed no evidence of tumorigenicity at dietary doses of up to 50 mg/kg (approximately 8 times the maximum recommended daily oral dose for adults on a mg/m$^2$ basis, or, approximately 7 times the maximum recommended daily oral dose for children on a mg/m$^2$ basis).

Albuterol sulfate was not mutagenic in the Ames test with or without metabolic activation using tester strains *Salmonella typhimurium* TA1537, TA1538, and TA98 or *Escherichia coli* WP2, WP2uvrA, and WP67. No forward mutation was seen in yeast strain *Saccharomyces cerevisiae* S9 nor any mitotic gene conversion in yeast strain *S. cerevisiae* JD1 with or without metabolic activation. Fluctuation assays in *S. typhimurium* TA98 and *E. coli* WP2, both with metabolic activation, were negative. Albuterol sulfate was not clastogenic in a human peripheral lymphocyte assay or in an AH1 strain mouse micronucleus assay at intraperitoneal doses of up to 200 mg/kg.

Reproduction studies in rats demonstrated no evidence of impaired fertility at oral doses up to 50 mg/kg (approximately 15 times the maximum recommended daily oral dose for adults on a mg/m$^2$ basis).

**PREGNANCY** *TERATOGENIC EFFECTS. PREGNANCY CATEGORY C.* Albuterol has been shown to be teratogenic in mice. A study in CD-1 mice at subcutaneous (sc) doses of 0.025, 0.25, and 2.5 mg/kg (approximately 3/1000, 3/100, and 3/10 times, respectively, the maximum recommended daily oral dose for adults on a mg/m$^2$ basis), showed cleft palate formation in 5 of 111 (4.5%) fetuses at 0.25 mg/kg and in 10 of 108 (9.3%) fetuses at 2.5 mg/kg. The drug did not induce cleft palate formation at the lowest dose, 0.025 mg/kg. Cleft palate also occurred in 22 of 72 (30.5%) fetuses from females treated with 2.5 mg/kg of isoproterenol (positive control) subcutaneously (approximately 3/10 times the maximum recommended daily oral dose for adults on a mg/m$^2$ basis).

A reproduction study in Stride Dutch rabbits revealed cranioschisis in 7 of 19 (37%) fetuses when albuterol was administered orally at a 50 mg/kg dose (approximately 25 times the maximum recommended daily oral dose for adults on a mg/m$^2$ basis).

There are no adequate and well-controlled studies in pregnant women. Albuterol should be used during pregnancy only if the potential benefit justifies the potential risk to the fetus.

During worldwide marketing experience, various congenital anomalies, including cleft palate and limb defects, have been rarely reported in the offspring of patients being treated with albuterol. Some of the mothers were taking multiple medications during their pregnancies. No consistent pattern of defects can be discerned, and a relationship between albuterol use and congenital anomalies has not been established.

*USE IN LABOR AND DELIVERY*   Because of the potential for beta-agonist interference with uterine contractility, use of albuterol tablets for relief of bronchospasm during labor should be restricted to those patients in whom the benefits clearly outweigh the risk.

*TOCOLYSIS*   Albuterol has not been approved for the management of preterm labor. The benefit/risk ratio when albuterol is administered for tocolysis has not been established. Serious adverse reactions, including maternal pulmonary edema, have been reported during or following treatment of premature labor with beta$_2$-agonists, including albuterol.

*NURSING MOTHERS*   It is not known whether this drug is excreted in human milk. Because of the potential for tumorigenicity shown for albuterol in some animal studies, a decision should be made whether to discontinue nursing or to discontinue the drug, taking into account the importance of the drug to the mother.

*PEDIATRIC USE*   Safety and effectiveness in children below 6 years of age have not been established.

#### Chapter 9

**ADVERSE REACTIONS**

In clinical trials, the most frequent adverse reactions to albuterol tablets were:

### PERCENT INCIDENCE OF ADVERSE REACTIONS

| *REACTION* | *PERCENT INCIDENCE* |
|---|---|
| Central nervous system | |
| Nervousness | 20% |
| Tremor | 20% |
| Headache | 7% |
| Sleeplessness | 2% |
| Weakness | 2% |
| Dizziness | 2% |
| Drowsiness | <1% |
| Restlessness | <1% |
| Irritability | <1% |
| Cardiovascular | |
| Tachycardia | 5% |
| Palpitations | 5% |
| Chest discomfort | <1% |
| Flushing | <1% |
| Musculoskeletal | |
| Muscle cramps | 3% |
| Gastrointestinal | |
| Nausea | 2% |
| Genitourinary | |
| Difficulty in micturition | <1% |

Rare cases of urticaria, angioedema, rash, bronchospasm, and oropharyngeal edema have been reported after the use of albuterol.

In addition, albuterol, like other sympathomimetic agents, can cause adverse reactions such as hypertension, angina, vomiting, vertigo, central nervous system stimulation, unusual taste, and drying or irritation of the oropharynx.

The reactions are generally transient in nature, and it is usually not necessary to discontinue treatment with albuterol tablets. In selected cases, however, dosage may be reduced temporarily; after the reaction has subsided, dosage should be increased in small increments to the optimal dosage.

**OVERDOSAGE**

The expected symptoms with overdosage are those of excessive beta-adrenergic stimulation and/or occurrence or exaggeration of any of the symptoms listed under section Adverse Reactions, for example, seizures, angina, hypertension or hypotension, tachycardia with rates up to 200 beats/min, arrhythmias, nervousness, headache, tremor, dry mouth, palpitation, nausea, dizziness, fatigue, malaise, and sleeplessness. Hypokalemia may also occur. As with all sympathomimetic medications, cardiac arrest and even death may be associated with abuse of albuterol tablets. Treatment consists of discontinuation of albuterol tablets together with appropriate symptomatic therapy. The judicious use of a cardioselective beta-receptor blocker may be considered, bearing in mind that such medication can produce bronchospasm. There is insufficient evidence to determine if dialysis is beneficial for overdosage of albuterol tablets. The oral median lethal dose of albuterol sulfate in mice is greater than 2000 mg/kg (approximately 250 times the maximum recommended daily oral dose for adults on a mg/m$^2$ basis, or, approximately 200 times the maximum recommended daily oral dose for children on a mg/m$^2$ basis). In mature rats, the sc median lethal dose of albuterol sulfate is approximately 450 mg/kg (approximately 110 times the maximum recommended daily oral dose for adults on a mg/m$^2$ basis, or, approximately 90 times the maximum recommended daily oral dose for children on a mg/m$^2$ basis). In small young rats, the sc median lethal dose is approximately 2000 mg/kg (approximately 500 times the maximum recommended daily oral dose for adults on a mg/m$^2$ basis, or, approximately 400 times the maximum recommended daily oral dose for children on a mg/m$^2$ basis).

**DOSAGE AND ADMINISTRATION**

The following dosages of albuterol tablets are expressed in terms of albuterol base.

### USUAL DOSAGE

- Adults and children over 12 years of age: The usual starting dosage for adults and children 12 years and older is 2 or 4 mg three or four times a day.
- Children 6–12 years of age: The usual starting dosage for children 6–12 years of age is 2 mg three or four times a day.

**DOSAGE ADJUSTMENT**

- Adults and children over 12 years of age: For adults and children 12 years and older, a dosage above 4 mg four times a day should be used only when the patient fails to respond. If a favorable response does not occur with the 4 mg initial dosage, it should be cautiously increased stepwise up to a maximum of 8 mg four times a day as tolerated.
- Children 6–12 years of age who fail to respond to the initial starting dosage of 2 mg four times a day: For children from 6 to 12 years of age who fail to respond to the initial starting dosage of 2 mg four times a day, the dosage may be cautiously increased stepwise, but not to exceed 24 mg/day (given in divided doses).

**ELDERLY PATIENTS AND THOSE SENSITIVE TO BETA-ADRENERGIC STIMULATORS**   An initial dosage of 2 mg three or four times a day is recommended for elderly patients and for those with a history of unusual sensitivity to beta-adrenergic stimulators. If adequate bronchodilation is not obtained, dosage may be increased gradually to as much as 8 mg three or four times a day.

The total daily dose should not exceed 32 mg in adults and children 12 years and older.

**HOW SUPPLIED**     Albuterol tablets, USP, contain albuterol sulfate equivalent to 2 or 4 mg of albuterol.

The tablets containing albuterol sulfate equivalent to 2 mg of albuterol are white, scored, round tablets debossed with **M255** on the scored side. They are available as follows:

- NDC 0378-0255-01: bottles of 100 tablets
- NDC 0378-0255-05: bottles of 500 tablets

The tablets containing albuterol sulfate equivalent to 4 mg of albuterol are white, scored, round tablets debossed with **M572** on the scored side. They are available as follows:

- NDC 0378-0572-01: bottles of 100 tablets
- NDC 0378-0572-05: bottles of 500 tablets

Store at 20–25°C (68–77°F) (See USP for controlled room
  temperature).
Protect from light.
Dispense in a tight, light-resistant container as defined in the USP
  using a child-resistant closure.

Mylan Pharmaceuticals Inc.
Morgantown, WV 26505
ALB:R14
Revision date: 03/28/2006

---

## ALBUTEROL (ALBUTEROL SULFATE)

### PRODUCT INFORMATION

| | | | |
|---|---|---|---|
| Product code | 0378-0255 | Dosage form | Tablet |
| Route of administration | Oral | DEA schedule | |

### INGREDIENTS

| NAME (ACTIVE MOIETY) | TYPE | STRENGTH |
|---|---|---|
| Albuterol sulfate (albuterol) | Active | 2 mg in 1 tablet |
| Lactose | Inactive | |
| Magnesium stearate | Inactive | |
| Pregelatinized (corn) starch | Inactive | |
| Sodium lauryl sulfate | Inactive | |

### IMPRINT INFORMATION

| CHARACTERISTIC | APPEARANCE | CHARACTERISTIC | APPEARANCE |
|---|---|---|---|
| Color | White (white) | Score | 2 |
| Shape | Round (round) | Symbol | False |
| Imprint code | M;255 | Coating | False |
| Size | 6 mm | | |

### PACKAGING

| # | NDC | PACKAGE DESCRIPTION | MULTILEVEL PACKAGING |
|---|---|---|---|
| 1 | 0378-0255-01 | 100 tablets in 1 bottle, plastic | None |
| 2 | 0378-0255-05 | 500 tablets in 1 bottle, plastic | None |

## ALBUTEROL (ALBUTEROL SULFATE)

### PRODUCT INFO

| | | | |
|---|---|---|---|
| Product code | 0378-0572 | Dosage form | Tablet |
| Route of administration | Oral | DEA schedule | |

### INGREDIENTS

| NAME (ACTIVE MOIETY) | TYPE | STRENGTH |
|---|---|---|
| Albuterol sulfate (albuterol) | Active | 4 mg in 1 tablet |
| Lactose | Inactive | |
| Magnesium stearate | Inactive | |
| Pregelatinized (corn) starch | Inactive | |
| Sodium lauryl sulfate | Inactive | |

### IMPRINT INFORMATION

| | | | |
|---|---|---|---|
| Size | 9 mm | | |
| Imprint code | M;572 | Coating | False |
| Size | 9 mm | | |

### PACKAGING

| # | NDC | PACKAGE DESCRIPTION | MULTILEVEL PACKAGING |
|---|---|---|---|
| 1 | 0378-0572-01 | 100 tablets in 1 bottle, plastic | None |
| 2 | 0378-0572-05 | 500 tablets in 1 bottle, plastic | None |

### SUGGESTED READINGS

Center for Drug Evaluation and Research (CDER). U.S. Food and Drug Administration Web site. www.fda.gov/cder/regulatory/physLabel. Accessed December 15, 2006.

iPLEDGE Web site. www.ipledgeprogram.com. Accessed December 15, 2006.

National Library of Medicine, DailyMed Web site. http://dailymed.nlm.nih.gov/dailymed/about.cfm. Accessed December 15, 2006.

S.T.E.P.S.® 3.0 Celgene's Innovative Restricted Distribution Program. Thalomid® Web site. www.thalomid.com/steps_program.aspx. Accessed December 15, 2006.

United States National Library of Medicine, National Institutes of Health Web site. www.nlm.nih.gov. Accessed December 15, 2006.

United States National Library of Medicine, National Institute of Health DailyMed Current Medication Information.

# 10 Antitampering and Poison Prevention Packaging

## Drug Tampering History

Deliberate contamination of Tylenol capsules in 1982 with cyanide prompted the Federal Antitampering Act (P.L. 98-127) (18 U.S.C. 1365). This act applies to all consumer products, including any food, drug, device, or cosmetic. If a product is not packaged according to the Food, Drug, and Cosmetic Act, the product is considered misbranded or adulterated. For the purpose of consumer products, tampering refers to any alteration of the product with the intent to make the product objectionable without the authority to make the alteration.

## Legal Recognition of Drug Tampering

There are five areas that the law identifies as tampering with a product:

1. Tampering with a consumer product or its labeling that affects interstate or foreign commerce, with reckless disregard for the risk of death or bodily injury
2. Tampering with a consumer product with the intent of injuring a business
3. Communicating false information that a consumer product has been tainted

4. Threatening to tamper with a consumer product
5. Conspiring to tamper

The Antitampering Act established fines and imprisonment for convictions.

## Tamper-Resistant Packaging

Tamper-resistant packaging refers to packaging that contains an indicator or barrier that if missing can reasonably be expected to alert the consumer to the possibility that tampering has occurred. Tamper proof packaging does not exist and would be unrealistic to attain. All over-the-counter (OTC) human drug products, cosmetic liquid oral hygiene products, vaginal products, and contact lens must be packaged in tamper-resistant packaging. Exceptions to tamper-resistant packaging requirements include dermatologics, dentifrices, insulin, throat lozenges, and prescriptions dispensed by a pharmacist. Tamper-resistant packaging can be distinctive by design such as an aerosol container or contain a symbol that when missing would alert the consumer to the possibility of tampering. All packaging must contain a statement that alerts the consumer to the tamper-resistant packaging. The statement must remain intact after the consumer has opened the package. Exceptions to the statement requirement include crushable glass ampules, aerosols, and compressed medical oxygen. OTC products that consist of two-piece hard gelatin capsules must have two tamper-resistant mechanisms in the packaging, unless the manufacturer utilizes tamper-resistant technology.

Tamper-resistant technology may include some or all of the following:

1. Film wrappers that tightly adhere to the container
2. Blister packs, bubble packs, heat shrink bands, and wrapper
3. Foil, paper, or plastic pouches
4. Container with inner seals; tape seals, breakable caps; sealed metal tubes or plastic blind-end heat-sealed tubes
5. Sealed cartons
6. Aerosol containers
7. Cans composed of all metal or composite

The tamper-resistant labeling must state what form of tamper-resistant packaging was utilized in the packaging of the product.

# Poison Prevention Packaging Act

The U.S. Consumer Protection Safety Commission enforces the Poison Prevention Packaging Act (15 U.S.C. 1471–1476). The purpose of the Poison Prevention Act was to protect children under the age of 5 from poisoning. The Poison Prevention Packaging Act requires that packaging for oral medication be difficult for children to open. All hazardous household substances are required to be packaged in child-resistant containers. This packaging requirement applies to prescription drugs. Waivers of the packaging requirement may be affected by a prescriber or a patient. Prescribers have the authority to exempt a specific prescription for a patient from the child-resistant packaging. The prescriber is required to make a notation on the prescription. This waiver is valid for the duration of that specific prescription but does not carry over to subsequent prescriptions for that patient written by that prescriber. Patients have the authority to request a non-child-resistant container per prescription or they may make a blanket request to have all of their prescriptions placed in a non-child-resistant container. Either request should be in writing with the patient's signature included with the request. The pharmacy dispensing medication for the patient who has signed the waiver must maintain a record of the waiver in the pharmacy. Blanket waivers are permissible upon patient request only. A single request should not be confused with a blanket request. A prescriber cannot make a blanket request for a waiver. It is the responsibility of the pharmacist to ensure that all prescriptions are dispensed in a child-resistant container unless a specific waiver is initiated by a prescriber/prescription or the patient. Medications for patients who are in hospitals and institutions are not in the custody of the patient, therefore, the child-resistant container is not a requirement for the hospitals and institutions. OTC products must meet certain packaging requirements. The container need not be completely childproof. However, 80% of children must find the container difficult to open while 90% of adults must be able to open the container. Manufacturers of OTC products may designate one size of their product as a noncompliant container, provided the product contains a conspicuous warning label that states, "This package for households without young children or package not child resistant for small packages." Products supplied to pharmacies in quantities of 100, 500, or larger need not meet the child-resistant packaging requirement. A violation of the Poison Prevention Packaging Act would deem the product to be misbranded.

## Packaging Exemptions

Manufacturers can apply for an exemption to the child-resistant packaging. They must show that the toxicity of the product is low. Some products that are exempt from child-resistant packing include hormone replacement therapy, conjugated estrogen, oral contraceptives, powdered unflavored aspirin, effervescent aspirin, sublingual nitroglycerine, powdered iron preparations, effervescent acetaminophen, sublingual and chewable isosorbide dinitrate in doses of 10 mg or less, potassium supplements in unit dosing, sodium fluoride containing not more than 264 mg of NaFl, anhydrous cholestyramine, sacrosidase, and aerosols. When refilling prescriptions, the entire container, vial, bottle, and cap should be replaced unless the vial or bottle is made of glass. The integrity of the plastic vial, bottle, or cap may be compromised with repeated use. Therefore, visible inspections should be made if the plastic pieces are used repeatedly. The child-resistant requirement applies to oral medication, only not topical products. Some manufacturers require that their products be dispensed in their original container.

Prescribers who dispense drugs and samples from their practice are required to utilize child-resistant packaging also.

## Unit-of-Use Drug Products

Unit-of-use products such as Cytotec and Urocit contain information necessary for the safe administration of the product to the patient requiring that the product remain in the original packaging.

### Suggested Readings

Antitampering Act. U.S. Food and Drug Administration Web site. www.fda.gov/opacom/laws/fedatact.htm. Accessed December 15, 2006.

United States Consumer Protection Safety Commission Web site. www.cpsc.gov. Accessed December 15, 2006.

# Good Manufacturing Practices and Expiration Dating

## Good Manufacturing Practices

Good Manufacturing Practices (GMP) are minimum standards used in the manufacturing process that assure that the product meets requirements of safety, identity, strength, quality, and purity. If a product does not meet these requirements the product may be considered adulterated or misbranded. Manufacturers are required to register with the Food and Drug Administration (FDA) and their manufacturing process is described in the new drug application. The FDA attempts to inspect manufacturers every 2 years.

## Expiration Dating

Expiration dating (21 CFR § 211) refers to the date after which the product's stability is not guaranteed. Products must meet standards of identity, strength, quality, and purity at the time of use. Expiration dates may be dependent upon specific storage requirements as specified in the labeling of the product. Homeopathic drug products, allergenic abstracts labeled "No U.S. Standard of

Potency," and new drug products for investigational use are exempt from expiration dating.

## Beyond Use Dating

Beyond use dating is used for those products that are changed by the addition of another substance thereby affecting the stability of the product. For these products the pharmacist should include the date beyond which the product would not be deemed to be stable and effective. An example of this is an amoxicillin suspension that is stable for 10 days in the refrigerator. The manufacturer's expiration date of the amoxicillin suspension is greater than 10 days; however, the addition of water to the product makes the product unstable after 10 days. Compounded products are intended for immediate use and should contain a beyond use date that does not extend beyond the manufacturer's expiration date of the products.

Pharmacists dispensing solid oral medication may use their discretion as to the beyond use dating for the product. It cannot exceed the expiration date stated on the manufacturer's label. There is no Federal requirement that expiration dates be included on the prescription label prior to dispensing to the consumer. The FDA does require beyond use dating for drug products dispensed to patients in long-term care facilities.

Manufacturer expiration dating is specific to stability testing. The date is specified as month/year. If a product is labeled with an expiration date of 1/08, the product will be stable through January 31, 2008.

Unit dose expiration dating is 1 year maximum or 50% of the remaining time on the original package of the bulk drug product, whichever is less.

## United States Pharmacopeia (USP) Storage Temperature Guideline

- Cold—not exceeding 8°C (46°F)
- Cool—between 8 and 15°C (46–59°F)
- Room temperature—temperature prevailing in working area
- Controlled room temperature—maintained between 15 and 30°C (59–86°F)
- Warm—between 30 and 40°C (86–104°F)

- Excessive heat—above 40°C (104°F)
- Refrigerator—maintained between 2 and 8°C (36–46°F)
- Freezer—maintained between −20 and −10°C (−4 and 14°F)

Expired products should be removed from the operating stock in the pharmacy to prevent dispensing of expired products.

### SUGGESTED READING

U.S. Pharmacopeia Web site. www.usp.org. Accessed December 15, 2006.

# 12 Omnibus Budget Reconciliation Act of 1990

## Medicaid Review

Medicaid is a cooperative state-federal program that provides medical care to those individuals who cannot obtain or afford the medical care through other insurance avenues. The states provide the care and the federal government oversees the administration of the care and contributes matching funds for approved state programs.

The federal agency responsible for the Medicaid program is the Centers for Medicare and Medicaid Services (CMS, formerly known as the Health Care Financing Administration or HCFA), which is part of the Department of Health and Human Services. A state may receive between 50 and 77% of the cost of providing Medicaid care from the federal government depending on the state's per capita income.

## Implementation of Omnibus Reconciliation Act

The Omnibus Reconciliation Act of 1990 (OBRA) (P.L. 101-508) included a Medicaid initiative. The Medicaid rebate provisions of OBRA 1990 granted the Medicaid program "most-favored customer" status, requiring that drug manufacturers sell their drugs to Medicaid at the "best price" available to any other purchaser. In return for accepting the pricing provisions, drug companies would be assured that their products would be covered under each state's

Medicaid prescription drug program. The drug manufacturer's drug would then become part of the state Medicaid preferred drug list.

## Drug Utilization Review

Omnibus Reconciliation Act required that states engage in drug utilization review (DUR) for all Medicaid patients if that wanted to receive federal monies. This review looked into underutilization of drugs, prescribing errors and adverse drug effects, and generic substitution. The DUR program required a prospective review that examines future drug use and a retrospective review that examines past drug use. In performing a prospective DUR, the pharmacist reviews the patient's written medication profile prior to dispensing. It is the pharmacist's responsibility to obtain and update the patient's medication profile including disease state information, recreational drug use, over-the-counter drug use, herbal and homeopathic drug use, and allergy information. A patient's refusal to provide this information should be documented in the patient's medication profile. The DUR should consist of review of all of the patient's prescription records in conjunction with a review of the patient's disease states looking for under and over utilization of drug products. The review should include therapeutic duplication, incorrect dose or dosing regimen, and patient compliance. A verbal offer to counsel the patient on his or her medication should be made for each Medicaid patient. Each individual state will be responsible for determining if the counseling requirement will be a requirement for all patients not just Medicaid patients. Most states have extended the counseling requirement to all patients. Some states require counseling on all prescriptions and some states require counseling only on new patients and new prescriptions for existing patients.

## Counseling

Pharmacists should use their professional judgment to determine what information should be disseminated to the patient. When appropriate, the pharmacist should review the following information with the patient:

1. Name and use of the drug product
2. Route of administration

3. Duration of therapy
4. Action to be taken if necessary for a missed dose
5. Contraindications, precautions, and warning
6. Common adverse side effects
7. Drug-drug interactions
8. Food-drug interactions
9. Storage of the medication
10. Refill information

Studies have shown that patient counseling reduces medication errors. Since medication errors are always an issue for all health care providers, every effort that can be taken to reduce medication errors is important whether state or federally mandated.

### SUGGESTED READING

Centers for Medicare and Medicaid Services Web site. www.cms.hhs.gov. Accessed December 15, 2006.

# 13

# Labeling of Over-the-Counter Drug Products

## General Product Labeling

The purpose of labeling for over-the-counter (OTC) drug products and cosmetic-drug products is to provide the consumer with information necessary for safe and effective self-medication. The information needs to be conspicuous. The standards for safety, effectiveness, and labeling for OTC products are described in 21 CFR § 330.10 (a) (4). Safety refers to a low incidence of adverse reactions or significant side effects when used according to the directions for self-administration as well as low potential for harm associated with any abuse that may occur. Effectiveness refers to a reasonable expectation that when the drug is self-medicated by the consumer the drug will provide a clinically significant benefit as claimed in the labeling of the drug product.

Since no drug is considered totally safe, the benefit versus risk ratio of the drug product needs to be assessed. Do the benefits of the drug outweigh the risks associated with the drug? As the risks increase, there needs to be a significant benefit to match the risk. Drugs that are associated with more significant safety problems are expected to have sufficiently greater benefits to justify the increased risk.

The labeling of the container of the OTC drug product shall contain the title, headings, and subheadings (see Figure 13-1).

1. The title shall state the name of the product and the words "Drug Facts."

2. Active ingredient(s) followed by the established name of each active ingredient and the quantity of each active ingredient per dosage unit.
3. Purpose or purposes followed by the general pharmacologic category or the principal intended action.
4. Uses followed by the indications for the product.

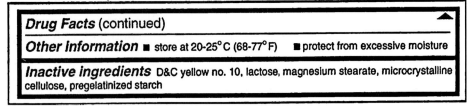

# Drug Facts

**Active ingredient (in each tablet)**                                    **Purpose**
Chlorpheniramine maleate 2 mg...................................................................Antihistamine

**Uses** temporarily relieves these symptoms due to hay fever or other upper respiratory allergies: ■ sneezing   ■ runny nose   ■ itchy, watery eyes   ■ itchy throat

**Warnings**
**Ask a doctor before use if you have**
■ glaucoma      ■ a breathing problem such as emphysema or chronic bronchitis
■ trouble urinating due to an enlarged prostate gland

**Ask a doctor or pharmacist before use if you are taking tranquilizers or sedatives**

**When using this product**
■ drowsiness may occur     ■ avoid alcoholic drinks
■ alcohol, sedatives, and tranquilizers may increase drowsiness
■ be careful when driving a motor vehicle or operating machinery
■ excitability may occur, especially in children

**If pregnant or breast-feeding,** ask a health professional before use.
**Keep out of reach of children.** In case of overdose, get medical help or contact a Poison Control Center right away.

**Directions**

| | |
|---|---|
| adults and children 12 years and over | take 2 tablets every 4 to 6 hours; not more than 12 tablets in 24 hours |
| children 6 years to under 12 years | take 1 tablet every 4 to 6 hours; not more than 6 tablets in 24 hours |
| children under 6 years | ask a doctor ▼ |

**Drug Facts** (continued)                                                      ▲

**Other Information** ■ store at 20-25°C (68-77°F)   ■ protect from excessive moisture

**Inactive Ingredients** D&C yellow no. 10, lactose, magnesium stearate, microcrystalline cellulose, pregelatinized starch

***Figure 13-1:*** Drug facts—chlorpheniramine maleate 2 mg. (The new Drug Facts labeling requirements do not apply to dietary supplements, which are regulated as food products, and are labeled with a Supplement Facts panel.)

5. Warning followed by one or more of the following if applicable:
   - For external use
   - Any of the following applicable warnings
     - Reye syndrome
     - Allergic reactions
     - Flammability
     - Water soluble gums
     - Alcohol
     - Sore throat
     - Contains sodium phosphates
     - Do Not Use followed by contraindications
     - Consult with your physician before using if you have . . . or for use in children under 12 years of age
     - Consult with a physician or pharmacist before using if you are . . . or for use in children under 12 years of age
     - When using this product the following side effects may occur
     - Stop use and consult with a physician with notation about signs of toxicity
     - Any applicable warnings listed in the drug's monograph
     - Pregnancy/breast-feeding warning
6. Keep out of reach of children.
7. Directions.
8. Other information that is not listed elsewhere but is required by the drug monograph.
   - Required information about ingredients contained in the product such as sodium, calcium, magnesium, and potassium
   - Phenylalanine/aspartame content if applicable
9. Inactive ingredients including the established name of each inactive ingredient.
10. Questions with the telephone number and days and hours of operation of the service.

# Pregnancy and Nursing Labeling (21 CFR § 210.63)

All products intended for OTC systemic absorption, unless exempt, shall contain in the Warning section the warning, "If pregnant or breast-feeding, ask a health professional before use."

The words "if pregnant or breast-feeding" must be in bold type. Exemptions include: drugs intended to benefit the fetus or nursing infant and drugs that are labeled specifically for pediatric use. Labeling for orally or rectally administered aspirin-containing drug products must contain second warning after the general warning that states, "It is especially important not to use "*drug name*" during the last 3 months of pregnancy unless definitely directed to do so by a doctor because it may cause problems in the unborn child or complications during delivery."

## Over-the-Counter Labeling of Sodium Content (21 CFR § 201.64)

The labeling of OTC products intended for oral ingestion shall contain the sodium content per dosage unit if the sodium content of a single maximum recommended dose of the product is 5 mg or more. Gum and lozenges are included in the products that require sodium content labeling. It does not include dentifrices, mouthwashes, or mouth rinses. The sodium content shall be expressed in milligrams per dosage unit and shall include the total amount of sodium regardless of the source. The source could be active and inactive ingredients. The content should be rounded up to the nearest whole number. Sodium content information should be listed under the heading of "Other Information."

Under the heading of "Warning" the following statement should be included if the amount of sodium is more than a maximum daily dose of 140 mg, "Ask a doctor before use if you have **a sodium restricted diet**."

The term "sodium free" is used when the maximum daily dose of sodium in the product is 5 mg or less and the amount of sodium per dosage unit is 0 mg.

The term "very low sodium" is used when the maximum daily dose of sodium in the product is 140 mg or less.

The term "salt" is not synonymous with the term "sodium" and should not be used interchangeably.

When using terms such as sodium free, very low sodium, or low sodium, the font size cannot exceed the size used in the products statement of identity and should not be any more prominent.

Rectal products containing dibasic sodium phosphate and/or monobasic sodium phosphate shall list the sodium content per delivered dose if the content is more than 5 mg or more. This information shall be listed under the heading "Other Information."

## Calcium Labeling (21 CFR § 201.70)

The labeling of OTC products intended for oral ingestion shall contain the calcium content per dosage unit if the calcium content of a single maximum recommended dose of the product is 20 mg or more. Gum and lozenges are included in the products that require calcium content labeling. It does not include dentifrices, mouthwashes, or mouth rinses. The calcium content shall be expressed in milligrams or grams per dosage unit and shall include the total amount of calcium regardless of the source. The source could be active and inactive ingredients. The content should be rounded up to the nearest 5 mg or nearest tenth of a gram of over 1 g. Calcium content information should be listed under the heading of "Other Information." The following statement should be included under the heading of Warning, "Ask a doctor before use if you have **kidney stones and are on a calcium restricted diet**."

## Magnesium Labeling (21 CFR § 210.71)

The labeling of OTC products intended for oral ingestion shall contain the magnesium content per dosage unit if the magnesium content of a single maximum recommended dose of the product is 8 mg or more. Gum and lozenges are included in the products that require magnesium content labeling. It does not include dentifrices, mouthwashes, or mouth rinses. The magnesium content shall be expressed in milligrams or grams per dosage unit and shall include the total amount of magnesium regardless of the source. The source could be active and inactive ingredients. The content should be rounded up to the nearest 5 mg or nearest tenth of a gram of over 1 g. Magnesium content information should be listed under the heading of "Other Information." The following statement under the heading of Warning should be included if the magnesium content in the maximum daily dose is more than 600 mg, "Ask a doctor before use if you have **kidney disease and are on a magnesium restricted diet**."

## Potassium Labeling (21 CFR § 201.71)

The labeling of OTC products intended for oral ingestion shall contain the potassium content per dosage unit if the potassium content of a single maximum recommended dose of the product is 5 mg or more. Gum and lozenges are included in the products that require potassium content labeling. It does not include dentifrices, mouthwashes, or mouth rinses. The potassium content shall be expressed in milligrams or grams per dosage unit and shall include the total amount of potassium regardless of the source. The source could be active and inactive ingredients. The content should be rounded up to the nearest 5 mg or nearest tenth of a gram of over 1 g. Potassium content information should be listed under the heading of "Other Information." The following statement under the heading of Warning should be included if the potassium content in the maximum daily dose is more than 975 mg, "Ask a doctor before use if you have **kidney disease and are on a potassium restricted diet**."

## Professional Labeling

Professional labeling provides specific information for health care professionals for uses not included in the OTC labeling. OTC drug monographs with professional labeling include the following drug categories:

- Antacid
- Antiflatulent
- Topical antifungal
- Antiemetic
- Cough and cold
- Internal analgesics
- Ophthalmic
- Anticaries
- Anthelmintic
- Cholecystokinetic

## SUGGESTED READINGS

Center for Drug Evaluation and Research (CDER). U.S. Food and Drug Administration Web site. www.fda.gov/cder/otc/label/default.htm. Accessed December 15, 2006.

Division of Over-the-Counter Drug Products Web site. http://www.fda.gov/cder/otc/index.htm. Accessed December 15, 2006.

FDA Consumer Magazine. U.S. Food and Drug Administration Web site. http://www.fda.gov/fdac/features/2002/402_otc.html. Accessed December 15, 2006.

# 14 Federal Controlled Substance Law

## History of Controlled Substance Regulation

The regulation of controlled substances is under the authority of the Drug Enforcement Administration (DEA) at <<www.dea.gov>>. The purpose of the controlled substance laws in the United States is to prevent diversion and abuse of controlled substances. The Controlled Substances Act (CSA), Title II and Title III of the Comprehensive Drug Abuse Prevention and Control Act of 1970, is the legal foundation of the government's fight against the abuse of drugs and other substances. The CSA is a consolidation of numerous laws regulating the manufacture and distribution of narcotics, stimulants, depressants, hallucinogens, anabolic steroids, and chemicals used in the illicit production of controlled substances.

The Federal Comprehensive Drug Abuse and Prevention Control Act established five schedules of controlled substances. In determining what schedule a drug product is placed into, a review of the medical use, abuse potential, and safety and dependence liability is conducted. The key issue in determining if a drug product should be scheduled is the product's potential for abuse. The following items are evaluated to assess the potential for abuse of a drug product:

1. Are individuals taking the drug product in amounts that are or may be hazardous to their health or the safety of others?
2. Is there significant diversion of the drug product through legitimate drug channels?
3. Are individuals self-administering the drug without the advice of practitioners and without legal prescribing?
4. Is the drug a new drug related to another drug that is scheduled because of abuse potential?

The CSA (21 U.S.C. § 811 I) lists the following factors for determining whether a drug product should be controlled and which schedule the drug product should be placed in:

1. The drug's actual or relative potential for abuse.
2. Scientific evidence of the drug's pharmacologic effects. Does the drug have hallucinogenic effects?
3. Scientific knowledge regarding the substance.
4. The history and pattern of abuse. What are the socioeconomic characteristics of the population using the substance?
5. The scope, duration, and significance of the abuse. Is the abuse widespread? What effect will regulation have on the population? What are the economic ramifications?
6. What risks, if any, are there to the public health?
7. The drug's psychic or physiologic dependence liability. Is the drug physically addictive or psychologically habit forming?
8. Is the substance an immediate precursor of a substance already controlled? The CSA allows inclusion of immediate precursors on this basis alone into the appropriate schedule and thus safeguards against possibilities of clandestine manufacture.

## Controlled Substances Schedules

**SCHEDULE I CONTROLLED SUBSTANCES**  Those drugs with a high potential for abuse, with no currently accepted medical use in treatment in the United States and no accepted information on the safety of their use, even under medical supervision. Research is allowed for Schedule I controlled substances provided the entity is registered with DEA as a researcher.

Examples of Schedule I drugs are opiates; opium derivatives—heroin; hallucinogenic substances—lysergic acid, marijuana, mescaline; depressants—methaqualone and gamma-hydroxybutyrate (GHB); stimulants—methcathinone and temporary listing of substances subject to emergency scheduling.

**SCHEDULE II CONTROLLED SUBSTANCES**  Those drugs with a high potential for abuse less than Schedule I, with accepted medical use in treatment in the United States and abuse of the drug may lead to severe physical or psychological dependence.

Examples of Schedule II drugs are opiates and opioids (narcotics)—straight opiates of codeine, morphine, meperidine; stimulants—amphetamine, methylphenidate; depressants—amobarbital, pentobarbital, secobarbital, or any combination, that is, Tuinal; hallucinogenic substances and any immediate precursors.

**SCHEDULE III CONTROLLED SUBSTANCES**

Those drugs with an abuse potential less than that of Schedule I and Schedule II, with accepted medical use in treatment in the United States and abuse of the drug may lead to moderate or low physical dependence or high psychological dependence.

Examples of Schedule III drugs are drugs not previously listed in another category; stimulants; depressants; nalorphine; narcotic drugs in various amounts; anabolic steroids; buprenorphine (Subutex); buprenorphine + naloxone (Suboxone); dronabinol (Marinol); ketamine or drug products containing less than 15 mg of hydrocodone per dosage unit (i.e., Vicodin, Lorcet, Tussionex) and products containing not more than 90 mg of codeine per dosage unit (i.e., codeine with acetaminophen, aspirin, or ibuprofen); and Schedule II barbiturates such as amobarbital, secobarbital, and pentobarbital when combined with noncontrol drugs, such as aspirin or acetaminophen or if they are in suppository form.

**SCHEDULE IV CONTROLLED SUBSTANCES**

Those drugs with an abuse potential less than Schedule III with accepted medical use in treatment in the United States and abuse of the drug may lead to limited physical or psychological dependence less than Schedule III.

Examples are the benzodiazepines, phenobarbital, Darvon, Darvocet.

**SCHEDULE V CONTROLLED SUBSTANCES**

Those drugs with a low abuse potential less than Schedule IV, with accepted medical use in treatment in the United States and abuse of the drug may lead to limited physical or psychological dependence less than Schedule IV.

Examples are cough syrups containing codeine; diphenoxylate preparations; opium preparations 100 mg/mL; and antidiarrheal and analgesics. Some examples are cough preparations containing not more than 200 mg of codeine per 100 mL or per 100 g (Robitussin AC), Phenergan with codeine.

The Code of Federal Regulations (CFR) publishes the drugs classified in each schedule in Title 21, Section 1308:

<<http://www.deadiversion.usdoj.gov/21cfr/cfr/2108cfrt.htm>>.
The *Federal Register* publishes all new scheduling information.
If the DEA Administrator has determined that a drug or other substance should be controlled, decontrolled, or rescheduled, a pro-
posal to take action is published. There is a comment period and
any party may request a hearing with the DEA. Upon evaluation,
the DEA will publish a final order in the *Federal Register* establishing effective dates for scheduling of the drugs.

## DEA Registration

A DEA registration grants the registrant the authority to possess
and handle controlled substances in the manner specified in the
registration. The activities that the registrant is authorized to
engage in is limited by both state and federal law. The more stringent law always applies. The following must register with the
DEA if they engage in activities utilizing controlled substances
(see Figures 14-1, 14-2, and 14-3):

1. Researchers (New application: DEA Form 224)
2. Manufacturers (New application: DEA Form 225)
3. Distributors (New application: DEA Form 225)
4. Laboratories (New application: DEA Form 225)
5. Exporters (New application: DEA Form 225)
6. Importers (New application: DEA Form 225)
7. Educational institutions (New application: DEA Form 224)
8. Narcotic treatment programs or dispensing location (New
   application: DEA Form 363)
9. Pharmacies (New application: DEA Form 224)

Every manufacturer, distributor, or dispenser must have its
own DEA registration except: warehouses used by registrants to
store controlled substances; practitioner's office; common carri-
ers; and offices where sales of controlled substances are solicited,
made, or supervised but not stored. All DEA registrants are responsible for maintaining records on all controlled substances received,
distributed, destroyed, or disposed of. DEA Form 224 is used for
Application for Registration (Figure 14-1). Online forms and application are available at <<http://www.deadiversion.usdoj.gov/
online_forms.htm>>. Renewal is available online for the following entities: Retail Pharmacy (DEA Form 224a), Hospital/Clinic

U.S.DEPARTMENT OF JUSTICE - Drug Enforcement Administration

# APPLICATION FOR REGISTRATION
## Under Controlled Substances Act of 1970

### INSTRUCTIONS FOR COMPLETING FORM DEA-224

▲ This form is for new applicants only and not for renewal of registration.
This application is for a three year registration period. See form for fee amount.

*ADDRESS BLOCK* - Information must be TYPED or PRINTED in the blocks provided. The manner in which information is placed on the application is the way your Certification of Registration will read. Please use the street address of proposed business. *WHEN USING A P.O. BOX YOU MUST ALSO PROVIDE A STREET ADDRESS.*

*TAX IDENTIFYING NUMBER AND/OR SOCIAL SECURITY NUMBER* - Indicate only one. *The Debt Collection Improvement Act of 1996 (PL 104-134) requires that you furnish your Federal Taxpayer Identifying Number to DEA. This number is required for debt collection procedures should your fee become uncollectable.*

Item 1 - **BUSINESS ACTIVITY** - Indicate only one.

| | |
|---|---|
| **Retail Pharmacy:** | Name of Pharmacy must appear in address block. |
| **Hospital/Clinic:** | Applicants applying for Hospital/Clinic registration should check with local state licensing authority to ensure they meet state requirements for that activity. |
| **Practitioner:** | Furnish professional degree in the space provided, next to Practitioner business activity (e.g., DDS, DO, DVM, MD, etc.) |
| **Teaching Institution:** | Registration as a Teaching Institution authorizes purchase and possession of controlled substances for instructional purposes only. Practitioners or Teaching Institutions desiring to conduct research with any Schedule I substance must obtain a "Researcher" registration by submitting Form DEA-225 with applicable fee. |
| **Mid-Level Practitioner:** | Furnish professional degree in the space provided, next to Mid-Level Practitioner business activity (e.g., PA, NP, OD, NH AMB, AS, etc.) |

Item 2 - **ORDER FORM BOOKS** - Indicate only if you intend to purchase or transfer Schedule II substances. Order form books will be issued to you upon issuance of your DEA registration.

Item 3 - **DRUG SCHEDULES** - Indicate schedule(s) of controlled substance(s) pertaining to your business activity and those that you intend to handle.

Item 4 - **STATE LICENSURE** - Federal registration by DEA is based upon the applicant being in compliance with applicable state and local laws. Applicants should contact the local state licensing authority prior to completing this application. If your state requires a separate controlled substance license, provide the number. If you have applied for state license and it has not been issued, indicate "Pending". If state licensing authority is not required, indicate "NA". All applicants must answer Items 4 (a), (b). (c). (d), and (e). If any are answered "YES", except 4(a), include a statement using the space provided in item 5 on the reverse of the application. Mid-Level Practitioners (Nurse Practitioners, Physicians Assistants, etc.) must also complete Item 4(f).

Item 5 - **EXPLANATION FOR ANSWERING "YES" TO ITEM(S) 4 (b), (c), (d), (e).**

Item 6 - **METHOD OF PAYMENT** - Indicate desired method of payment. Make check or money order payable to Drug Enforcement Administration. Checks or money orders drawn on foreign banks will not be accepted. If a credit card is used, provide the number, type of card (VISA or MasterCard), signature, and expiration date. *Application fees are not refundable.*

Item 7 - **FEE EXEMPTION** - Exemption from payment of application fee is limited to federal, state, or local government operated hospitals, institutions, or officials. The address on the application must be that of the affiliated federal, state, or local government; the signature and title of a supervisor *(other than applicant)* must appear on the application.

Item 8 - **APPLICANT SIGNATURE** - Must be completed with an original signature in ink.

**NOTE:** Initial registration period will not be less than 28 months nor more than 39 months. Once your DEA registration is issued, a renewal application is automatically mailed to you 45 days prior to your expiration date. Any change of address must be reported to the DEA. Renewal applications are *not* forwarded.

**WARNING:** *Section 843(a)(4)(A) of Title 21, United States Code, states that any person who knowingly or intentionally furnishes false or fraudulent information in the application is subject to imprisonment for not more than four years, a fine of not more than $30,000.00 or both.*

▼ *PRINT YOUR NUMBERS AND LETTERS AS INDICATED BELOW* ▼

| A | B | C | D | E | F | G | H | I | J | K | L | M | N | O | P | Q | R | S | T | U | V | W | X | Y | Z | 0 | 1 | 2 | 3 | 4 | 5 | 6 | 7 | 8 | 9 |

In accordance with the Paperwork Reduction Act of 1995, no person is required to respond to a collection of information unless it displays a valid OMB control number. The valid OMB control number for this collection of information is 111-0014. Public reporting burden for this collection of information is estimated to average 12 minutes per response , including the time for review-ing instructions, searching existing data sources, gathering and maintaining  the data needed, and completing and reviewing the collection of information.

*Figure 14-1.* DEA Form 224.

Listed below are examples of the schedules with assigned drug code numbers. If you are in need of additional information, see 21 cfr 1308 or contact the DEA Office serving your area

## SCHEDULE I

### NARCOTIC & NON NARCOTIC BASIC CLASSES

| | CODE |
|---|---|
| Acetorphine | 9319 |
| Acetylmethadol | 9601 |
| Allylprodine | 9602 |
| Alphacetylmethadol ( except LAAM) | 9603 |
| Bufotenine | 7433 |
| Dextromoramide | 9613 |
| Diethyltryptamine (DET) | 7434 |
| 2,5-Dimethoxyamphetamine (DMA) | 7396 |
| Dimethyltryptamine (DMT) | 7435 |
| Etorphine (except HCL) | 9056 |
| Heroin | 9200 |
| Ibogaine | 7260 |
| Ketobemidone | 9628 |
| Lysergic acid diethylamide (LSD) | 7315 |
| Marihuana | 7360 |
| Mescaline | 7381 |
| Methaqualone | 2565 |
| 3,4-Methylenedioxyamphetamine (MDA) | 7400 |
| 3,4-Methylenedioxymethamphetamine (MDMA) | 7405 |
| N-Ethyl-1-Phenylcyclohexylamine (PCE) | 7455 |
| Peyote | 7415 |
| 1-(1-Phenylcyclohexyl)pyrrolidine (PCPy) | 7458 |
| Psilocybin | 7437 |
| Psilocyn | 7438 |
| Tetrahydrocannabinols (THC) | 7370 |
| 1-[-1-(2-Thienyl)-cyclohexyl]-piperidine (TCP) | 7470 |

## SCHEDULE II

### NARCOTIC BASIC CLASSES

| | CODE |
|---|---|
| Alphaprodine | 9010 |
| Anileridine | 9020 |
| Cocaine | 9041 |
| Codeine | 9050 |
| Dextropropoxyphene (bulk) | 9273 |
| Diphenoxylate | 9170 |
| Diprenorphine (M50-50) | 9058 |
| Ethylmorphine | 9190 |
| Etorphine Hydrochloride (M-99) | 9059 |
| Glutethimide | 2550 |
| Hydrocodone | 9193 |
| Hydromorphone | 9150 |
| Levo-alphacetylmethadol (LAAM) | 9648 |
| Levorphanol | 9220 |
| Meperidine | 9230 |
| Methadone | 9250 |
| Morphine | 9300 |
| Opium, powdered | 9639 |
| Opium, raw | 9600 |
| Oxycodone | 9143 |
| Oxymorphone | 9652 |
| Poppy Straw | 9671 |
| Poppy Straw Concentrate | 9670 |
| Thebaine | 9333 |

### NON NARCOTIC BASIC CLASSES

| | CODE |
|---|---|
| Amobarbital | 2125 |
| Amphetamine | 1100 |
| Methamphetamine | 1105 |
| Methylphenidate | 1724 |
| Pentobarbital | 2270 |
| Phencyclidine (PCP) | 7471 |
| Phenmetrazine | 1631 |
| Phenyacetone | 8501 |
| Secobarbital | 2315 |

## SCHEDULE III

### NARCOTIC BASIC CLASSES

| | CODE |
|---|---|
| Codeine up to 90mg/du + other ingred. | 9804 |
| Dihydrocodeine up to 90mg/du + other | 9807 |
| Ethl/morphine up to 15mg/du + other | 9808 |
| Hydrocodone up to 15mg/du + other | 9806 |
| Morphine up to 50mg/100ml or gm + other | 9810 |
| Opium up to 500mg/100ml + other active ingred. | 9809 |

### NON NARCOTIC BASIC CLASSES

| | CODE |
|---|---|
| Anabolic Steroids | 4000 |
| Benzphetamine | 1228 |
| Butalbital | 2100 |
| Dronabinol Pharmaceutical Product | 7369 |
| Ketamine | 7285 |
| Methyprylon | 2575 |
| Pentobarbital + noncontrolled active ingred. | 2271 |
| Pentobarbital suppository | 1615 |
| Phendimetrazine | 2316 |
| Secobarbital + noncontrolled active ingred. | 2316 |
| Secobarbital suppository | 2316 |
| Thiopental | 2329 |
| Vinbarbital | 2335 |

## SCHEDULE IV

### NARCOTIC BASIC CLASSES

| | CODE |
|---|---|
| Dextropropoxyphene du | 9278 |
| Difenoxin 1mg/25ug atropine SO4/du | 9167 |

### NON NARCOTIC BASIC CLASSES

| | CODE |
|---|---|
| Alprazolam | 2882 |
| Barbital | 2145 |
| Chloral Hydrate | 2465 |
| Chlordiazepoxide | 2744 |
| Clorazepate | 2768 |
| Diazepam | 2765 |
| Diethylpropion | 1610 |
| Fenfluramine | 1670 |
| Flurazepam | 2767 |
| Halazepam | 2762 |
| Lorazepam | 2885 |
| Mazindol | 1605 |
| Mebutamate | 2800 |

## SCHEDULE IV (cont'd)

| | CODE |
|---|---|
| Mephobarbital | 2250 |
| Meprobamate | 2820 |
| Methohexital | 2264 |
| Midazolam | 2884 |
| Oxazepam | 2835 |
| Paraldehyde | 2585 |
| Pemoline | 1530 |
| Pentazocine | 9709 |
| Phenobarbital | 2285 |
| Phentermine | 1640 |
| Prazepam | 2764 |
| Quazepam | 2881 |
| Temazepam | 2925 |
| Triazolam | 2887 |
| Zolpidem | 2783 |

## SCHEDULE V

| | CODE |
|---|---|
| Buprenorphine | 9064 |
| Codeine Cough Preparation | 9100 |

***Figure 14-1.*** *(Continued)*

APPROVED OMB NO. 1117-0014
FORM DEA-224 (11-00)
*Previous editions are obsolete*

No registration will be issued unless a completed application form has been received (21 CFR 1301.13).

**The Debt Collection Improvement Act of 1996 (PL 104-134) requires that you furnish your Taxpayer Identifying Number and/or Social Security Number to DEA. This number is required for debt collection procedures should your fee become uncollectable.**

## APPLICATION FOR REGISTRATION
### UNDER CONTROLLED SUBSTANCES ACT OF 1970

READ INSTRUCTIONS BEFORE COMPLETING
USE BLACK INK

NAME: APPLICANT OR BUSINESS (LAST)

(First, MI)

TAX IDENTIFYING NUMBER          and/or          SOCIAL SECURITY NUMBER

PROPOSED BUSINESS ADDRESS   *(When using a P.O. Box you must also provide a street address)*

CITY

STATE          ZIP CODE

APPLICANT'S BUSINESS PHONE NUMBER

APPLICANT'S FAX NUMBER

FOR DEA USE ONLY

ATTACH CHECK HERE

2. INDICATE HERE IF YOU REQUIRE ORDER FORM BOOKS.

## REGISTRATION CLASSIFICATION

**1. BUSINESS ACTIVITY:** (Fill-in Circle)

A. ○ RETAIL PHARMACY   B. ○ HOSPITAL/CLINIC   C. ○ PRACTITIONER - ( Specify professional degree. e.g., DDS, DO, DVM, MD, etc. )

D. ○ TEACHING INSTITUTION   M. ○ MID-LEVEL PRACTITIONER (MLP)   (Specify professional degree, e.g. PA, NP, OD, NH, AMB, AS, etc.)

*(Instructional purposes only)*

**3. DRUG SCHEDULES:**   (Fill-in all circles that apply)

○ SCHEDULE II NARCOTIC   ○ SCHEDULE II NON NARCOTIC   ○ SCHEDULE III NARCOTIC   ○ SCHEDULE III NON NARCOTIC   ○ SCHEDULE IV   ○ SCHEDULE V

**4. ALL APPLICANTS MUST ANSWER THE FOLLOWING:**

(a) Are you currently authorized to prescribe, distribute, dispense, conduct research, or otherwise handle the controlled substances in the schedules for which you are applying under the laws of the **state** or jurisdiction in which you are operating or propose to operate?

○ YES   ○ NO

○ Yes - State License No.

○ Yes - State Controlled Substance No.

(b) Has the applicant ever been convicted of a crime in connection with controlled substances under state or federal law?   ○ YES   ○ NO

(c) Has the applicant ever surrendered or had a federal controlled substance registration revoked, suspended, restricted or denied?   ○ YES   ○ NO

(d) Has the applicant ever surrendered or had a state professional license or controlled substance registration revoked, suspended, denied, restricted, or placed on probation? Is any such action pending?   ○ YES   ○ NO

(e) If the applicant is a corporation (other than a corporation whose stock is owned and traded by the public), association, partnership, or pharmacy, has any officer, partner, stockholder or proprietor been convicted of a crime in connection with controlled substances under state or federal law, or ever surrendered or had a federal controlled substance registration revoked, suspended, restricted or denied, or ever had a state professional license or controlled substance registration revoked, suspended, denied, restricted, or place on probation?   ○ YES   ○ NO   ○ N/A

○ PENDING   ○ N/A

○ PENDING   ○ N/A

Continued on Reverse ▶

**ATTENTION ▶ FEE IS $210. FOR 3 YRS**

*Figure 14-1. (Continued)*

**4. CONTINUED**

**(f) MLP** only: Applicant is authorized to engage in the following controlled substance activities by the **state** in which applicant practices. (Fill-in all circles that apply.)

| | Prescribe | Administer | Dispense | Procure* |
|---|---|---|---|---|
| SCHEDULE II NARCOTIC | ○ | ○ | ○ | ○ |
| SCHEDULE II NON NARCOTIC | ○ | ○ | ○ | ○ |
| SCHEDULE III NARCOTIC | ○ | ○ | ○ | ○ |
| SCHEDULE III NON NARCOTIC | ○ | ○ | ○ | ○ |
| SCHEDULE IV | ○ | ○ | ○ | ○ |
| SCHEDULE V | ○ | ○ | ○ | ○ |

*Procure means to individually obtain controlled substances by purchase or receipt of samples from a manufacturer or distributor. It does not include receipt of controlled substances from, or pursuant to an order from a collaborating or supervising physician.

**5. EXPLANATION FOR ANSWERING "YES" TO ITEM(S) 4(b), (c), (d), OR (e).** Applicants who have answered "YES" to item(s) 4(b), (c), (d), or (e) are required to submit a statement explaining such response(s). The space provided below should be used for this purpose. If additional space is needed, use a separate sheet and return with application.

**FEES ARE NOT REFUNDABLE**

**6. PAYMENT METHOD (Fill-in only one circle)**

○ VISA   ○ MASTER CARD   ○ CHECK   ○ U.S. MONEY ORDER

CREDIT CARD NUMBER

EXPIRATION DATE

SIGNATURE OF CARD HOLDER

**7. CERTIFICATION FOR FEE EXEMPTION (Fill-in Circle)**

○ FILL-IN CIRCLE IF APPLICANT NAMED HEREON IS A FEDERAL, STATE, OR LOCAL GOVERNMENT OPERATED HOSPITAL, INSTITUTION, OR OFFICIAL. The undersigned hereby certifies that the applicant named hereon is a federal, state or local government operated hospital, institution, or official, and is exempt from payment of the application fee.

SIGNATURE OF CERTIFYING OFFICIAL (Other than applicant)   DATE

PRINT OR TYPE NAME OF CERTIFYING OFFICIAL   PRINT OR TYPE TITLE OF CERTIFYING OFFICIAL

**8. APPLICANT SIGNATURE** *(must be an original signature in ink)*   ▶ Remove form from package before signing

SIGNATURE   DATE

I hereby certify that the foregoing information furnished on this application is true and correct.

Print or Type Name

Print or Type Title (e.g., President, Dean, Procurement Officer, etc...)

**RETURN COMPLETED APPLICATION WITH FEE IN ATTACHED ENVELOPE**

*MAKE CHECK OR MONEY ORDER PAYABLE TO*

**DRUG ENFORCEMENT ADMINISTRATION**

UNITED STATES DEPARTMENT OF JUSTICE
DRUG ENFORCEMENT ADMINISTRATION
CENTRAL STATION
P.O. BOX 28083
WASHINGTON, D.C. 20038-8083

For information, call 1 (800) 882-9539
See "Privacy Act" Information on last page of application.

**MAKE A COPY FOR YOUR RECORDS.**

*Figure 14-1.* (*Continued*)

# DEA OFFICES (800, 877 and 888 are toll free numbers)

**ATLANTA DIVISION OFFICE**
Attn: Registration
75 Spring Street, SW, Room 740
Atlanta, GA  30303

| | |
|---|---|
| Georgia | (888) 219-7898 |
| North Carolina | (888) 219-8689 |
| South Carolina | (888) 219-8689 |
| Tennessee | (888) 219-7898 |

**BOSTON DIVISION OFFICE**
JFK Federal Bldg., Room E-400
15 New Sudbury Street
Boston, MA  02203-0131

| | |
|---|---|
| Connecticut | (617) 557-2200 |
| Maine | (617) 557-2200 |
| Massachusetts | (617) 557-2200 |
| New Hampshire | (617) 557-2200 |
| Rhode Island | (617) 557-2200 |
| Vermont | (617) 557-2200 |

**CARIBBEAN DIVISION OFFICE**
P.O. Box 2167
San Juan, PR, 00922-2167

| | |
|---|---|
| Puerto Rico | (787) 775-1766 |
| U.S. Virgin Islands | (787) 775-1766 |

**CHICAGO DIVISION OFFICE**
230 S. Dearborn Street, Suite 1200
Chicago, IL 60604

| | |
|---|---|
| Illinois | (312) 353-1234 |
| Indiana | (312) 353-1236 |
| Minnesota | (312) 353-9166 |
| North Dakota | (312) 353-9166 |
| Wisconsin | (312) 353-1236 |

**DALLAS DIVISION OFFICE**
10160 Technology Blvd, East
Dallas, TX 75220

| | |
|---|---|
| Oklahoma | (888) 336-4704 |
| Texas (Northern) | (888) 336-4704 |

**DENVER DIVISION OFFICE**
115 Inverness Drive East
Englewood, CO 80112

| | |
|---|---|
| Colorado | (800) 326-6900 |
| Montana | (800) 326-6900 |
| Utah | (800) 326-6900 |
| Wyoming | (800) 326-6900 |

**DETROIT DIVISION OFFICE**
431 Howard Street
Detroit, MI 48226

| | |
|---|---|
| Kentucky | (800) 230-6844 |
| Michigan | (800) 230-6844 |
| Ohio | (800) 230-6844 |

**HOUSTON DIVISION OFFICE**
1433 West Loop South, Suite 600
Houston, TX 77027

| | |
|---|---|
| New Mexico | (800) 743-0595 |
| Texas (South + Central) | (800) 743-0595 |

**LOS ANGELES DIVISION OFFICE**
255 East Temple Street, 20th Floor
Los Angeles, CA 90012

| | |
|---|---|
| California (So. Central) | (213) 621-6960 |
| Hawaii | (213) 621-6960 |
| Nevada | (213) 621-6960 |
| Trust Territory | (213) 621-6960 |

**MIAMI DIVISION OFFICE**
8400 N.W. 53rd Street
Miami, FL 33166

| | |
|---|---|
| Florida | (800) 667-9752 |

**NEWARK DIVISION OFFICE**
80 Mulberry Street
Newark, NJ 07102

| | |
|---|---|
| New Jersey | (888) 356-1071 |

**NEW ORLEANS DIVISION OFFICE**
Three Lake Way
3838 N. Causeway Boulevard, Suite 1800
Metairie, LA 70002

| | |
|---|---|
| Alabama | (888) 514-7302 or 8051 |
| Arkansas | (888) 514-7302 or 8051 |
| Louisana | (888) 514-7302 or 8051 |
| Mississippi | (888) 514-7302 or 8051 |

**NEW YORK DIVISION OFFICE**
99 Tenth Avenue
New York, NY 10011

| | |
|---|---|
| New York | (877) 883-5789 |

**PHILADELPHIA DIVISION OFFICE**
William J Green Federal Building
600 Arch Street, Room 10224
Philadelphia, Pa 19106

| | |
|---|---|
| Delaware | (888) 393-8231 |
| Pennsylvania | (888) 393-8231 |

**PHOENIX DIVISION OFFICE**
3010 N. 2nd Street, Suite 301
Phoenix, AZ 85012

| | |
|---|---|
| Arizona | (800) 741-0902 |

**SAN DIEGO DIVISION OFFICE**
4560 Viewridge Avenue
San Diego, CA 92123-1672

| | |
|---|---|
| California (Southern) | (800) 284-1152 |

**SAN FRANCISCO DIVISION OFFICE**
450 Golden Gate Avenue
P.O. Box 36035
San Francisco, CA 94102

| | |
|---|---|
| California (Northern) | (888) 304-3251 |

**SEATTLE DIVISION OFFICE**
400 Second Avenue West
Seattle, WA 98119

| | |
|---|---|
| Alaska | (888) 219-4261 |
| Idaho | (888) 219-4261 |
| Oregon | (888) 219-4261 |
| Washington | (888) 219-1418 |

**ST LOUIS DIVISION OFFICE**
United Missouri Bank Building
7911 Forsyth Boulevard, Suite 500
St. Louis, MO 63105

| | |
|---|---|
| Iowa | (888) 803-1179 |
| Kansas | (888) 803-1179 |
| Missouri | (888) 803-1179 |
| Nebraska | (888) 803-1179 |
| South Dakota | (888) 803-1179 |

**WASHINGTON, D.C. DIVISION OFFICE**
Techworld Plaza
800 K Street, N.W., Suite 500
Washington, D.C. 20001

| | |
|---|---|
| District of Columbia | (877) 801-7974 |
| Maryland | (410) 962-7580 |
| Virginia | (877) 801-7974 |
| West Virginia | (410) 962-7580 |

**HEADQUARTERS**
United States Department of Justice
**Drug Enforcement Administration**
Central Station
P.O. Box 28083
Washington, D.C. 20038-8083

**(800) 882-9539**

**NOTE:** Additional information can be found on the Internet,
www.deadiversion.usdoj.gov

Title 21, United States Code, Section 827(g) requires all registrants to report any changes of professional or business address to the DEA. Notification of address changes must be made in writing to the DEA office which has jurisdiction for your registered location. Direct requests for the following actions to the address listed for your state. 1. Request a modification to your DEA Registration (address change), 2. Request order form books, 3. Status of pending application.

## PRIVACY ACT INFORMATION

**AUTHORITY:** Section 302 and 303 of the Controlled Substances Act of 1970 (PL 91-513) and Debt Collection Improvement Act of 1996 (PL 104-134) (for federal taxpayer identifying number and/or social security number).

**PURPOSE:** To obtain information required to register applicants pursuant to the Controlled Substances Act of 1970.

**ROUTINE USES:** The Controlled Substances Act Registration Records produces special reports as required for statistical analytical purposes. Disclosures of information from this system are made to the following categories of users for the purposes stated:
A.  Other federal law enforcement and regulatory agencies for law enforcement and regulatory purposes.
B.  State and local law enforcement and regulatory agencies for law enforcement and regulatory purposes.
C.  Persons registered under the Controlled Substances Act (PL 91-513) for the purpose of verifying the registration of customers and practitioners.

**EFFECT:** Failure to complete form will preclude processing of the application

*Figure 14-1.* (*Continued*)

APPROVED OMB NO. 1117-0012

FORM DEA-225 (11-00)
Previous editions are obsolete

# APPLICATION FOR REGISTRATION
## UNDER CONTROLLED SUBSTANCES ACT OF 1970

READ INSTRUCTIONS BEFORE COMPLETING
USE BLACK INK

No registration will be issued unless a completed application form has been received (21 CFR 1301.13).

**The Debt Collection Improvement Act of 1996 (PL 104–134) requires that you furnish your Taxpayer Identifying Number and/or Social Security Number to DEA. This number is required for debt collection procedures should your fee become uncollectable.**

FOR DEA USE ONLY

NAME: APPLICANT OR BUSINESS(LAST)

(First, MI)

TAX IDENTIFYING NUMBER          and/or          SOCIAL SECURITY NUMBER

PROPOSED BUSINESS ADDRESS          (When using a P.O. Box you must also provide a street address)

CITY

STATE          ZIP CODE

APPLICANT'S BUSINESS PHONE NUMBER          APPLICANT'S FAX NUMBER

1. **BUSINESS ACTIVITY:** (Fill-in Circle)
E. ◯ MANUFACTURER   F. ◯ DISTRIBUTOR   G. ◯ RESEARCHER
H. ◯ ANALYTICAL LAB   J. ◯ IMPORTER   K. ◯ EXPORTER

2. **DRUG SCHEDULES:** (Fill-in all circles that apply)
◯ SCHEDULE I      ◯ SCHEDULE III NARCOTIC      ◯ SCHEDULE IV
◯ SCHEDULE II      ◯ SCHEDULE III NON NARCOTIC      ◯ SCHEDULE V

3. **INDICATE HERE IF YOU REQUIRE ORDERFORM BOOKS** ◯

| SCHEDULES |
| I | II | III | IIINon | IV | V |
| ◯ | ◯ | ◯ | ◯ | ◯ | ◯ |
| ◯ | ◯ | ◯ | ◯ | ◯ | ◯ |
| ◯ | ◯ | ◯ | ◯ | ◯ | ◯ |
| ◯ | ◯ | ◯ | ◯ | ◯ | ◯ |

4. **SUPPLY ANY OTHER DEA REGISTRATION NUMBERS FOR ANY CLASS OF BUSINESS AT THE ADDRESS SHOWN ON THIS APPLICATION**

5. **MANUFACTURERS ONLY**
Mark category and Schedules applicable in the circles to the right (Definitions on reverse of instruction sheet)

MANUFACTURES CATEGORIES

A ◯ Bulk, Synthesizer-Extractor

B ◯ Dosage Form

C ◯ Repacker-Relabeler

D ◯ Non-Human Consumption

6. **ALL APPLICANTS MUST ANSWER THE FOLLOWING:**

(a) Are you currently authorized to prescribe, distribute, dispense, conduct research, or otherwise handle the controlled substances in the schedules for which you are applying under the laws of the **state** or jurisdiction in which you are operating or propose to operate?

◯ YES - State License No.          ◯ PENDING   ◯ N/A

◯ YES - State Controlled Substance No.          ◯ PENDING   ◯ N/A

► ATTENTION ►    **Researcher, LAB $130;   Dist., Importer, Exporter $813;   Manuf $1,625;   For 1 YR** Continue on Reverse►

*Figure 14-2.*   DEA Form 225.

**6. CONTINUED**

**(b)** Has the applicant ever been convicted of a crime in connection with controlled substances under state or federal law?   ○ YES   ○ NO

**(c)** Has the applicant ever surrendered or had a federal controlled substance registration revoked, suspended, restricted or denied?   ○ YES   ○ NO

**(d)** Has the applicant ever surrendered or ever had a state professional license or controlled substance registration revoked, suspended, denied, restricted, or placed on probation? Is any such action pending?   ○ YES   ○ NO

**(e)** If the applicant is a corporation (other than a corporation whose stock is owned and traded by the public), association, partnership, or pharmacy, has any officer, partner, stockholder or proprietor been convicted of a crime in connection with controlled substances under state or federal law, or ever surrendered or had a federal controlled substance registration revoked, suspended, restricted or denied, or ever had a state professional license or controlled substance registration revoked, suspended, denied, restricted, or placed on probation?   ○ YES   ○ NO   ○ N/A

**7. EXPLANATION FOR ANSWERING "YES" TO ITEM(S) 6(b), (c), (d), OR (e).** Applicants who have answered "yes" to item(s) 6(b), (c), (d), or (e) are required to submit a statement explaining such response(s). The space provided below should be used for this purpose. If additional space is needed, use a separate sheet and return with application.

**8. DRUG CODE NUMBERS** must coincide with the schedules requested. Listed below are the Drug Code requirements for each business activity:

Analytical Lab-Not required to list drug codes
Distributor-Schedule I
Importer-Schedule I thru V
Exporter-Schedule I thru V

Researcher-Schedule I an II (See Item I, Researcher on Instruction Sheet)
Manufacturer-Schedule I, II, III, IIIN in addition to codes furnished, bulk manufacturer (synthesizer/extractor) applicants MUST Circle Below those "Basic Classes" of controlled substances in Schedule I and II which you propose to "Manufacture in Bulk" "If additional space is required, use a separate sheet and return with application.

**FEES ARE NOT REFUNDABLE**

**9. PAYMENT METHOD (Fill-in only one circle)**

○ VISA   ○ MASTER CARD   ○ CHECK

CREDIT CARD DATE

**EXPIRATION DATE**

SIGNATURE OF CARD HOLDER

**10. CERTIFICATION FOR FEE EXEMPTION (Fill-in Circle)**

○ FILL-IN CIRCLE IF APPLICANT NAMED HEREON IS A FEDERAL, STATE, OR LOCAL GOVERNMENT OPERATED HOSPITAL, INSTITUTION, OR OFFICIAL. The undersigned hereby certifies that the applicant named hereon is a federal, state, or local government operated analytical lab or researcher, and is exempt from payment of the application fee.

SIGNATURE OF CERTIFYING OFFICIAL (Other than applicant)    DATE

PRINT OR TYPE NAME OF CERTIFYING OFFICIAL    PRINT OR TYPE TITLE OF CERTIFYING OFFICIAL

**11. APPLICANT SIGNATURE (must be an original signature in ink)** ▶ Remove form from package before signing

SIGNATURE    DATE

I hereby certify that the foregoing information furnished on this application is true and correct.

Print or Type Name

Print or Type Title (e.g., President, Dean, Procurement Officer, etc...)

**MAKE A COPY FOR YOUR RECORDS.**

**RETURN COMPLETED APPLICATION WITH FEE IN ATTACHED ENVELOPE**

*DRUG ENFORCEMENT ADMINISTRATION*

UNITED STATES DEPARTMENT OF JUSTICE
DRUG ENFORCEMENT ADMINISTRATION
CENTRAL STATION
P.O. BOX 28083
WASHINGTON, D.C. 20038-8083

For information, call 1 (800) 882-9539
See "Privacy Act" Information on last page of application.

*Figure 14-2.* (*Continued*)

101

| Form-363 | **APPLICATION FOR REGISTRATION**<br>Under the Narcotic Addict Treatment Act of 1974 | APPROVED OMB NO 1117-0015<br>FORM DEA-363 (10-06)<br>Previous editions are obsolete |
|---|---|---|

**INSTRUCTIONS**

**Save time - apply on-line at *www.deadiversion.usdoj.gov***

1. To apply by mail complete this application.  Keep a copy for your records.
2. Print clearly, using black or blue ink, or use a typewriter.
3. Mail this form to the address provided in Section 7 or use enclosed envelope.
4. Include the correct payment amount.  FEE IS NON-REFUNDABLE.
5. If you have any questions call 800-882-9539 prior to submitting your application.
IMPORTANT:  DO NOT SEND THIS APPLICATION **AND** APPLY ON-LINE.

DEA OFFICIAL USE :

Do you have other DEA registration numbers?
☐ NO            ☐ YES

**MAIL-TO ADDRESS**   Please print mailing address changes to the right of the address in this box.

FEE FOR ONE (1) YEAR IS $184
**FEE IS NON-REFUNDABLE**

**SECTION 1**   APPLICANT IDENTIFICATION

Name 1      (Business or Facility Name)

Name 2      (Continuation of business name)

Street Address Line 1 (if applying for fee exemption, this must be the address of the fee exempt institution)

Address Line 2

City                                                                 State    Zip Code

Business Phone Number          Point of Contact

Business Fax Number            Email Address

**DEBT COLLECTION INFORMATION**

Mandatory pursuant to Debt Collection Improvements Act

Tax Identification Number

See additional information note #3 on page 4.

**SECTION 2**

**BUSINESS ACTIVITY**

Check one business activity box only

☐ NTP - Maintenance                    ☐ NTP - Compounder / Maintenance

☐ NTP - Detoxification                 ☐ NTP - Compounder / Detoxification

☐ NTP - Maintenance and Detoxification ☐ NTP - Compounder / Maintenance and Detoxification

**SECTION 3**

**DRUG SCHEDULES**

Check all that apply

☐ Schedule II Narcotic (9250 Methadone)    ☐ Schedule III Narcotic (9064 Buprenorphine)

☐ Check this box if you require official order forms - for purchase or transfer of schedule II controlled substances

NEW - Page 1

*Figure 14-3.*   DEA Form 363.

**SECTION 4**
**STATE LICENSE**

You MUST be currently authorized to prescribe, distribute, dispense, conduct research, or otherwise handle the controlled substances in the schedules for which you are applying under the laws of the **state** or jurisdiction in which you are operating or propose to operate.

State
License Number

Expiration
Date    /    /
MM - DD - YYYY

What state was this license issued in? _____

**SECTION 5**
**LIABILITY**

**IMPORTANT**

All questions in this section must be answered.

YES   NO
☐    ☐

1. Has the applicant ever been **convicted of a crime** in connection with controlled substance(s) under state or federal law, or is any such action pending?

Date(s) of incident MM-DD-YYYY: ☐☐-☐☐-☐☐☐☐

YES   NO
☐    ☐

2. Has the applicant ever surrendered (for cause) or had a **federal** controlled substance registration revoked, suspended, restricted, or denied, or is any such action pending?

Date(s) of incident MM-DD-YYYY: ☐☐-☐☐-☐☐☐☐

YES   NO
☐    ☐

3. Has the applicant ever surrendered (for cause) or had a **state** professional license or controlled substance registration revoked, suspended, denied, restricted, or placed on probation, or is any such action pending?

Date(s) of incident MM-DD-YYYY: ☐☐-☐☐-☐☐☐☐

YES   NO
☐    ☐

4. If the applicant is a **corporation** (other than a corporation whose stock is owned and traded by the public), association, partnership, or pharmacy, has any officer, partner, stockholder, or proprietor been **convicted of a crime** in connection with controlled substance(s) under state or federal law, or ever surrendered, for cause, or had a **federal** controlled substance registration revoked, suspended, restricted, denied, or ever had a **state** professional license or controlled substance registration revoked, suspended, denied, restricted or placed on probation, or is any such action pending?

Date(s) of incident MM-DD-YYYY: ☐☐-☐☐-☐☐☐☐    *Note: If question 4 does not apply to you, be sure to mark 'NO'. It will slow down processing of your application if you leave it blank.*

**EXPLANATION OF "YES" ANSWERS**

Applicants who have answered "YES" to any of the four questions above **must provide a statement to explain each "YES" answer.**

Use this space or attach a separate sheet and return with application

Liability question # _____    Location(s) of incident: _____

Nature of incident:

Disposition of incident:

**SECTION 6**   **EXEMPTION FROM APPLICATION FEE**

☐ Check this box if the applicant is a federal, state, or local government official or institution. Does not apply to contractor-operated institutions.

Business or Facility Name of Fee Exempt Institution. **Be sure to enter the address of this exempt institution in Section 1.**

The undersigned hereby certifies that the applicant named hereon is a federal, state or local government official or institution, and is exempt from payment of the application fee.

**FEE EXEMPT CERTIFIER**

Provide the name and phone number of the certifying official

_____   _____
Signature of certifying official (**other than applicant**)       Date

_____   _____
Print or type name and title of certifying official       Telephone No. (required for verification)

**SECTION 7**
**METHOD OF PAYMENT**

Check one form of payment only

☐ Check   Make check payable to: **Drug Enforcement Administration**
See page 4 of instructions for important information.

☐ American Express   ☐ Discover   ☐ Master Card   ☐ Visa

Credit Card Number                    Expiration Date

Sign if paying by credit card

_____
Signature of Card Holder

_____
Printed Name of Card Holder

*Mail this form with payment to:*

U.S. Department of Justice
Drug Enforcement Administration
P.O. Box 28083
Washington, DC  20038-8083

**FEE IS NON-REFUNDABLE**

**SECTION 8**
**APPLICANT'S SIGNATURE**

Sign in ink

I certify that the foregoing information furnished on this application is true and correct.

_____   _____
**Signature of applicant (sign in ink)**       Date

_____
Print or type name and title of applicant

**WARNING:** Section 843(a)(4)(A) of Title 21, United States Code states that any person who knowingly or intentionally furnishes false or fraudulent information in the application is subject to imprisonment for not more than four years, a fine of not more than $30,000, or both.

NEW - Page 2

*Figure 14-3.*   (*Continued*)

---

| Form-363 | **APPLICATION FOR REGISTRATION** | Supplementary Instructions and Information |

**SECTION 1.** **APPLICANT IDENTIFICATION** - Information must be typed or printed in the blocks provided to help reduce data entry errors. A physical address is required in address line 1; a post office box or continuation of address may be entered in address line 2. Fee exempt applicant must list the address of the fee exempt institution. The email address and point of contact are new data items that are in the process of OMB approval and will soon be mandatory. They are requested in order to facilitate communication or as required by inter-agency data sharing requirements. Applicant must enter a valid tax identification number (TIN).

*Debt collection information is mandatory pursuant to the Debt Collection Improvement Act of 1996.*

**SECTION 2.** **BUSINESS ACTIVITY** - Indicate only one.

**SECTION 3.** **DRUG SCHEDULES** - Applicant should check all drug schedules to be handled. However, applicant must still comply with state requirements; federal registration does not overrule state restrictions. Check the order form box only if you intend to purchase or to transfer schedule 2 controlled substances. Order forms will be mailed to the registered address following issuance of a Certificate of Registration.

**SECTION 4.** **STATE LICENSE** - Federal registration by DEA is based upon the applicant's compliance with applicable state and local laws. Applicant should contact the local state licensing authority prior to completing this application.

**SECTION 5.** **LIABILITY** - Applicant must answer all four questions for the application to be accepted for processing. If you answer "Yes" to a question, provide an explanation in the space provided. If you answer "Yes" to several of the questions, then you must provide a separate explanation describing the location, nature, and result of incident for each "Yes" answer. If additional space is required, you may attach a separate page.

**SECTION 6.** **EXEMPTION FROM APPLICATION FEE** - Exemption from payment of application fee is limited to federal, state or local government official or institution. The applicant's superior or agency officer must certify exempt status. The signature, authority title, and telephone number of the certifying official (other than the applicant) must be provided. The address of the fee exempt institution must appear in Section 1.

**SECTION 7.** **METHOD OF PAYMENT** - Indicate the desired method of payment. Make checks payable to "Drug Enforcement Administration". Third-party checks or checks drawn on foreign banks will not be accepted.

*FEES ARE NON-REFUNDABLE.*

**SECTION 8.** **APPLICANT'S SIGNATURE** - Applicant MUST sign in this section or application will be returned. Card holder signature in section 7 does not fulfill this requirement.

NEW INST - Page 3

---

***Figure 14-3.*** (*Continued*)

| Form-363 | APPLICATION FOR REGISTRATION<br>- CONTINUED - | Supplementary Instructions and Information |
|---|---|---|

## Notice to Registrants Making Payment by Check

*Authorization to Convert Your Check:* If you send us a check to make your payment, your check will be converted into an electronic fund transfer. "Electronic fund transfer" is the term used to refer to the process in which we electronically instruct your financial institution to transfer funds from your account to our account, rather than processing your check. By sending your completed, signed check to us, you authorize us to copy your check and to use the account information from your check to make an electronic fund transfer from your account for the same amount as the check. If the electronic fund transfer cannot be processed for technical reasons, you authorize us to process the copy of your check.

*Insufficient Funds:* The electronic funds transfer from your account will usually occur within 24 hours, which is faster than a check is normally processed. Therefore, make sure there are sufficient funds available in your checking account when you send us your check. If the electronic funds transfer cannot be completed because of insufficient funds, we may try to make the transfer up to more two times.

*Transaction Information:* The electronic fund transfer from your account will be on the account statement you receive from your financial institution. However, the transfer may be in a different place on your statement than the place where your checks normally appear. For example, it may appear under "other withdrawals" or "other transactions". You will not receive your original check back from your financial institution. For security reasons, we will destroy your original check, but we will keep a copy of the check for record-keeping purposes.

*Your Rights:* You should contact your financial institution immediately if you believe that the electronic fund transfer reported on your account statement was not properly authorized or is otherwise incorrect. Consumers have protections under Federal law called the Electronic Fund Transfer Act for an unauthorized or incorrect electronic fund transfer.

### ADDITIONAL INFORMATION

1. No registration will be issued unless a completed application form has been received (21 CFR 1301.13).
2. In accordance with the Paperwork Reduction Act of 1995, no person is required to respond to a collection of information unless it displays a valid OMB control number. The OMB number for this collection is 1117-0015. Public reporting burden for this collection of information is estimated to average 15 minutes per response, including the time for reviewing instructions, searching existing data sources, gathering and maintaining the data needed, and completing and reviewing the information.
3. The Debt Collection Improvements Act of 1996 (PL 104-134) requires that you furnish your Taxpayer Identification Number and/or Social Security Number on this application. This number is required for debt collection procedures if your fee is not collectible.
4. PRIVACY ACT INFORMATION
   AUTHORITY:      Section 302 and 303 of the Controlled Substances Act of 1970 (PL91-513) and
                           Debt Collection Improvements Act of 1966 (PL 104-134) for SSN and/or TIN
   PURPOSE:         To obtain information required to register applicants pursuant to the
                           Controlled Substances Act of 1970
   ROUTINE USES: The Controlled Substances Act registration system produces special reports as required for
                           statistical analytical purposes. Disclosures of information from this system are made to the
                           following :
                           A. Other federal law enforcement and regulatory agencies
                               for law enforcement and regulatory purposes
                           B. State and local law enforcement and regulatory agencies
                               for law enforcement and regulatory purposes
                           C. Persons registered under the Controlled Substances Act (PL 91-513)
                               for the purpose of verifying registration
   EFFECT:            Failure to complete form will preclude processing of the application

INTERNET:
www.deadiversion.usdoj.gov

TELEPHONE:
HQ Call Center (800)882-9539

WRITTEN INQUIRIES:
DEA
P.O. Box 28083
Washington, D C 20038-8083

NEW INST - Page 4

**Figure 14-3.** (*Continued*)

(DEA From 224a), Practitioner (DEA Form 224a), Teaching Institution (DEA Form 224a) or MidLevel Practitioner (DEA Form 224a), Manufacturer (DEA Form 225a), Distributor (DEA Form 225a), Researcher (DEA Form 225a), Analytical Laboratory (DEA Form 225a), Importer (DEA Form 225a), Exporter (Form 225a), Domestic Chemicals (DEA Form 510a), Narcotic Treatment Programs (DEA Form 363a).

## Pharmacy DEA Registration

Any pharmacy that dispenses controlled substances must register with the DEA. Pharmacists do not register with the DEA; however, pharmacists must comply with their own state regulation for the handling of controlled substances. New pharmacy applicants must complete Form 224 and submit to DEA, Registration Unit, Central Station. P.O. Box 28083, Washington, DC 20038-8083 (see Figure 14-1). Registrations must be renewed every 3 years. Each registered location must maintain the DEA registration certificate at that location. Each renewal will be sent to the address noted on the registration certificate. DEA registrations are sent to the registrants at least 45 days prior to the expiration of the registration. DEA registration renewals are done on DEA Form 224a. If the registrant does not receive the registration renewal notice 30 days prior to expiration of the registration, the registrant should contact the DEA office of his or her state and request a DEA registration renewal. In the event of a pharmacy changing its business address, a new DEA registration must be applied for in advance of the move of the pharmacy. The DEA registration certificate must reflect the current address of the registrant. DEA registration should not be forwarded to a different address.

## Denial, Revocation, or Suspension of DEA Registration

The law provides the federal government with the authority to take action against registrants who engage in controlled substance drug diversion. The United States Attorney General has the authority to suspend or revoke a DEA registration upon a finding that the registrant has:

1. Filed an application with falsified material.
2. Committed and been convicted of a felony involving a controlled substance or a List I Chemical that results in revocation, suspension, or denial of state license or registration.
3. Committed an act which would render the registration contrary to the public interest.
4. Been excluded from participation in a Medicaid or Medicare program.

## Denial of DEA Registration in the Public Interest

The United States Attorney General has the authority to deny any application for DEA registration or renewal if the granting of the DEA registration/renewal would create a threat to the health and safety of the public. In determining whether there is a public threat, the following factors are considered:

1. The recommendation of the appropriate state licensing board or state professional disciplinary authority.
2. The applicant's experience and past history in dispensing or conducting research with respect to controlled substances.
3. The applicant's conviction record under federal or state laws relating to the manufacture, distribution, or dispensing of controlled substances.
4. Compliance with applicable state, federal, or local laws regulating controlled substances.
5. Such other conduct which may threaten the health and safety of the public.

The DEA Office of Diversion Control publishes a list of drugs and chemicals of concern at <<http://www.deadiversion.usdoj.gov/drugs_concern/index.html>>.

## Ordering of Controlled Substances

Schedule I and II controlled substances can be ordered only by a DEA registrant on the official DEA Form 222. Schedule III–V controlled substances are ordered through the normal ordering process for noncontrolled substances. No special forms are necessary for ordering Schedule III–V controlled substances. The registrant (pharmacy) must keep a record on the receipt (i.e., invoice or packing slip) indicating the date the drugs were received and confirming that the order is accurate. These receipts must be maintained in a readily retrievable manner for inspection by the DEA. DEA Form 222 is a triplicate form used for ordering, transferring, and distributing Schedule I and II controlled substances. Once a registrant has received the initial order of Form 222, Form 222a is used for all subsequent ordering of forms. The address on the Form 222 must be the same as the one on the DEA registration for that particular establishment. Each book of forms contains seven sets of order forms. Each pharmacy is allowed a maximum of six books unless they can demonstrate a need for more. The form is a triplicate numbered in sequence. Each part of the triplicate is numbered also. Each part of the triplicate is numbered in the lower right hand corner in red: 1, 2, or 3. Copy 3 contains instructions on the back. Copy 2 is sent to the nearest DEA office by the pharmaceutical supplier. Copy 1 stays with the pharmaceutical supplier and Copy 3 stays with the pharmacy or ordering entity. Only a DEA registrant may execute the Form 222. The signature on the Form 222 must be by the same person who signed the most recent application for the DEA registration or by a person who has executed a Power of Attorney.

## Power of Attorney (21 CFR § 1305)

In many cases, the DEA registrant may not be the same person who oversees the day-to-day operation of the pharmacy or business entity and may not be responsible for ordering Schedule I and II controlled substances. If that is the case, the DEA registrant utilizes a Power of Attorney that authorizes one or more individuals to obtain and execute the Form 222 on behalf of the registrant. The Power of Attorney requires two signatures for validation. The most recent DEA registrant must sign the form as well as the person to whom authority is being granted. Once a person other than the DEA registrant is granted Power of Attorney, that person has the authority to execute DEA Form 222. The executed Power of Attorney should be kept with all order forms executed under the signature of the person being given the authority to execute the forms. These records must be kept on file for 2 years from the date of execution of the order forms. When a pharmacist is no longer practicing in the location where the Power of Attorney was executed for, a Notice of Revocation needs to be executed by the person who most recently signed the DEA registration or reregistration and two witnesses. The Notice of Revocation must be filed with the revoked Power of Attorney at the designated location. These records need to be kept for the required 2 years and be made available for inspection (Figure 14-4).

The DEA Form 222 contains the name, address, and registration number of the DEA registrant. The form also specifies the type of authorized activity, that is, research, educational institution, pharmacy, and the schedules of controlled substances that the registrant is permitted to work with. The DEA Form 222 cannot be changed or altered by the recipient. If the information on the DEA Form 222 is incorrect, the form must be sent back to the DEA for correction. If the form contains minor misspellings in the name and address of the purchaser, the supplier can accept the form. However, the purchaser should contact the DEA office to obtain corrections in the name and address for future use. No supplier will accept an order form that has erasures, cross outs, or any handwritten or typewritten information on it other than the actual order. When completing the order form, the form is completed by the pharmacy or practitioners office in triplicate by pen, indelible pencil, or typewriter. There are only 10 numbered lines on each order form. Execution of DEA Form 222:

1. One item is ordered per numbered line. An item is one or more commercial or bulk containers of the same finished or bulk form and quantity of the same substance. Multiple units of the same item may be ordered per line.
2. Upon completion of the order form, the DEA registrant makes a notation of the number of lines completed on the order form at the bottom of the DEA Form 222 in the space provided on the left of the form.
3. The registrant completes the name and address of the supplier on the order form. Only one supplier may be listed per form. If the registrant uses more than one supplier, the registrant must complete a separate form for each supplier.
4. The registrant signs the form and dates the form as of the date that the form is completed. Execution of the order is done by the most recent person to register or reregister with DEA or an individual who has been given Power of Attorney. It is not advisable to sign and predate forms because of theft and diversion.

Unexecuted order forms may be kept and may be executed in a location other than the DEA registered location printed on the

**Power of Attorney for DEA Order Forms**

_____(Name of registrant)

_____(Address of registrant)

_____(DEA registration number)

I, _____ (name of person granting power), the undersigned, who is authorized to sign the current application for registration of the above-named registrant under the Controlled Substances Act or Controlled Substances Import and Export Act, have made, constituted, and appointed, and by these presents, do make, constitute, and appoint

_____(name of attorney-in-fact), my true and lawful attorney for me in my name, place, and stead, to execute applications for books of official order forms and to sign such order forms in requisition for Schedule I and II controlled substances, in accordance with section 308 of the Controlled Substances Act (21 U.S.C. 828) and part 1305 of Title 21 of the Code of Federal Regulations. I hereby ratify and confirm all that said attorney shall lawfully do or cause to be done by virtue hereof.

_____

(Signature of person granting power)

I, _____(name of attorney-in-fact), hereby affirm that I am the person named herein as attorney-in-fact and that the signature affixed hereto is my signature.

_____

(Signature of attorney-in-fact)

   Witnesses:
   1. _____

   2. _____

Signed and dated on the _____ day of _____, _____(year),

at _____

**Notice of Revocation**

The foregoing power of attorney is hereby revoked by the undersigned, who is authorized to sign the current application for registration of the above-named registrant under the Controlled Substances Act of the Controlled Substances Import and Export Act.
Written notice of this revocation has been given to the attorney-in-fact

_____ this same day.

_____

(Signature of person revoking power)
Witnesses:
   1. _____

   2. _____

Signed and dated on the _____ day of _____, _____(year).

*Figure 14-4.* Power of Attorney Form.

form. All unused forms must be promptly delivered to the DEA registered site when any federal, state, or local inspector inspects the DEA registered site. The DEA Form 222 must be kept in an area separate from the pharmacy's business records.

Only those manufacturers or distributors that have a valid DEA registration may fill orders for Schedule I and II controlled substances except for the following:

1. Pharmacist discontinuing a pharmacy.
2. Registrant's DEA registration is expiring and the registrant does not intend to reregister.
3. Registrant is returning a Schedule I or II controlled substance to the supplier from whom the Schedule I or II controlled substance was ordered from.
4. Registrant is authorized to conduct chemical analysis or research with Schedule I or II controlled substances.
5. Registered compounder of narcotic substances for use at off-site locations in conjunction with a narcotic treatment program.

When a registered pharmacy transfers Schedule I or II controlled substances to another registered pharmacy, a DEA Form 222 must be used to transfer the stock.

A registered pharmacy completes the DEA Form 222 in triplicate. The pharmacy submits Copy 1 and Copy 2 to the supplier/wholesaler and retains Copy 3 in the pharmacy. The supplier completes the order and records on Copy 1 and Copy 2, the number of commercial or bulk containers supplied on each ordered item and the date the containers were shipped to the pharmacy. DEA policy does not preclude the substitution of identical products differing in packaging size from those initially ordered provided the actual quantity does not exceed the amount initially ordered and the National Drug Code (NDC) number reflected is that of the actual product shipped. For example, if the pharmacy ordered 1 bottle of 500, 10 mg tablets, the supplier can send 5 bottles of 10 mg tablets for a total of 500 as was ordered.

## Defective Order Forms: Errors or Omissions on DEA Form 222

If the purchaser makes an error or an omission on the order form, the supplier may correct the error and send the ordered products provided the error relates to the following:

1. Misspellings of the drug's name. If there is no question as to what the purchaser intended, then the supplier can complete the order without requiring a new order.
2. Date of order is missing. Supplier may fill in the date as of the date of delivery provided the date of delivery is not 60 days or more after the date of receipt.
3. Package size is missing. If the product is supplied in only one size then the supplier may either supply the product without completion of that section of the order form or the supplier may complete the order by including the size of the product. If there are multiple sizes then the supplier will have to void that particular line item with notification to the purchaser.
4. Strength of drug is missing. If the product is supplied as only one strength, then it is not necessary to designate the strength in the "Name of Drug" section of the DEA Form 222. If there are multiple sizes then the supplier will void that particular line item with notification to the purchaser.
5. Number of line items completed is missing. The supplier may not complete this section of the order form. The form is invalid if the purchaser does not complete this section. If the section is completed incorrectly by the purchaser the form is also invalid.
6. Incorrect placement of items on the order form. That is, size is placed in the section for strength or vice versa. The form is acceptable provided there is no question as to what was ordered. If it is unclear then a new order form would have to be executed upon notification by the supplier.

If the order form is illegible, is not executed or endorsed, or the order form shows signs of alteration, erasure, or change, the supplier will not fill the order. If a supplier receives a defective order form that cannot be completed, the supplier will return Copies 1 and 2 of the order form to the purchaser with a statement as to the reason the order was not filled. The supplier has the right to refuse to fill an order for any reason. The supplier does not have to state a reason on the returned order form as to why the form was rejected and returned to the purchaser. It is sufficient for the supplier to state that the order is not acceptable. When the purchaser receives the rejected, returned order forms, the purchaser must attach Copies 1 and 2 to Copy 3 and retain these copies in a file.

The incorrect order form may not be corrected. A new order form must be executed by the purchaser.

## Partial Filling of DEA Form 222

Partial filling of DEA Form 222 orders is permissible under certain circumstances. The balance of the order must be supplied in subsequent shipments within 60 days of the original date of the order. If the order cannot be completed within 60 days of the original date of the order then the order becomes invalid. In this case, the pharmacy would have to execute a new order form for the products listed on the original order form. The order will be shipped to the purchaser at the address listed on the order form. The supplier still retains Copy 1 of the order form and sends Copy 2 to the regional DEA office at the close of the month during which final shipment is made or within the 60-day expiration period. The purchaser must record on Copy 3 the number of commercial or bulk containers received on each item and the dates on which it was received.

## Endorsement of DEA Form 222 Order

Endorsement refers to a situation where a supplier cannot fill all or part of an order within the 60-day limitation and the original supplier endorses the original order over to another supplier for completion of the order. The endorsement must state on the reverse side of Copies 1 and 2 the name and address of the second supplier and must be signed by a person authorized to obtain and execute order forms on behalf of the first supplier. The first supplier may not fill any part of an endorsed order form. The second supplier must fill the order, if possible, and ship the order directly to the purchaser. Orders filled by the second supplier are reported in the same manner except where the name of the supplier is requested; the second supplier must record the name, address, and registration number of the first supplier.

## Lost or Stolen DEA Form 222

If a purchaser executes an order form and the order is not received by the purchaser, the purchaser should call the supplier to whom the order was submitted to inquire as to the status of the order. If the purchaser discerns that the order was never received by the supplier, the purchaser should then prepare a statement with the following information:

1. Serial number of order form executed by purchaser
2. Date of order
3. Statement that the items listed in the order were not received because the form was lost or stolen

Since the purchaser requires the items listed on the lost or stolen order form, the purchaser will execute a second order form in triplicate for the supplier to fill. The statement about the lost order is attached to Copies 1 and 2 of the second order. The purchaser retains a copy of the statement with Copy 3 from the first and second order forms. If the first order form is subsequently received by the supplier, the supplier must write "Not Accepted" on the face of the order form and return Copies 1 and 2 to the purchaser who must attach to Copy 3 of the first order form with the statement about the lost or stolen form.

Used or unused forms that are stolen or lost by the purchaser or supplier must be reported immediately upon discovery of the theft or loss to the Special Agent in Charge of the DEA in the Divisional Office responsible for the area where the registrant is located. The report must contain the serial number for each stolen form. If the serial number is not known, then the date of receipt of the forms and the name and address for the purchaser should be provided. In the event that forms that were lost are found, the DEA should be notified immediately of the discovery of the forms. It is recommended that each purchaser have a mechanism for recoding the serial numbers of the DEA Form 222 that are stored in the facility. The DEA Form 222 should be stored in an area separate from the storage of the serial number documentation.

## Storage of Executed and Unexecuted Order Forms

All orders forms must be kept on file for 2 years from the date of execution. For the purchaser, these records include Copy 3 of the DEA Form 222, all unaccepted or defective order forms received from the supplier, and any statements associated with lost or stolen order forms executed by the purchaser. The supplier will retain Copy 1 for the required 2-year period. All DEA Form 222 must be maintained separately from all other records that the registrant maintains. A supplier of carfentanil, etorphine HCl, and diprenorphine must keep these records separate from all other DEA Form 222 records. All orders for carfentanil, etorphine HCl, and diprenorphine must be kept separate from other Schedule I and II controlled substance orders.

## Return of Unused Order Forms

When a registrant's DEA registration is terminated, revoked, suspended, or the name or address changes, all unused forms must be returned to the nearest DEA office.

## Cancellation and Voiding of Order Forms

A purchaser may cancel part or all of an order by notifying the supplier in writing of the cancellation. The supplier will indicate the cancellation on Copy 1 and 2 of the order form by drawing a line through the canceled items and printing canceled in the space provided for the number of items shipped.

A supplier may void part or all of an order on a DEA Form 222 by notifying the purchaser in writing of the cancellation voiding all or part of the order. The supplier will indicate the void on Copy 1 and 2 of the order form by drawing a line through the voided items and printing void in the space provided for the number of items shipped.

## Electronic 222 (CFR § 1305.21 & 1311)

The DEA's rationale for establishing an electronic process for the ordering of Schedule I and II controlled substances was to provide a means for legal distribution that deters diversion of the controlled substances for illegitimate purposes and to ensure an adequate drug supply of controlled substances. Two significant pieces of legislation have led to this process. The Government Paperwork Elimination Act of 1988 and the Electronic Signatures in Global and National Commerce Act of 2000 required Federal agencies to accept electronic record keeping and reporting and recognized electronic signatures. Electronic versions of DEA Form 222, known as e222 allows registrants to order Schedule I or II controlled substances electronically at <<www.deadiversion.usdoj.gov>>. The DEA Certification Authority issues digital certificates, which serve as an electronic equivalent to DEA Form 222. The digital certificates will not be limited to Schedule I and II controlled substances but will be available for ordering all controlled substances, also. The electronic process will assist suppliers in verifying purchases. DEA issues electronic forms to registrants with information specific to the registrant and the registrant's location. The supplier's software performs the necessary validation confirming the purchaser is authorized by DEA to place orders for Schedule I and/or II controlled substances. The DEA encourages all registrants to use the certificates to order controlled substances. The use of e222 is not mandatory. The DEA Form 222 is still available for those who prefer the paper method. e222 also allows for the maintenance of records electronically. Digital certificates are renewed at the same time as the DEA registration and are valid for the same 3-year period of time that the DEA registration is valid for. Digital certificates cannot be valid beyond the life of a DEA registration because the certificate's validity is based on having an active DEA registration. Practically, therefore, manufacturers, distributors, exporters, researchers, chemical analysts, and narcotic treatment programs would have to renew annually because their DEA registrations are valid for 1 year.

The DEA requires certain information for the e222:

1. Unique number generated by purchaser to track order— 9 character format, last 2 digits of the year, the character "X," and 6 numbers of the purchaser's choice
2. Name of supplier
3. Complete address of supplier
4. Supplier's DEA number
5. Date order is signed
6. Name of controlled substance
7. NDC number
8. Quantity in a single package or container
9. Number of packages or containers of each item ordered

The digital certificate is attached to the order and provides the purchaser's name, registered location, DEA number, business activity, and authorized schedules. The supplier reports to the DEA the following information:

1. Supplier's name, complete address, and DEA number
2. Purchaser's name, address, and DEA number
3. Schedules purchaser is authorized to receive

4. Purchaser's business activity
5. Unique tracking number
6. Date order was signed
7. Name of controlled substance and NDC number
8. Quantity, number of packages ordered, and number of packages shipped
9. Date shipped

The supplier reports this information to the DEA every other business day. Monthly reporting is too long a period in the event of diversion.

## Annotation of Electronic 222 Orders

Once an electronic order is submitted, the original order cannot be altered because it contains an electronic signature. Therefore, the supplier and purchaser have to create separate records that are electronically linked to the original order with information about what the supplier shipped and what the purchaser received. The supplier's linked file would have to contain identification of packages shipped including the date shipped and any other item that the supplier shipped. The purchaser's linked file would have to contain the number of packages received including the date received. All partially filled orders, endorsed orders, or canceled orders must have records linked to the original order also.

## Endorsement of an Electronic 222 Order

Endorsement of electronic orders is permissible. To endorse the whole order to a second supplier, the initial supplier would make a copy of the incoming order, link the copy to a record of the name and address of the secondary supplier, then digitally sign the copy of the order and the linked file using the DEA issued digital certificate. The initial supplier may then transmit the original order and linked endorsement record to the secondary supplier. As an alternative, the initial supplier could fill part of the order, create a linked record indicating what had been filled, then endorse the remainder of the order to a second supplier, adding a second linked record with the second supplier's name and address, and digitally signing the order and linked records. The secondary supplier would have to validate both the purchaser's and the initial supplier's digital certificates before filling the order.

Because the customer can easily generate a new electronic order, the supplier may simply choose to notify the purchaser that the order cannot be filled or filled in its entirety, allowing the purchaser to directly place the order electronically with another supplier. The supplier would then create a linked record voiding all or part of the order.

## Revocation of the Digital Certificate

There are a number of circumstances that would require the revocation of a digital certificate. The Certification Authority would automatically revoke a certificate upon notice of the following:

1. The smart card or other hardware storage device has been lost, stolen, or compromised in any fashion.
2. The password has been forgotten.
3. The private key can no longer be accessed.
4. The certificate would also be revoked if the Certification Authority is notified that any of the information in the certificate changed (e.g., name or address, or new schedules added).
5. Registrant's Power of Attorney has been revoked.

If a DEA registration is revoked or terminated for any reason, all digital certificates linked to that registration would be revoked because the validity of the certificate is linked to the validity of the DEA registration.

## Veterinarian Orders of Carfentanil, Etorphine HCl, or Diprenorphine

When these three substances are ordered for use in a veterinary practice or exotic animal practice, the order form may contain these items only on the form. The quantities ordered must be reasonable and the products must be shipped under secure conditions using secure packaging with no indication on the outside of the packaging as to the contents of the package.

## Pharmacy Termination of DEA Registration

When a pharmacy decides to terminate its pharmacy business, the pharmacy is required to notify the nearest DEA Registration Field Office in *writing* prior to termination. By taking the following action, the pharmacy should be compliant with the CSA and DEA regulations:

1. Send the businesses' DEA Certificate of Registration to the nearest DEA Field Office upon termination of the pharmacy.
2. Send any unused DEA Order Forms (DEA Form 222) to the nearest DEA Field Office.
3. Write or stamp "VOID" across the face of all unused DEA Form 222.
4. Indicate where the controlled substance inventories and records will be maintained upon termination of the pharmacy.
5. Indicate how the controlled substances will be transferred or destroyed.
6. Indicate where all records will be maintained for the required 2-year period from the date of the pharmacy termination.

## Transferring Controlled Substances When Terminating a Pharmacy

Upon termination of a pharmacy, the drug products must be accounted for and disposed of properly. For controlled substances there must be an accounting and a record of the disposition of the drug products. Controlled substances may be transferred to another pharmacy, a supplier, a manufacturer, or a distributor registered to dispose of controlled substances. To transfer Schedule I and II controlled substances, the receiving registrant must issue a DEA Form 222 to the registrant transferring the drugs.

The transfer of Schedule III–V controlled substances must be documented in writing including the drug name, dosage form, strength, quantity, and date transferred. The document must include the names, addresses, and DEA registration numbers of the parties involved in the transfer of the controlled substances.

## Transfer of Business to Another DEA Registrant

A registrant transferring a pharmacy business to another registrant shall notify the nearest DEA Registration Field Office at least 14 days before the date of the proposed transfer and provide the following information:

1. The name, address, registration number of the registrant discontinuing business.
2. The name, address, registration number of the registrant acquiring the pharmacy.

3. Whether the business activities will be continued at the location registered by the current business owner or moved to another location. If the latter, give the address of the new location.
4. The date on which the controlled substances will be transferred to the person acquiring the pharmacy.

On the day of the transfer of the controlled substances, a complete controlled substance inventory must be conducted. A record of the inventory must remain with the pharmacy transferring the controlled substance. A copy of the inventory must accompany the transfer of the controlled substances to the person acquiring the pharmacy.

If the transfer is to a new pharmacy, the new pharmacy should obtain a state pharmacy license to facilitate the process. If the registrant acquiring the pharmacy owns at least one other pharmacy licensed in the same state as the pharmacy being transferred, the registrant may apply for a new DEA registration prior to the date of transfer. DEA will issue a registration which will authorize the registrant to obtain controlled substances at the time of transfer. But the registrant may not dispense controlled substances until the pharmacy has been issued a valid state pharmacy license. If the transfer is to an existing pharmacy, the DEA registration process can be expedited if the applicant includes an affidavit verifying that the pharmacy has been registered by the state licensing agency. The affidavit verifying the existence of the state license should be attached to the initial application for registration.

## Day of Controlled Substance Transfer to Another Pharmacy

On the day the controlled substances are transferred, a complete inventory must be taken which documents the drug name, dosage form, strength, quantity, and date transferred. In addition, DEA Form 222 must be prepared to document the transfer of Schedule I and II controlled substances. This inventory will serve as the final inventory for the registrant going out of business and transferring the controlled substances. It will also serve as the initial inventory for the registrant acquiring the controlled substances. A copy of the inventory must be included in the records of each registrant. It is not necessary to send a copy of the inventory to the DEA. The registrant acquiring the controlled substances must maintain all records involved in the transfer of the controlled substances for 2 years and the registrant terminating the business must maintain a record of the transfer for 2 years.

## Day of Controlled Substance Transfer to Another Supplier or Manufacturer

If the transfer of the controlled substance is to a supplier or manufacturer, the pharmacist must maintain a written record of the transfer showing the following:

1. The date of the transaction.
2. The name, strength, form, and quantity of the controlled substance.
3. The supplier's or manufacturer's name, address, and, if known, registration number.
4. The DEA Form 222 will be the official record for the transfer of Schedule I and II controlled substances.

## Disposal and Destruction of Controlled Substances

A pharmacy may return unused controlled substances to the supplier from which the substances were obtained. The pharmacy may also hire an outside firm to inventory, package, and arrange for the transfer of its controlled substances to another pharmacy, supplier, or manufacturer. The pharmacy is responsible for the actual transfer of the controlled substances and for the accuracy of the inventory and records. The pharmacy may also transfer the drugs to a distributor registered with DEA to destroy drugs (reverse distributor). The pharmacy may not turn over any controlled substances to a distributor unless the reverse distributor is registered to destroy controlled substances. The pharmacy is responsible for verifying that the reverse distributor is registered with DEA. The records involving the transfer or destruction of controlled substances must be kept readily available for 2 years for inspection and copying by the DEA. The two primary methods for disposing of controlled substances are transfer to another registrant or destruction as explained below in the section entitles "Transfer of controlled substances to a Reverse Distributor Registered to Dispose of Controlled Substances."

## Transfer of Controlled Substances to a Reverse Distributor Registered to Dispose of Controlled Substances

Any pharmacy may forward controlled substances to a DEA registered reverse distributor who handles the disposal of drugs. DEA recommends that any pharmacy seeking to dispose of controlled substances first contact the nearest DEA Diversion Field Office for disposal instructions. Controlled substances for disposal are not to be sent to the DEA without prior approval from the DEA. The laws of each state must also be complied with. Registrants who request authorization from the DEA to dispose of controlled substances may have to follow the procedures set forth in state law especially if the disposal is to be done outside of the presence of the DEA. In many cases, the registrant may have to obtain both DEA approval for disposal of controlled substances and state approval before any action can be taken.

## Once-a-Year DEA Authorization for Destruction of Controlled Substances

Once a year, the DEA grants retail pharmacies, if requested, the authority to destroy damaged, outdated, or otherwise unwanted controlled substances. The pharmacy must complete DEA Form 41 (Registrants Inventory of Drugs Surrendered; Figure 14-5), listing all drugs to be destroyed. In addition, the pharmacy must prepare a letter requesting permission to destroy the controlled substances, proposing a date and method of destruction, and listing the names of at least two people who will witness the destruction. The witnesses should be a licensed physician, pharmacist, midlevel practitioner, nurse, or a state or local law enforcement officer. Both documents must be received by the nearest DEA Diversion Field Office at least 2 weeks prior to the proposed destruction date. After reviewing all available information, the DEA office will then notify the registrant in writing of its decision. During the same time period, the pharmacy should also contact the state authority responsible for overseeing the proper handling of controlled substances to obtain its authority. Once the controlled substances have been destroyed, signed copies of the DEA Form 41 must be forwarded to DEA (and in most probability to the state authority as well). The pharmacy should maintain all records associated with the destruction for at least 2 years from the date of destruction.

| OMB Approval No. 1117 - 0007 | U.S. Department of Justice Drug Enforcement Administration **REGISTRANTS INVENTORY OF DRUGS SURRENDERED** | PACKAGE NO. |
|---|---|---|

The following schedule is an inventory of controlled substances which is hereby surrendered to you for proper disposition.

FROM: (Include Name, Street, City, State and ZIP Code in space provided below.)

Signature of applicant or author ized agent

Registrant's DEA Number

Registrant's Telephone Number

NOTE: CERTIFIED MAIL (Return Receipt Requested) IS REQUIRED FOR SHIPMENTS OF DRUGS VIA U.S. POSTAL SERVICE. See instructions on reverse (page 2) of form.

| NAME OF DRUG OR PREPARATION — Registrants will fill in Columns 1,2,3, and 4 ONLY. | Number of Containers | CONTENTS (Number of grams, tablets, ounces or other units per container) | Controlled Substance Content, (Each Unit) | FOR DEA USE ONLY DISPOSITION | QUANTITY GMS. | MGS. |
|---|---|---|---|---|---|---|
| 1 | 2 | 3 | 4 | 5 | 6 | 7 |
| 1 | | | | | | |
| 2 | | | | | | |
| 3 | | | | | | |
| 4 | | | | | | |
| 5 | | | | | | |
| 6 | | | | | | |
| 7 | | | | | | |
| 8 | | | | | | |
| 9 | | | | | | |
| 10 | | | | | | |
| 11 | | | | | | |
| 12 | | | | | | |
| 13 | | | | | | |
| 14 | | | | | | |
| 15 | | | | | | |
| 16 | | | | | | |

FORM DEA-41 (9-01)    Previous edition dated **6-86** is usable    See instructions on reverse (page 2) of form

***Figure 14-5.*** DEA Form 41.

DEA-41 (6/1986) Pg. 2

| NAME OF DRUG OR PREPARATION | Number of Containers | CONTENTS (Number of grams, tablets, ounces or other units per container) | Controlled Substance Content, (Each Unit) | FOR DEA USE ONLY | | |
|---|---|---|---|---|---|---|
| | | | | DISPOSITION | QUANTITY | |
| | | | | | GMS. | MGS. |
| Registrants will fill in Columns 1, 2, 3, and 4 ONLY.<br>1 | 2 | 3 | 4 | 5 | 6 | 7 |
| 17 | | | | | | |
| 18 | | | | | | |
| 19 | | | | | | |
| 20 | | | | | | |
| 21 | | | | | | |
| 22 | | | | | | |
| 23 | | | | | | |
| 24 | | | | | | |

The controlled substances surrendered in accordance with Title 21 of the Code of Federal Regulations, Section 1307.21, have been received in _____packages purporting to contain the drugs listed on this inventory and have been:  ** (1) Forwarded tape-sealed without opening; (2) Destroyed as indicated and the remainder forwarded tape-sealed after verifying contents; (3) Forwarded tape-sealed after verifying contents.

DATE _____     DESTROYED BY: _____

** Strike out lines not applicable.

WITNESSED BY: _____

## INSTRUCTIONS

1. List the name of the drug in column 1, the number of containers in column 2, the size of each container in column 3, and in column 4 the controlled substance content of each unit described in column 3; e.g., morphine sulfate tabs., 3 pkgs., 100 tabs., 1/4 gr. (16 mg.) or morphine sulfate tabs.,1 pkg., 83 tabs., 1/2 gr. (32mg.), etc.

2. All packages included on a single line should be identical in name, content and controlled substance strength.

3. Prepare this form in quadruplicate. Mail two (2) copies of this form to the Special Agent in Charge, under separate cover. Enclose one additional copy in the shipment with the drugs. Retain one copy for your records. One copy will be returned to you as a receipt. No further receipt will be furnished to you unless specifically requested. Any further inquiries concerning these drugs should be addressed to the DEA District Office which serves your area.

4. There is no provision for payment for drugs surrendered.  This is merely a service rendered to registrants enabling them to clear their stocks and records of unwanted items.

5. Drugs should be shipped tape-sealed via prepaid express or certified mail (**return receipt requested**) to Special Agent in Charge, Drug Enforcement Administration, of the DEA District Office which serves your area.

### PRIVACY ACT INFORMATION

AUTHORITY: Section 307 of the Controlled Substances Act of 1970 (PL 91-513).
PURPOSE: To document the surrender of controlled substances which have been forwarded by registrants to DEA for disposal.
ROUTINE USES: This form is required by Federal Regulations for the surrender of unwanted Controlled Substances. Disclosures of information from this system are made to the following categories of users for the purposes stated.
  A. Other Federal law enforcement and regulatory agencies for law enforcement and regulatory purposes.
  B. State and local law enforcement and regulatory agencies for law enforcement and regulatory purposes.
EFFECT:  Failure to document the surrender of unwanted Controlled Substances may result in prosecution for violation of the Controlled Substances Act.

Under the Paperwork Reduction Act, a person is not required to respond to a collection of information unless it displays a currently valid OMB control number.  Public reporting burden for this collection of information is estimated to average 30 minutes per response, including the time for reviewing instructions, searching existing data sources, gathering and maintaining the data needed, and completing and reviewing the collection of information.  Send comments regarding this burden estimate or any other aspect of this collection of information, including suggestions for reducing this burden, to the Drug Enforcement Administration, FOI and Records Management Section, Washington, D.C. 20537; and to the Office of Management and Budget, Paperwork Reduction Project no. 1117-0007, Washington, D.C. 20503.

*Figure 14-5.*  *(Continued)*

The pharmacist should contact local environmental authorities prior to implementing the proposed method of destruction to ascertain that hazards are not associated with the destruction.

## Exception to DEA Authorization for Destruction of Controlled Substances

Prior DEA authorization to destroy controlled substances is not necessary when an authorized member of a state law enforcement authority or regulatory agency witnesses the destruction. Copies of DEA Form 41 or state controlled substance destruction form must still be forwarded to the local DEA Diversion Office after the destruction. The pharmacy should maintain a copy of the form as well for 2 years from the date of destruction.

## Reverse Distributors Authorized to Destroy Controlled Substances

A pharmacy may at any time forward controlled substances to DEA registered reverse distributors who handle the disposal of drugs. The pharmacist may contact the local DEA Diversion Field Office for an updated list of those reverse distributors in his or her area. When a pharmacy transfers Schedule I and II controlled substances to a reverse distributor for destruction, the distributor must issue a DEA Form 222 to the pharmacy. When Schedule III–V controlled substances are transferred to a reverse distributor for destruction, the pharmacy should document in writing the drug name, dosage form, strength, quantity, and date transferred. The DEA registered reverse distributor who will destroy the controlled substances is responsible for submitting a DEA Form 41 to the DEA when the drugs have been destroyed. A DEA Form 41 should not be used to record the transfer of controlled substances between the pharmacy and the registered reverse distributor disposing of the drugs.

## "Blanket Authorization" for Destruction of Controlled Substances

The DEA issues "Blanket Authorizations" for destruction of controlled substances on a very limited basis. The only registrants who the DEA issues this authorization to are associated with hospitals, clinics, or other registrants having to dispose of used needles, syringes, or other injectable objects only. The reason for the limited exception is there is a high probability that those objects have been contaminated by hazardous bodily fluids and destruction of the objects is in the best interest of all. A request of blanket authorization is initiated by the pharmacist. The DEA evaluate the following in determining whether to grant the request or not:

1. The frequency of destruction (i.e., daily, weekly) and the quantity of drugs requiring destruction.
2. The method of destruction. All drugs must be rendered unusable.
3. The registrant's past history with destroying controlled substances.
4. The security in place at the pharmacy or registered location.
5. The name and position of the individual responsible for the destruction.

Once a blanket authorization is granted, the registrants will complete DEA Form 41.

## Controlled Substance Theft or Loss

The pharmacy is responsible for notifying the DEA, the appropriate State agency, and the Local Police of any suspected theft or significant loss of any controlled substances, regardless of the schedule. This should be done immediately upon the discovery of the suspected theft or loss. If the pharmacy is unsure of whether a theft or significant loss has occurred, the pharmacy should err on the side of caution and let the DEA know of the possibility. The DEA will investigate and make a determination as to whether the theft or loss was real and significant. If the pharmacy is part of a larger entity such as a corporation, the DEA still needs to be notified. It is the pharmacy's responsibility to notify the DEA not the corporate headquarters. It is not a good idea to assume that by notifying the corporate headquarters of the suspected theft or loss that the corporate headquarters will notify the DEA. Again this is another case of erring on the side of caution. Therefore, it is recommended that the pharmacy notify the DEA first and then notify the corporate headquarters Documentation of all action taken by the pharmacy would be prudent with records maintained for 2 years. DEA Form 106 (Report of Theft or Loss of Controlled Substances) must be completed. This form is used to report the theft or loss of controlled substances. The form will document the circumstances of the theft or loss and the identification and quantities of the drugs involved. This form is not to be used to report minor inventory adjustments to the DEA. The original DEA Form 106 and a copy of it are sent to the DEA Diversion Field Office and the pharmacy retains a copy for its records for 2 years. Failure to report theft or loss of controlled substances may result in penalties under Section 402 and 403 of the CSA.

DEA Form 106 (Figure 14-6) should contain the following information:

1. Name and address of registered establishment
2. DEA registration number of establishment
3. Date of theft
4. Name and telephone number of local police notified
5. Descriptions of the theft, that is, robbery, break in at night, internal
6. Listing of special markings or codes used by the registered establishment for cost identification or storage (if any)
7. Listing of controlled substance missing from theft or significant loss

(See also the U.S. Department of Justice's web site for the DEA at http://www.deadiversion.usdoj.gov/21cfr_reports/theft/index.html.)

If the investigation reveals that there was no theft or significant loss, DEA Form 106 does not need to be filed with the DEA. The registrant should notify the DEA in writing that there was no finding of theft or significant loss so that the initial case can then be closed. Records associated with the suspected theft or loss should be maintained by the registered establishment for 2 years.

Significant loss is a judgment call on the part of the registrant and it is better to err on the side of caution by letting the DEA know of any suspicion. What may be a significant loss to one registrant may not be a significant loss to another. Some considerations when determining if a loss is significant or not:

1. The schedule of the missing items.
2. The abuse potential of the missing items.
3. The abuse potential in the local area of the missing substance.
4. The quantity missing (one tablet vs. one bottle or container).
5. Whether this was the first time or a recurring problem.
6. Whether the loss was reported to local law enforcement authorities or not.
7. Always err on the side of caution and report to DEA.

## REPORT OF THEFT OR LOSS OF CONTROLLED SUBSTANCES

Federal Regulations require registrants to submit a detailed report of any theft or loss of Controlled Substances to the Drug Enforcement Administration.

Complete the front and back of this form in triplicate. Forward the original and duplicate copies to the nearest DEA Office. Retain the triplicate copy for your records. Some states may also require a copy of this report.

OMB APPROVAL
No. 1117-0001

| 1. Name and Address of Registrant (include ZIP Code) | 2. Phone No. (Include Area Code) |
|---|---|

ZIP CODE

3. DEA Registration Number

2 ltr. prefix          7 digit suffix

4. Date of Theft or Loss

5. Principal Business of Registrant (Check one)
- 1 ☐ Pharmacy
- 2 ☐ Practitioner
- 3 ☐ Manufacturer
- 4 ☐ Hospital/Clinic
- 5 ☐ Distributor
- 6 ☐ Methadone Program
- 7 ☐ Other (Specify)

6. County in which Registrant is located

7. Was Theft reported to Police?
☐ Yes   ☐ No

8. Name and Telephone Number of Police Department (Include Area Code)

9. Number of Thefts or Losses Registrant has experienced in the past 24 months

10. Type of Theft or Loss (Check one and complete items below as appropriate)
- 1 ☐ Night break-in
- 2 ☐ Armed robbery
- 3 ☐ Employee pilferage
- 4 ☐ Customer theft
- 5 ☐ Other (Explain)
- 6 ☐ Lost in transit (Complete Item 14)

11. If Armed Robbery, was anyone:
Killed? ☐ No   ☐ Yes (How many) _____
Injured? ☐ No   ☐ Yes (How many) _____

12. Purchase value to registrant of Controlled Substances taken?
$

13. Were any pharmaceuticals or merchandise taken?
☐ No   ☐ Yes (Est. Value)
$

14. IF LOST IN TRANSIT, COMPLETE THE FOLLOWING:

A. Name of Common Carrier

B. Name of Consignee

C. Consignee's DEA Registration Number

D. Was the carton received by the customer?
☐ Yes   ☐ No

E. If received, did it appear to be tampered with?
☐ Yes   ☐ No

F. Have you experienced losses in transit from this same carrier in the past?
☐ No   ☐ Yes (How Many) _____

15. What identifying marks, symbols, or price codes were on the labels of these containers that would assist in identifying the products?

16. If Official Controlled Substance Order Forms (DEA-222) were stolen, give numbers.

17. What security measures have been taken to prevent future thefts or losses?

### PRIVACY ACT INFORMATION

AUTHORITY: Section 301 of the Controlled Substances Act of 1970 (PL 91-513).
PURPOSE: Report theft or loss of Controlled Substances.
ROUTINE USES: The Controlled Substances Act authorizes the production of special reports required for statistical and analytical purposes. Disclosures of information from this system are made to the following categories of users for the purposes stated:

A. Other Federal law enforcement and regulatory agencies for law enforcement and regulatory purposes.

B. State and local law enforcement and regulatory agencies for law enforcement and regulatory purposes.

EFFECT: Failure to report theft or loss of controlled substances may result in penalties under Section 402 and 403 of the Controlled Substances Act.

In accordance with the Paperwork Reduction Act of 1995, no person is required to respond to a collection of information unless it displays a ly valid OMB control number. The valid OMB control number for this collection of information is 1117-0001. Public reporting burden for this collection of information is estimated to average 30 minutes per response, including the time for reviewing instructions, searching existing data sources, gathering and maintaining the data needed, and completing and reviewing the collection of information.

**FORM DEA** - 106 (11-00) *Previous editions obsolete*

CONTINUE ON REVERSE

***Figure 14-6.*** DEA Form 106.

**FORM DEA-106 (Nov. 2000) Pg. 2**

## LIST OF CONTROLLED SUBSTANCES LOST

| Trade Name of Substance or Preparation | Name of Controlled Substance in Preparation | Dosage Strength and Form | Quantity |
|---|---|---|---|
| **Examples:** Desoxyn | Methamphetamine Hydrochloride | 5 mg Tablets | 3 x 100 |
| Demerol | Meperidine Hydrochloride | 50 mg/ml Vial | 5 x 30 ml |
| Robitussin A-C | Codeine Phosphate | 2 mg/cc Liquid | 12 Pints |
| 1. | | | |
| 2. | | | |
| 3. | | | |
| 4. | | | |
| 5. | | | |
| 6. | | | |
| 7. | | | |
| 8. | | | |
| 9. | | | |
| 10. | | | |
| 11. | | | |
| 12. | | | |
| 13. | | | |
| 14. | | | |
| 15. | | | |
| 16. | | | |
| 17. | | | |
| 18. | | | |
| 19. | | | |
| 20. | | | |
| 21. | | | |
| 22. | | | |
| 23. | | | |
| 24. | | | |
| 25. | | | |
| 26. | | | |
| 27. | | | |
| 28. | | | |
| 29. | | | |
| 30. | | | |
| 31. | | | |
| 32. | | | |
| 33. | | | |
| 34. | | | |
| 35. | | | |
| 36. | | | |
| 37. | | | |
| 38. | | | |
| 39. | | | |
| 40. | | | |
| 41. | | | |
| 42. | | | |
| 43. | | | |
| 44. | | | |
| 45. | | | |
| 46. | | | |
| 47. | | | |
| 48. | | | |
| 49. | | | |
| 50. | | | |

I certify that the foregoing information is correct to the best of my knowledge and belief.

_____     _____     _____
Signature                   Title                       Date

***Figure 14-6.*** *(Continued)*

## Federal Investigation of Thefts and Robberies

The Controlled Substances Registrant Protection Act of 1984 grants authority for the federal investigation of pharmaceutical thefts and robberies under the following circumstances:

1. Replacement cost of the controlled substances taken is $500 or more.
2. A registrant or other person is killed or suffers "significant" bodily injury during the commission of the robbery or theft of a controlled substance.
3. Interstate or foreign commerce is involved in planning or executing the crime.

## Penalties for Conviction under the Controlled Substances Registrant Protection Act

Penalties for conviction under Controlled Substances Registrant Protection Act:

1. Commission of burglary or robbery—maximum $25,000 fine and/or 20 years imprisonment.
2. Use of a dangerous weapon in the commission of the crime—maximum $35,000 fine and/or 25 years imprisonment.
3. Death resulting from the crime—maximum $50,000 fine and/or life imprisonment.

## In Transit Loss of Controlled Substances

In the event an order for controlled substances is not received by the pharmacy or other registered establishment after the order has been filled by the supplier, the order is considered to have been lost in transit. Under these circumstances, the supplier is responsible for notification of the DEA of the loss. Once the purchaser receives the controlled substances from the supplier, then the responsibility shifts to the purchaser.

## Breakage/Spillage of Controlled Substance

The DEA does not consider breakage and spillage of controlled substances a loss. This is considered a form of destruction. The DEA considers the product to be damaged thereby requiring destruction or disposal of the product. Recovered product and damaged product may be returned to a reverse distributor or a DEA-approved process using DEA Form 41. This is considered a minor inventory adjustment and DEA does not view it as a theft or loss.

# Controlled Substance Record Keeping Requirements

The diversion and abuse potential associated with controlled substances warrants extensive record keeping involving every aspect of the controlled substances, from manufacturing to acquisition to dispensing to disposal/destruction. Purchasers are required to keep complete and accurate records for each controlled substance manufactured, purchased, received, distributed, dispensed, or otherwise disposed of for 2 years. All records must be available to the DEA for inspection and copying. All records and inventories of Schedule II controlled substances must be maintained separately from *all* other records of the registrant. All records and inventories of Schedule III–V controlled substances must be maintained either separately from all other records or in such a form that the information is *readily retrievable* from the ordinary business records at the time of DEA inspection.

Readily retrievable means that:

1. Records can be accessed in a reasonable time regardless of the system used to store the records.
2. Records are easily accessed through the use of an identification symbol or character that distinguishes the records from the other business records.

# Controlled Substance Records That Must be Maintained

The purchaser must maintain the following records:

1. DEA Form 222—the official Schedule I and II order form
2. Power of Attorney authorization to sign DEA Form 222
3. Receipts and invoices for Schedule III–V controlled substances
4. All inventory records of controlled substances, including the initial and biennial inventories
5. Records of controlled substances distributed or dispensed (i.e., prescriptions)

6. Report of theft or significant loss—DEA Form 106
7. Inventory of drugs surrendered for disposal—DEA Form 41
8. Records of transfers of controlled substances between pharmacies
9. DEA registration certificate

## Central Record Keeping of Controlled Substances (21 CFR § 1304.04)

Registrants, who have multiple registered locations, that is, chain pharmacies, may determine that it is better to maintain controlled substance records at a central location. The registrants must notify the nearest DEA Diversion Filed Office of their interest in housing records for the associated registered establishments centrally as opposed to housing the records at each individual location. This is one case where inaction on the part of the DEA grants the registrant permission. If the DEA does not respond to the request, the registrant is thereby granted permission to keep the records at the central location beginning 14 days from the date of request. The DEA no longer issues central record keeping permits.

## Prescription Records of Controlled Substances

A pharmacy may utilize one of three available options for storing controlled substance prescription records. These records must be stored for 2 years from the date of last fill. The CFR recognizes the following three options:

1. *Option 1* (three separate files):
   • One file for Schedule II controlled substances dispensed.
   • One file for Schedule III–V controlled substances dispensed.
   • One file for prescription orders for all noncontrolled drugs dispensed.
2. *Option 2* (two separate files):
   • One file for all Schedule II controlled substances dispensed.
   • One file for all other drugs dispensed (noncontrolled and those controlled substances in Schedule III–V). If this method is used, a prescription for a Schedule III–V

controlled substance must be made readily retrievable by use of a red "C" stamp not less than 1 in. high. If a pharmacy has an electronic record keeping system for prescriptions which permits identification by prescription number and retrieval of original documents by the prescriber's name, patient's name, drug dispensed, and date filled, then the requirement to mark the hard copy prescription with a red "C" is waived.

3. *Option 3* (two separate files):
   - One file for all Schedule II–V controlled substances. If this method is used, a prescription for a Schedule II–V controlled substance must be made readily retrievable by use of a red "C" stamp not less than 1 in. high. If a pharmacy has an electronic record keeping system for prescriptions which permits identification by prescription number and retrieval of original documents by the prescriber's name, patient's name, drug dispensed, and date filled, then the requirement to mark the hard copy prescription with a red "C" is waived.
   - One file for prescription orders for all noncontrolled drugs dispensed.

All prescription records must be readily retrievable for DEA inspection.

## Computer Use for the Storage of Controlled Substance Records

Computers have made record storage much more manageable. An alternative to the three options listed above is to store records in a computer system. This is valid only for Schedules III–V controlled substances. Schedule II controlled substances must be stored separately.

This system can be utilized for online retrieval of original prescription information for prescriptions with authorized refills. The original prescription information retrieved should include at least the following:

1. Original prescription number
2. Date of issue
3. Full name and address of the patient
4. Prescriber's name, address, and DEA registration number

5. Name, strength, dosage form, and quantity of the controlled substance prescribed
6. Total number of refills authorized by the prescriber

The refill information retrieved should include at least the following:

1. Name of controlled substance
2. Date of refill
3. Quantity dispensed
4. Dispensing pharmacist's name/initials for each refill
5. Total number of refills dispensed to date for that prescription

The pharmacist is responsible for verifying the accuracy of the data contained in the computer system, for the original prescription information, and the refills. At the close of business, the pharmacy computer system should provide a hard copy of the each day's controlled substances prescriptions. The hard copy should be reviewed, verified, and signed by *each* pharmacist who was responsible for filling the prescriptions noted on the report. The hard copy report must be maintained in a separate file for 2 years from the date of last fill. The pharmacy must have an auxiliary procedure for downtime in the event that the computer is not functioning. A pharmacy may use only one of the two systems described (i.e., manual or computer).

## Controlled Substance Inventory Requirements

The CFR requires that all registrants conduct an inventory of all controlled substances. The inventory is not sent to the DEA but is maintained at the registered location in a readily retrievable manner for copying and inspection by the DEA for 2 years from the date of the inventory. The inventory of Schedule II controlled substances must be kept separate from those for all other controlled substances.

**INITIAL INVENTORY**

Once a pharmacy has been issued a registration by the DEA, the pharmacy must conduct a controlled substance initial inventory. The inventory includes an actual physical count of all controlled substances in the possession of the pharmacy. If the pharmacy does not have any controlled substances in its possession at the time that the DEA registration is issued then the registrant records a zero inventory on the inventory form. The inventory is maintained in a readily retrievable manner at the registered location for copying and inspection by the DEA.

The CFR requires that the inventory include:

1. The inventory date
2. The time the inventory is taken (i.e., opening or close of business)
3. The drug name
4. The drug strength
5. The drug form (e.g., tablet, capsule, and so forth)
6. The number of units/volume
7. The total quantity

DEA recommends that the inventory record also include:

1. The name, address, and DEA registration number of the registrant
2. The signature of the person or persons responsible for taking the inventory

**BIENNIAL INVENTORY**

An operating pharmacy must conduct a biennial inventory (every 2 years) after the initial inventory. The biennial inventory requires the same information as the initial inventory. The inventory may be taken at any time within the 2-year period from the initial inventory or previous inventory provided it is within the 2-year time period not after. The biennial inventory is not sent to the DEA but is maintained at the registrant's location for 2 years for copying and inspection by the DEA.

All Schedule II controlled substances must be counted. No estimation of Schedule II controlled substances is permissible. Inventory of Schedule III–V controlled substances may be estimated unless the container is opened and holds a quantity of more than 1000 dosage units.

The biennial inventory must contain the following information:

1. Time of inventory, either beginning or close of business
2. Names of controlled substances
3. Each finished form of the substances (i.e., 10 mg tablet)
4. Number of dosage units of each finished form in the commercial container (100 tablet bottle)
5. The number of commercial containers of each finished form (i.e., five 100 tablet bottles)
6. Disposition of the controlled substance

A practitioner who maintains an office supply of controlled substances, must conduct a biennial inventory also including any samples received from pharmaceutical companies.

## Inventorying Newly Scheduled Controlled Substances

When a new drug is scheduled, all registrants must inventory the drug as of the effective date of scheduling. The new controlled substance is added to the previous inventory including all of the information for the new drug as specified above.

## Inventory of Controlled Substances for Destruction or No Longer Saleable

An inventory must be made by each registrant for every controlled substance that is (1) damaged, defective, or impure and is awaiting disposal, (2) held for quality control purposes, or (3) maintained for extemporaneous compoundings.

The CFR requires that the inventory of controlled substances for destruction or no longer saleable include:

1. The inventory date
2. The drug name
3. The drug strength
4. The drug form (e.g., tablet, capsule, and so forth)
5. The total quantity or total number of units/volume
6. The reason why the substance is being maintained
7. Whether substance could be used in the manufacture of any controlled substance in finished form

## Prescription Requirements for Controlled Substances

Upon presentation of a controlled substance prescription by a patient, the pharmacist must determine if the prescription is valid prior to dispensing the drug product. The prescription must meet the legal requirements of both federal and state law for controlled substance prescriptions. A distinction is made between a prescription and a medication order. A prescription is intended for dispensing medication to an ultimate user. A medication order is intended to be administered to a patient in a hospital. Since the medication order is not intended for self-administration, the medication order is not considered a prescription.

Prescriptions must be signed and dated on the date of issue. Prescriptions should not be pre- or postdated. This can lead to diversion and abuse. The prescription must contain the following information:

1. Patient's full name and address
2. Practitioner's name, address, and DEA number
3. Drug name and strength, dosage form, reason prescribed
4. Directions for use
5. Number of refills, with a zero if there are no refills intended

The practitioner should write the prescription using indelible pencil, ink, or a typewriter with the signature in the practitioner's own hand. The practitioner may delegate a staff member to prepare the prescription. The practitioner is ultimately responsible for the contents of the prescription. The practitioner must insure that the prescription is correct and that the prescription meets the laws, rules, and regulations for a controlled substance prescription, regardless of whether he or she delegated the preparation of the prescription to a staff member or not.

Prescriptions may be issued by physicians, dentists, podiatrists, veterinarians, midlevel practitioners, and any other registered practitioner who is authorized to prescribe controlled substances by the jurisdiction in which the practitioner practices. The practitioner must be licensed with the DEA or must be recognized by the DEA as an exempt practitioner (i.e., Public Health Service, Bureau of Prisons).

## Use of a Hospital's DEA Number

A hospital's DEA number may be used by authorized practitioners who cannot obtain their own DEA number. An intern, resident, staff physician, or midlevel practitioner who is an employee of a hospital or other institution may use the hospital's DEA number to prescribe controlled substances provided the following circumstances are met:

1. Controlled substances are dispensed, administered, or prescribed in the usual course of practice.
2. Authority to prescribe controlled substances has been granted to the practitioner by the state that the practitioner is practicing in.

3. The hospital has verified that the practitioner has the authority to dispense, administer, or prescribe in the state.
4. The practitioner acts only within his or her scope of employment.
5. The hospital authorizes the practitioner to dispense or prescribe under the hospital's DEA number with a code assigned to the practitioner that identifies the practitioner.
6. The hospital maintains a current list of the assigned codes and practitioners. The hospital must make the list of codes available to regulatory agencies, enforcement agencies, and other registrants for verification purposes.

## Practitioners Exempt from DEA Registration

Practitioners practicing in the Public Health Service and the Bureau of Prisons are exempt from registering with the DEA when they engage in prescribing, dispensing, or administering controlled substances. The exempt practitioners must include their agency and the service identification number of the issuing official in lieu of the DEA registration number for all controlled substance prescriptions.

## Military Registration Requirement

Military practitioners are also exempt from DEA registration for prescribing, dispensing, administering, or purchasing controlled substances. Military practitioners must indicate the branch of service or agency and their service identification number in lieu of the DEA registration number. These prescriptions may be filled off base at nonmilitary facilities. Because of problems with computer programs not recognizing service identification numbers at nonmilitary pharmacies, the DEA has started to issue DEA numbers to military practitioners to facilitate the pharmacy transaction off base. A military practitioner may have a service identification number or a DEA number depending on the area in which he or she practices.

Midlevel military practitioners will be issued DEA registration numbers only if they are allowed to dispense, prescribe, and administer controlled substances in the state in which they are stationed.

If a military practitioner engages in practice outside of the military, he or she must obtain a separate DEA number for the non-military practice.

## Midlevel Practitioners

21 CFR § 1300.01(b28) defines a "midlevel practitioner as an individual practitioner, other than a physician, dentist, veterinarian, or podiatrist, who is licensed, registered, or otherwise permitted by the United States or the jurisdiction in which he or she practices, to dispense a controlled substance in the course of professional practice." Examples of midlevel practitioners include, but are not limited to, health care providers such as nurse practitioners, nurse midwives, nurse anesthetists, clinical nurse specialists, and physician assistants who are authorized to dispense controlled substances by the state in which they practice. The state regulates whether midlevel practitioners have the authority to prescribe, dispense, or administer controlled substances. Some states may allow dispensing, prescribing, or administering of only certain schedules of controlled substances.

The following web site provides information about midlevel practitioner controlled substance authorization by state: <<http://www.deadiversion.usdoj.gov/drugreg/practioners/index.html>>.

Midlevel practitioners may receive individual DEA registrations granting controlled substance privileges. Midlevel practitioners' DEA registration will begin with the letter "M." Just because a midlevel practitioner has a DEA registration number does not mean that the midlevel practitioner is authorized to prescribe, administer, or dispense all schedules of controlled substance. Verification with the state authority is advisable.

## Who may Issue Prescriptions for Controlled Substances

Prescriptions may be issued only by an authorized registered practitioner, such as a physician, dentist, podiatrist, veterinarian, or midlevel practitioner who is:

1. Authorized to prescribe controlled substance by the jurisdiction in which the practitioner is licensed to practice
2. Registered with DEA or exempt from registration

3. An agent or employee of a hospital or other institution acting in the normal course of business or employment under the registration of the hospital

# Purpose of Issue (21 CFR § 1306.04(A))

A practitioner acting in the usual course of his or her professional practice may issue a prescription for a controlled substance. The controlled substance prescription is valid only if the prescription is issued for a legitimate medical purpose. The practitioner must document the purpose for issuing the controlled substance prescription. Practitioners are responsible for the proper prescribing and dispensing of controlled substances. Pharmacists have a corresponding responsibility for the proper dispensing of the controlled substance. If a valid controlled substance prescription is not issued in the usual course of professional practice, treatment, or research, for a legitimate purpose, the prescription is not a valid prescription within the meaning and intent of the CSA. The practitioner who knowingly issues the invalid prescription and/or the pharmacist who knowingly dispenses the invalid prescription will be subject to criminal and/or civil penalties and administrative sanctions.

Office supplies for controlled substances must be obtained by purchase through a legitimate DEA registered supplier. The practitioner cannot write a prescription for controlled substances for "office use." A prescription written for "office use" is not a valid prescription and would not be filled by a pharmacy.

# Schedule II Controlled Substances

Schedule II controlled substances are strictly controlled. They have a high abuse potential and they are highly addictive. Schedule II prescriptions must be written and signed by the practitioner on the date of issue. There is no date by which a prescription for a Schedule II controlled substance must be filled. There also is no limit on the days supply. Verify with your state authority what midlevel practitioners are authorized to prescribe Schedule II controlled substances. Your state may also have a requirement that a controlled substance prescription be filled within 30 days of issuance of the prescription and there may be a restriction as to the days supply that can be issued. A pharmacist should use his or her professional judgment in assessing whether a controlled substance prescription is necessary for the patient, especially if a long period of time has elapsed since the date the prescription was issued and the date of presentation for filling by the patient. If a determination is made by the pharmacist that the prescription is no longer necessary for the appropriate treatment of the patient, the pharmacist should call the prescribing practitioner before consulting with the patient.

## Emergency Dispensing of Schedule II Controlled Substances

Oral prescriptions for Schedule II controlled substances are permitted for emergency situations only. Emergency refers to situations where:

1. Immediate administration of the drug is necessary for proper treatment of the intended ultimate use.
2. No alternative treatment is available (including a drug which is not a Schedule II controlled substance).
3. The prescribing practitioner cannot provide a written prescription for the drug at that time.

In a bona fide emergency, a practitioner may telephone a Schedule II prescription to the pharmacy or transmit the prescription by facsimile to the pharmacy, and the pharmacist may dispense the prescription provided that:

1. The amount prescribed and ultimately dispensed is limited to the amount necessary to treat the patient during the emergency period. There is no limitation on the quantity that a practitioner can prescribe in the event of an emergency. It is the practitioner's professional judgment as to what quantity is sufficient to adequately treat the patient during the emergency. If the controlled substance is to be continued after the emergency period, the practitioner must issue a written prescription for the additional period of time.
2. The receiving pharmacist reduces the telephone prescription order to writing with all of the information required to make the prescription a valid order (except for the prescriber's signature).
3. The pharmacist makes a good faith effort to verify the identity of the practitioner if the practitioner is not known to the pharmacist and the patient if the patient is not known to the pharmacist.

4. The practitioner provides the pharmacy with a signed prescription within 7 days after authorizing an emergency telephone prescription. The prescription may be delivered in person by the practitioner or the patient. If delivered to the pharmacy by mail it must be postmarked within the 7-day period. The delivered (cover) prescription must have the following words written on the face of the prescription "Authorization for Emergency Dispensing." The receiving pharmacist must attach the written prescription (cover) to the oral prescription reduced to writing by the pharmacist. If the pharmacy does not receive the written prescription (cover) within the 7-day period, the law requires that the pharmacy notify the nearest DEA Diversion Field Office that the prescriber has failed to provide a written prescription within the required timeframe. Failure of the pharmacist to notify the DEA may invalidate the pharmacist's authority to accept and dispense oral Schedule II controlled substance prescriptions. State law may require that state agencies be notified also.

## Schedule II Controlled Substance Refills (21 U.S.C. § 829(A))

No refills are allowed on a Schedule II controlled substance prescription.

## Schedule II Controlled Substance Partial Dispensing

There are several circumstances where partial dispensing of Schedule II controlled substances is permissible:

1. The pharmacist is unable to supply the full quantity on a written prescription or emergency oral prescription. The pharmacist must make a notation on the front of the prescription of the quantity dispensed. The balance of the prescription may be dispensed within 72 hours of the initial partial dispensing. If the balance of the prescription cannot be dispensed within the 72 hours, the remainder of the prescription is forfeited. The pharmacist should notify the prescriber that a portion of the prescription was filled and that the prescription could not be filled to completion, so the patient does not have to go without the prescription. A new

prescription for the balance of the prescription will have to be written by the prescriber.

2. The patient is a resident of a Long-Term Care Facility (LTCF). A notation must be made on the prescription that the patient is a resident of a LTCF. If this notation is not made and the prescription is filled, the filling will be in violation of the CSA. A LTCF is a nursing home, retirement care, mental care, or other facility or institution which provides extended health care to resident patients. Most of these facilities are not registered with the DEA even though they maintain controlled substances for their residents. The controlled substances are considered to have been dispensed to their ultimate user even though the ultimate user is a resident of a LTCF. Since state agencies may have different requirements for the handling of Schedule II controlled substances, it would be prudent to verify state requirements also.

3. The patient has been diagnosed with a terminal illness. If there is any question regarding the patient's status, the pharmacist should contact the practitioner and verify prior to partially dispensing the prescription. This responsibility lies on both the pharmacist and the practitioner. There must be a notation made on the prescription that the patient is "terminally ill." The absence of this notation will cause a prescription to be filled in violation of the CSA.

When a pharmacist partially fills a prescription, the pharmacist must note on the prescription the date of the partial filling, the quantity dispensed on that date, the quantity remaining on that particular fill, and the initials or signature of the dispensing pharmacist. Partially filled prescriptions are valid for 60 days from the date of issue. Individual states may have stricter requirements so consult with your state agency prior to dispensing Schedule II controlled substances. The prescription is valid for 60 days from the date of issue unless the practitioner terminates the prescription or the patient expires.

## Facsimile Prescriptions for Schedule II Controlled Substances

Occasionally, prescriptions will be faxed to a pharmacy for expeditious filling for a patient in need. Under these circumstances, the patient is required to present the prescription to the pharmacist for verification against the faxed prescription prior to the pharmacist providing the filled prescription to the patient. The original prescription and the faxed prescription are filed together in the records for controlled substances. State law may be more restrictive and may prohibit this practice.

If the practitioner transmits an emergency prescription via fax to the pharmacy, the prescription is treated as a telephone order and the practitioner is required to send a written signed prescription to the pharmacy within 7 days of the date of the fax. This is a convenient method of transmission, however, the requirements for an emergency prescription apply and the practitioner must comply with the follow-up requirements set forth by the DEA.

The DEA recognizes three circumstances where the facsimile prescription for a Schedule II controlled substance prescription will be treated as the original prescription, thereby not requiring a follow-up prescription to the facsimile:

1. Prescriptions for patients receiving home infusion/ intravenous (IV) pain therapy.
2. Prescriptions for patients in LTCF. The practitioner's agent may also transmit the prescription to the pharmacy. The facsimile prescription serves as the original written prescription for the pharmacy. No further original prescription is required.
3. Prescriptions for patients in hospice care as certified by Medicare under Title XVIII or licensed by the state. Patients in hospice care may have prescriptions transmitted to the dispensing pharmacy by facsimile regardless of whether the patient resides in a hospice facility or other care setting.

In all of the three exceptions listed above, the practitioner's agent may transmit the prescription to the pharmacy. In this case, the practitioner will note on the prescription that it is for a hospice or LTCF patient. The facsimile will serve as the original written prescription.

## Transfer of Schedule II Controlled Substances

The transfer of Schedule II controlled substance prescriptions is not permissible.

# Schedule III, IV, or V Controlled Substances

Prescriptions for Schedule III, IV, or V controlled substances may be written, oral, or faxed. Refills may be authorized by the practitioner provided they are indicated on the face of the prescription. A Schedule III, IV, or V controlled substance prescription may be refilled up to a maximum of five times within a 6-month period of time after the date of issue. The key is the date of issue not the date of filling. The 6-month time period runs from the date the prescription was issued not the date that the pharmacy fills the prescription. After five refills have been exhausted or the 6-month timeframe has been expired, the patient must obtain a new prescription.

A pharmacist must record the following information on the back of a prescription when a pharmacist refills a Schedule III, IV, or V controlled substance prescription:

1. Dispensing pharmacist's initials
2. Date of refill
3. Amount of drug dispensed

In those cases where the pharmacists record only their initials and the date on the back of the prescription, the full amount of the originally filled prescription is the amount that is considered to have been refilled.

# Facsimile Prescriptions for Schedule III, IV, or V Substances

Fax prescriptions for Schedules III, IV, or V controlled substances are permissible and the fax is treated as the original prescription.

# Telephone Authorization for Schedule III, IV, or V Controlled Substance Prescriptions

Schedule III, IV, or V controlled substance prescriptions may be transmitted to the pharmacy via telephone by the practitioner or an agent or employee of the practitioner. The pharmacist is charged with the responsibility of verifying the validity of the telephone prescription orders.

## Transfer of Schedule III, IV, or V Controlled Substance Prescriptions

Provided state allows, Schedule III, IV, or V controlled substance refill prescriptions may be transferred between pharmacies on a onetime basis. For those pharmacies that electronically share a real time online database (i.e., chain pharmacies), the pharmacy may transfer up to the maximum number of refills allowed by the practitioner on the prescription. The requirements necessary for the transfer are as follows:

1.  The transfer must occur between two licensed pharmacists.
2.  The word VOID must be written on the face of the invalidated prescription. On the reverse side of the invalidated prescription, the name, address, and DEA registration number of the pharmacy to which the prescription was transferred and the name of the pharmacist receiving the prescription information must be recorded; the date of the transfer and the name of the pharmacist transferring the information.
3.  The pharmacist receiving the transferred prescription information must reduce to writing the prescription information including the date of issuance of original prescription; original number of refills; date of original dispensing; number of valid refills remaining; date(s) and location of previous refill(s); pharmacy name, address, DEA number, and prescription number from which the prescription information was transferred; name of pharmacist who transferred the prescription; pharmacy's name, address, DEA number, and prescription number from original.
4.  The original and transferred prescription must be maintained for 2 years from the date of last refill.

Those pharmacies that can electronically access the same prescription must include all of the necessary information as if the transfer was for manual prescriptions. The transfer of Schedule III, IV, or V controlled substance prescriptions is permissible only if state law allows.

## Emergency Dispensing of Schedule III, IV, or V Controlled Substance

Oral prescriptions for Schedule III, IV, or V controlled substances are permitted for emergency situations only. Emergency refers to situations where:

1. Immediate administration of the drug is necessary for proper treatment of the intended ultimate user.
2. No alternative treatment is available (including a drug which is not a Schedule II controlled substance).
3. The prescribing practitioner cannot provide a written prescription for the drug at that time.

In a bona fide emergency, a practitioner may telephone a Schedule III, IV, or V controlled substance prescription to the pharmacy or transmit the prescription by facsimile to the pharmacy, and the pharmacist may dispense the prescription provided that:

1. The amount prescribed and ultimately dispensed is limited to the amount necessary to treat the patient during the emergency period. There is no limitation on the quantity that a practitioner can prescribe in the event of an emergency. It is the practitioner's professional judgment as to what quantity is sufficient to adequately treat the patient during the emergency. If the controlled substance is to be continued after the emergency period, the practitioner must issue a written prescription for the additional period of time.
2. The receiving pharmacist reduces the telephone prescription order to writing with all of the information required to make the prescription a valid order (except for the prescriber's signature).
3. The pharmacist makes a good faith effort to verify the identity of the practitioner if the practitioner is not known to the pharmacist and the patient if the patient is not known to the pharmacist.
4. The practitioner provides the pharmacy with a signed prescription within 7 days after authorizing an emergency telephone prescription. The prescription may be delivered in person by the practitioner or the patient. If delivered to the pharmacy by mail it must be postmarked within the 7-day period. The receiving pharmacist must attach the written prescription (cover) to the oral prescription reduced to writing by the pharmacist. If the pharmacy does not receive the written prescription (cover) within the 7-day period, the pharmacy must make a notation on the back of the prescription that the written prescription (cover) was not received.

## Partial Filling of Schedule III, IV, or V Controlled Substances

Partial filling of Schedule III, IV, or V controlled substances is permissible. The pharmacist must initial the back of the prescription and record the date of the partial filling. The partial filling may not exceed the original quantity authorized on the prescription. All partial fillings expire 6 months from the date of issue of the prescription. Even though the number of partial fillings may exceed the number of authorized refills the partial fillings are considered one refill for each time period.

## Over-the-Counter Dispensing of Controlled Substances

There are still some states that permit the sale of Schedule II, III, IV, and V controlled substances over the counter. Only those controlled substances that are not a prescription item under the Federal Food, Drug and Cosmetic Act may be dispensed without a prescription at retail provided that:

1. They are dispensed by a pharmacist only. This responsibility cannot be delegated to a nonpharmacist.
2. The pharmacist must ensure the medical necessity or the need for the product since there is no medical supervision for Schedule V controlled substances.
3. Not more than 240 mL (8 fluid ounces) or not more than 48 solid dosage units of any substance containing opium, not more than 120 mL (4 fluid ounces) or not more than 24 solid dosage units of any other controlled substance, may be distributed at retail to the same purchaser in any given 48-hour period without a valid prescription.
4. The purchaser must be least 18 years of age.
5. The pharmacist must verify the identity and age of any customer the pharmacist does not know prior to the purchase.
6. The pharmacy must maintain a Schedule V bound record book, containing the name and address of the purchaser, the name and quantity of the controlled substance purchased, the date of each sale, and the initials of the dispensing pharmacist. The Schedule V bound book must be maintained for 2 years from the date of the last transaction entered.

State law should be checked to determine if the product requires a prescription.

## Dispensing Controlled Substances

The prescription label for a controlled substance must contain the following information:

1. Pharmacy name and address
2. Prescription number
3. Initial date of dispensing
4. Patient name
5. Prescribing practitioner name
6. Directions for use and any cautionary statements

The dispensed product must have a label affixed to it that states: "CAUTION: Federal law prohibits the transfer of this drug to any person other than the patient for whom it was prescribed."

## Controlled Substances and Internet Pharmacies

Internet pharmacies that offer controlled substances for sale must register their actual physical location with the DEA and any necessary state agency. If the Internet pharmacy maintains a central pharmacy warehouse site and offices where prescriptions are verified and controlled substances are shipped, the central pharmacy warehouse and office must be registered with DEA as a retail pharmacy. If an Internet site directs patients to pick up their prescriptions for controlled substances from a local pharmacy, then the local pharmacy must be registered with the DEA. If the Internet site does not have a physical location that handles controlled substances, then the Internet site does not have to register with the DEA. State law may require that the Internet site register with the state authority, also.

The concern with Internet pharmacies is the existence of a doctor-patient relationship. All controlled substances must be written for a legitimate medical purpose, hence the reason for the relationship. There are four elements that help to demonstrate the existence of a legitimate doctor-patient relationship:

1. Patient has a medical complaint.
2. Practitioner has taken a medical history.
3. Practitioner has performed a physical examination.
4. The medical complaint, the medical history, and the physical examination, all necessitate the use of a controlled substance.

## Electronic Transmission of Controlled Substance Prescriptions

The DEA is currently engaged in a project to establish the requirements for secure electronic transmission of all controlled substance prescriptions between the practitioner and the pharmacy. To date this has not been implemented.

Proposed security requirements include:

- Authentication of the prescriber
- Content integrity
- Nonrepudiation of involvement by parties to a transaction

## Schedule III, IV, *or* V Controlled Substance Prescriptions

A pharmacist may receive a controlled substance prescription for Schedule III, IV, or V as a written prescription; a facsimile transmitted by the practitioner; or an oral prescription. If the prescription is an oral prescription the pharmacist must immediately reduce the prescription to writing ensuring that the prescription contains all the necessary information required by the DEA and state law. At the printing of this book, the electronic transmission of controlled substance prescriptions is not considered valid. However, a prescription received via the Internet could be treated as an oral prescription. The pharmacist would be required to contact the practitioner and obtain the information from the practitioner including all the required information. The practitioner has 7 days to deliver a written follow-up prescription to the pharmacy. For oral Schedule III, IV, and V controlled substance prescriptions, the pharmacy is not responsible for notifying the DEA if a written follow-up prescription within the 7-day requirement is not received. The pharmacy does have an obligation to make a notation on the back of the oral prescription that it did not receive the written follow up within the 7-day period of time.

## Central Fill Pharmacies (21CFR § 1304.05)

Central fill pharmacies process requests from another pharmacy to fill or refill prescription drug orders. The central fill pharmacy may also perform drug utilization reviews, claim adjudications, refill authorizations, and therapeutic interventions. The prescriptions may be controlled substances. There must be a contract between the central fill pharmacy and the retail pharmacy or the owner of the central fill pharmacy and the retail pharmacy must be the same. Both the central fill pharmacy and the retail pharmacy must have a valid DEA registration number for the dispensing of controlled substances. Both pharmacies must maintain the required records for the handling of controlled substances. Security measures must be observed for the central fill pharmacy as well as the retail pharmacy. If a retail pharmacy acts as a central fill pharmacy, separate DEA registration, separate inventories, or separate records are not required.

A central fill pharmacy is not open for walk in pharmacy business. A patient cannot walk into the central fill pharmacy and request that a prescription be filled. The central fill pharmacy cannot accept phone prescriptions from a practitioner and it cannot deliver a filled prescription to a practitioner or a patient. The central fill pharmacy must receive the prescription from the retail pharmacy. There are two ways that the prescription can be transmitted to the central fill pharmacy. (1) Facsimile transmission the retail pharmacy can send a facsimile of the prescription. The retail pharmacy maintains the original prescription and the central fill pharmacy maintains the facsimile of the prescription. (2) Electronic transmission the DEA allows electronic transmission by the retail pharmacy to the central fill pharmacy. Both pharmacies must maintain the prescription information in a readily retrievable manner and must comply with all applicable federal and state record keeping requirements.

Every retail pharmacy that contracts with a central fill pharmacy must maintain records of all central fill pharmacies that are authorized to fill prescriptions on behalf of the retail pharmacy. These records must include the name, address, and DEA number of the central fill pharmacy. It is the responsibility of the retail pharmacy to verify the registration for each central fill pharmacy authorized to fill prescriptions on its behalf.

The central fill pharmacies have the same responsibility and must maintain records of all retail pharmacies that they contract with. These records must include the name, address, and DEA number for each of the contracted retail pharmacies. Likewise, the central fill pharmacies are responsible for verifying the registration of all retail pharmacies that they fill prescriptions for. All records must be made available to the DEA for inspection and copying.

# Emergency Kits for Long-Term Care Facilities

The DEA has issued a policy statement which provides individual state licensing and regulatory boards with general guidelines for establishing specific rules concerning controlled substances used in emergency kits at LTCF. Check with your state licensing board to determine what controlled substances are permissible in emergency kits in LTCF in your state.

# DEA Guidelines for Emergency Kits in Long-Term Care Facilities Not Registered with the DEA

The placement of emergency kits containing controlled substances in LTCF not registered with the DEA will be deemed in compliance with the Comprehensive Drug Abuse Prevention and Control Act of 1970, if the appropriate state agency or regulatory authority specifically approves such placement, and sets forth procedures that require the following:

1. *Source of supply*: The LTCF must obtain controlled substances for the emergency kits from a DEA registered hospital/clinic, pharmacy, or practitioner.
2. *Security safeguards*: Access to each emergency kit in the LTCF must be restricted and the type and quantity of controlled substances which may be placed in the emergency kit must be specifically limited.
3. *Proper control, accountability, and record keeping*: The LTCF and the DEA registered hospital/clinic, pharmacy, or practitioner providing the controlled substances must maintain complete and accurate records of the controlled substances placed in the emergency kit including the disposition of these controlled substances, including periodic physical inventories of the drugs.
4. *Administration of controlled substances*: In emergency medical situations when medication is needed from the emergency kit, only LTCF personnel who is authorized by an individual practitioner can administer the controlled substances.
5. *Prohibited activities*: Prohibited activities can result in the state revoking, suspending, or denying emergency kits containing controlled substances in a LTCF.

Refer to your state for laws regulating emergency medical kits in LTCF.

# Controlled Substance Distribution by a Pharmacy

A pharmacy registered to dispense controlled substances may distribute such substances (without being registered as a distributor) to another pharmacy or to a practitioner to dispense, provided that the following conditions are met:

1. The pharmacy or practitioner is registered under the CSA to dispense controlled substances.
2. The pharmacy records indicate that it distributed the controlled substances and the recipient pharmacy or practitioner records indicate that they received the controlled substances.
3. If a Schedule II controlled substance is distributed, the transfer must be documented on a DEA Form 222. The distributing pharmacy must record the following information on a DEA Form 222:
   - The name of the substance, the dosage form, and the quantity
   - The name, address, and DEA registration number of the pharmacy or practitioner to whom it is distributed
4. **Five Percent Rule**. The total number of dosage units of controlled substances distributed by a pharmacy may not exceed 5% of all controlled substances dispensed by the pharmacy during a calendar year. If at any time the controlled substances distributed exceeds 5%, the pharmacy is also required to register as a distributor

SUGGESTED READINGS

United States Drug Enforcement Administration Diversion Control Program Web site. www.deadiversion.usdoj.gov. Accessed December 15, 2006.

United States Department of Health and Human Services. Substance Abuse and Mental Health Services Administration (SAMHSA) Web site. dpt.samhsa.gov/regulation.htm. Accessed December 15, 2006.

# 15 FDA Authority and Internet Sales

## FDA Authority in Internet Sales

The Food and Drug Administration (FDA) under the Food, Drug and Cosmetic Act, has the legal authority to take action against:

1. The sale, distribution, or importation of an adulterated or misbranded drug
2. The sale, distribution, or importation of an unapproved new drug
3. Illegal promotion of a drug
4. The sale or dispensing of a prescription drug without a valid prescription
5. Counterfeit drugs

When the Internet is used for an illegal sale, the FDA works with the Department of Justice:

1. To establish the grounds for a case
2. To develop the same charges
3. To take the same actions

The action taken by the FDA and the Department of Justice is no different for an Internet pharmacy than a storefront. The FDA has investigated and referred numerous cases for criminal prosecution and initiated civil enforcement actions against online sellers of drugs and other FDA-regulated products, particularly sellers of drugs not approved by the FDA.

The National Association of Boards of Pharmacy (NABP) established the Verified Internet Pharmacy Practice Sites (VIPPS) in response to public safety concerns about Internet pharmacies. A pharmacy that wants to be VIPPS accredited must comply with the following requirements:

1. The pharmacies must meet the licensing and inspection requirements of the state in which they are located and each and every state that they distribute drug product to.
2. The pharmacies must demonstrate to NABP that their site includes patient rights to privacy, authentication, and security of prescription orders, adherence to a recognized quality assurance policy, and the provision of meaningful consultation between patients and pharmacists.

Internet pharmacy sites that have been accredited by VIPPS are identified by the VIPPS hyperlink seal displayed on their web site. The hyperlink seal allows access to the NABP VIPPS web site where verified information about the pharmacy is maintained by NABP. The VIPPS site has a section for consumers, one for pharmacists, and one for pharmacies. The site can be accessed at <<www.nabp.net/vipps>>.

## Electronic Transmission of Prescriptions

The Drug Enforcement Administration (DEA) is currently engaged in a project to establish the requirements for secure electronic transmission of all controlled substance prescriptions between the practitioner and the pharmacy. To date this has not been implemented.

Proposed security requirements include:

- Authentication of the prescriber
- Content integrity
- Nonrepudiation of involvement by parties to a transaction

### SUGGESTED READINGS

National Association of Boards of Pharmacy Web site. www.nabp.net. Accessed December 15, 2006.

U. S. Food and Drug Administration Web site. www.fda.gov. Accessed December 15, 2006.

# 16 Opioid Addiction Treatment and Methadone Use

## Opioid Addiction Treatment History

The Comprehensive Drug Abuse Prevention and Control Act of 1970 approved the use of methadone to wean narcotic-dependent individuals from opiates. The use of methadone for the treatment of addiction has always been controversial because of the potential for abuse and diversion. The Narcotic Addict Treatment Act of 1974 was the law that governed the use of narcotics and the treatment of addiction in the United States. In addition, the law designated which government agencies were responsible for narcotic treatment programs, defined the terms "maintenance" and "detoxification," placed more stringent controls on the use of methadone to treat addiction, and explained who had to register to treat patients for drug dependence. The dispensing of methadone was restricted to registered practitioners only. The Food and Drug Administration (FDA) in conjunction with the National Institute on Drug Abuse (NIDA) established recommended practices as guidelines.

Today the programs are referred to as Opioid Treatment Programs which are comprehensive maintenance programs for narcotic addicts.

Terms frequently used in Opioid Treatment Programs include:

- *Addiction*: Combination of physical dependence on, behavioral manifestations of the use of and subjective sense of the need of and craving for a psychoactive substance, leading to compulsive use of the substance either for its positive effects or to avoid negative effects associated with abstinence from the substance.

- *Comprehensive maintenance treatment*: Continuous therapy with medication in conjunction with a wide range of medical, psychiatric, and psychosocial services.
- *Dependence*: State of physical adaptation that is manifested by a drug class-specific withdrawal syndrome that can be produced by abrupt cessation, rapid dose reduction, decreasing blood level of a substance, and/or administration of an antagonist.
- *Detoxification*: Treatment for addiction to an illicit substance in which the substance is eliminated gradually from a patient's body while various types and levels of reinforcing treatment are provided to alleviate adverse physical and psychological reactions to the withdrawal process.
- *Interim maintenance treatment*: A time limited pharmacotherapeutic regimen in conjunction with appropriate medical services while a patient awaits transfer to an Opioid Treatment Program that provides comprehensive maintenance treatment.
- *Medication unit*: Facility established as part of, but geographically separate from an Opioid Treatment Program, from which certified private practitioners or community pharmacists may dispense or administer opioid agonist medications for observed ingestion.
- *Office-based opioid treatment*: Medication provided in a physician-based office or other approved health care setting.
- *Opioid addiction*: Cluster of cognitive, behavioral, and physiologic symptoms resulting from continuation of opioid use despite significant related problems.
- *Opioid addiction treatment*: Dispensing of approved medication to prevent withdrawal and craving during elimination of opioid use by a patient in medication-assisted treatment (MAT), with or without a comprehensive range of medical and rehabilitative services or medication prescribed when necessary to alleviate the adverse medical, psychological, or physical effects.

- *Opioid Treatment Program*: Substance Abuse and Mental Health Services Administration (SAMHSA) certified program, usually comprising a facility, staff, administration, patients, and services that engages in supervised assessment and treatment, using methadone, buprenorphine, L-α-acetylmethadol (LAAM), or naltrexone, of individuals who are addicted to opioids.
- *Withdrawal*: Reduction and elimination of substance use.
- *Withdrawal syndrome*: Predictable constellation of signs and symptoms after abrupt discontinuation of or rapid decrease in use of a substance that has been used consistently for a period of time.

Opioid addiction treatment pharmacotherapy is appropriate for persons who are currently addicted to an opioid and became addicted at least 1 year before admission to the program. Physicians can make exceptions to the 1-year rule if patients were recently released from prison, patients are pregnant, or patients were previously treated up to 2 years after discharge.

In 2001, the administrative responsibility and oversight of the use of narcotic drugs in the maintenance and detoxification treatment of opioid addiction was transferred from the FDA to the SAMHSA, a division of the United States Department of Health and Human Services. After the transfer, treatment of opioid addiction became focused on clinically driven MAT, with methadone, with an individualized patient care program. The goal was to treat the patient as a whole addressing his or her addiction as well as the ability to become or remain a functioning member of the community. The drugs used today to treat opioid addiction include methadone, LAAM, buprenorphine (Subutex), buprenorphine-naloxone (Suboxone), and naltrexone. In 2001, the use of LAAM was restricted to patients who were not responsive to methadone because cardiac arrhythmias were associated with the drug. Because of the restrictive use of LAAM and the reduced supply LAAM is no longer routinely used especially in new patients. Naltrexone patients should be abstinent from all short-acting opioids for at least 7 days and all long-acting opioids such as methadone for at least 10 days to avoid potential serious withdrawal symptoms. MAT for opioid addiction using methadone, LAAM, or buprenorphine involves the several phases as well as psychosocial and medical treatment.

## Treatment Plans

All treatment is individualized. Relapses are a common occurrence for patients in any of these programs.

Each patient must enter the program voluntarily with written program-specific informed consent. All information associated with the treatment program is confidential (42 CFR part 2). The program physician must document that treatment is medically necessary. The patient must meet the definition of opioid dependence. The patient's behavior should be indicative of addictive behavior including his or her continued use of opiates, obtaining illicit opiates, using prescribed opiates inappropriately, and one or more unsuccessful attempts to withdraw from opiates. The lack of physiologic dependence should not be a criterion for exclusion from a program.

The initial treatment phase includes a comprehensive physical examination, laboratory workup, psychosocial assessment, preliminary treatment plan, and patient orientation.

## Comprehensive Physical Assessment

*Physical examination*: The physician needs to assess the patient's degree of dependence. In examining the patient, the physician attempts to ascertain clinical signs of addiction, that is, fresh needle marks, constricted or dilated pupils, deviated nasal septum, and signs or symptoms of withdrawal or the absence of withdrawal, that is, rhinorrhea, chills, restlessness, irritability, perspiration, nausea, or diarrhea.

*Medical and family history*: Family information including sex and date of birth of children, parents, siblings with medical and drug use histories.

*Psychiatric history and mental status evaluation*: Is suicide an issue? Has the patient been previously evaluated for mental health issues?

*Vocational and educational evaluation*: Does the patient have a job? What job skills does the patient possess? Is the patient enrolled in school or college or vocational training?

*Laboratory evaluation*: Recommended tests include TB skin test, screening for syphilis, hepatitis B, HIV, and recent drug use. Other recommendations include complete blood count (CBC),

ECG, chest x-ray, Pap smear, sickle cell, and sexually transmitted diseases. Urine drug testing is sometimes utilized to test for opiates, methadone, amphetamines, cocaine, and barbiturates.

*Therapeutic dosages*: The goal of medication usage is:

1. Prevent the onset of withdrawal symptoms for 24 hours or more.
2. Reduce or eliminate the drug hunger or craving associated with addiction.
3. Inhibit the effects of illicit self-administered opioids, such as euphoria.
4. Ability to function normally.

*Use of methadone*: The initial recommended dose of methadone is 20–30 mg. If the program physician determines that a higher dosage is necessary to prevent the onset of withdrawal symptoms, the program physician must document the need for the higher dosage. If after 2 hours, the patient is still exhibiting withdrawal symptoms the program physician may increase the total dose to 40 mg, with appropriate documentation. Methadone is administered once a day. LAAM is a longer-acting drug and cannot be administered once a day. Methadone is administered orally unless the patient is admitted to a hospital for an emergency or a medical procedure. Hospitalized patients can be administered methadone intramuscularly. An adequate daily dose of methadone can suppress withdrawal symptoms for 24–36 hours. Methadone is always administered in a liquid formulation. LAAM is administered as a liquid, also. LAAM is colored so that it is easily distinguished from the liquid formulation of methadone.

Methadone is frequently used to treat heroin, codeine, hydrocodone, oxycodone, and morphine addictions. Methadone when used as prescribed, is safe and effective and does not cause euphoric sensations but does relieve physical withdrawal symptoms and reduces physiologic cravings. Methadone does have side effects which may be intolerable to some patients. They include: constipation, water retention, drowsiness, skin rash, excessive sweating, and change in sex drive. Methadone has been used successfully in the treatment of opioid addiction for over 30 years.

*Use of buprenorphine*: Buprenorphine is a sublingual tablet available as either Subutex, which is monotherapy, or Suboxone, which is a combination of 4 mg of buprenorphine and 1 mg of naloxone.

*Use of naltrexone*: Naltrexone has no narcotic effect and has poor patient compliance. Naltrexone is produced under the brand name of DePade in 25, 50, and 100 mg tablets.

Persons under 18 years of age are required to have had two documented attempts at short-term detoxification or psychosocial treatment within 12 months to be eligible for maintenance treatment. A parent, legal guardian, or responsible adult must sign the consent form for the person unless they are an emancipated minor. Age appropriate treatment is a requirement.

## Phases of Maintenance Treatment

The *Acute Phase* focuses on eliminating the use of illicit opioids for at least 24 hours and eliminating the abuse of other psychoactive substances. This phase looks into alcohol and drug use, any medical concerns such as infectious diseases, sickle cell anemia, or surgical needs, psychiatric disorders, basic living issues, therapeutic relationship, and motivation.

The *Rehabilitative Phase* focuses on providing patients with skills needed to cope with major life problems with a goal of enabling them to pursue and achieve life's long-term goals. The patient should be in the stabilization phase of the drug treatment plan. This phase looks into alcohol and drug use, medical concerns, psychiatric disorders, vocational and educational needs, family issues, and legal problems.

The *Supportive Care Phase* focuses on continued opioid therapy, counseling, medical care, and resumption of the patients' normal life. This phase continues to address treatment issues including alcohol and drug use, medical and mental health concerns, vocational and educational issues, family issues, and legal issues. Patients in this phase are eligible for take-home medications and less frequent visits to the treatment program or the physician's office.

The *Medical Maintenance Phase* focuses on patient's eligibility:

1. Patient has been in continuous treatment for 2 years.
2. Patient has been abstinent from illicit drug use and prescription drug abuse.
3. Patient has been abstinent from alcohol use.

4. Patient's living arrangements are stable and free from substance abuse.
5. Patient has a stable and legal source of income.
6. Patient is gainfully employed, successfully enrolled in school, or successfully running a household.
7. Patient has sufficient social support.

The *Tapering Phase* or medically supervised withdrawal phase is the gradual reduction and elimination of maintenance medication. As the medication is being tapered, intensified support services should be provided, including counseling and monitoring of behavioral and emotional situations. The risk of relapse is very high because of the physical and emotional stress of tapering the medication. If tapering is successful, the patient usually requires continued support for 3–12 months after the tapering.

The *Continuing Care Phase* focuses on medical follow up by a primary care physician with occasional check ups with the Opioid Treatment Program or Office-Based Opioid Treatment and involvement and participation in recovery support groups. Follow-up care usually continues for an additional 6–12 months.

# Drug Testing

Drug testing is utilized to detect substance abuse and to monitor patient compliance. At least eight random drug tests must be performed annually. Urine drug testing is used to test for opiates, methamphetamines, cocaine, and barbiturates. The test should be sensitive for the treatment medication so that compliance can be assured. No precise test is available for the testing of buprenorphine, therefore, drug testing for patients on buprenorphine should be for substance abuse not patient compliance. Urine drug testing is the most common testing of the Opioid Treatment Programs. Oral fluid testing and blood testing is also available but is not easily administered and is too costly. Urine drug testing is easy to do and cost-efficient. The clinic determines the frequency of urine drug testing. False results are a concern. As a result of false results, no clinical decisions are based solely on the results of urine drug testing.

## Take-Home Medication—Unsupervised Approved Use

Programs consider the following in determining whether a patient is a good candidate for take-home medication:

1. Cessation of illicit drug use
2. Program attendance
3. Length of time in program and dosage
4. Criminal activity
5. Serious behavioral problems
6. Drug abuse including alcohol
7. Other special needs such as pain management
8. At home security of medication
9. Stability of patient's home environment
10. Employment, enrollment in school, daily life activity
11. Difficulty associated with traveling to and from program

Take-home medication guidelines:

a. First 90 days of treatment (months 1–3)—maximum of one unsupervised dose per week
b. Second 90 days of treatment (months 4–6)—maximum of two unsupervised doses per week
c. Third 90 days (months 7–9)—maximum of three unsupervised doses per week
d. Remainder of year 1 (months 10–12)—maximum of six unsupervised doses per week
e. After 1 year of continuous treatment—maximum of 2 weeks' unsupervised doses
f. After 2 years of continuous treatment—a maximum of 30 unsupervised doses per month

No take-home medication is permissible for patients in short-tem detoxification or interim maintenance treatment. Emergencies are treated on a case-by-case basis. Usually, one time period not to exceed 3 days is sufficient to cover the emergency.

## Buprenorphine—Drug Addiction Treatment Act

The Drug Addiction Treatment Act of 2000 (DATA 2000), Title XXXV, Section 3502 of the Children's Health Act of 2000, permits physicians who meet certain qualifications to treat opioid addiction with Schedule III, IV, and V narcotic medications that have been specifically approved by the FDA for that indication. Such medications may be prescribed and dispensed by qualified physicians in treatment settings other than the traditional Opioid Treatment Program setting. Physicians are licensed under state law and board specialty certified. The physician is assigned an identification number, Drug Enforcement Administration (DEA) number with an "X." Only qualified office-based *physicians* are allowed to prescribe Schedule III, IV, and V medications to addicted persons. Midlevel practitioners are not qualified to participate in the DATA.

Buprenorphine is a Schedule III controlled substance available as Subutex buprenorphine sublingual tablets—2 mg and 8 mg; or Suboxone buprenorphine and naloxone sublingual tablets—2 mg/0.5 mg and 8 mg/2 mg to be administered as a single dose in the range of 12–16 mg/day. Subutex is usually used for the induction phase because it is monotherapy. Suboxone is usually used for the maintenance phase. Naloxone is added to Suboxone to prevent intravenous abuse. Buprenorphine has lower abuse potential than methadone. Buprenorphine is a Schedule III controlled substance, whereas methadone is a Schedule II controlled substance. This program works as a maintenance program through pharmacies. Patients receive monthly prescriptions from the pharmacy as opposed to the daily visit to a methadone clinic. The initial dose of buprenorphine monotherapy is 4 mg. If withdrawal symptoms continue after 2–4 hours, an additional 4 mg can be given for a total of 8 mg. Initial dosing with the buprenorphine/naloxone combination is a 4/1 ratio, with 12–16 mg of buprenorphine. Each dosing is patient specific.

## Program Withdrawal and Discharge

Administrative withdrawal is usually involuntary. Medical therapeutic withdrawal is considered a voluntary patient initiated withdrawal.

Administrative withdrawal may result from the following situations:

1. Nonpayment of fees
2. Disruptive behavior
3. Jail or other confinement

Medical withdrawal results when the patient and staff agree to the voluntary withdrawal. This is done in response to the request of the patient usually against medical advice. The dose reduction is done at a rate that is well tolerated by the patient. Counseling is increased prior to discharge and patients are encouraged to attend support groups once discharged.

The patient always has the right to withdraw from treatment. This is reviewed with the patient at the time of admission into the program along with the patient's bill of rights. If the patient leaves the program abruptly, the program may readmit the patient within 30 days without a formal reassessment procedure.

## Pregnant and Postpartum Patients

Addicted pregnant patients do not routinely receive prenatal care. Prenatal care is always offered at the onset of treatment. If the patient refuses treatment, the refusal should be documented when informed consent is sought. Detoxification is not recommended for pregnant patients. Detoxification is too abrupt for the fetus.

Methadone is the treatment of choice for pregnant patients. Buprenorphine is classified with a Category C Pregnancy Warning. Category C Pregnancy Warning states: "Animal studies have shown an adverse effect to the fetus and there are no adequate and well-controlled studies in pregnant women."

Comprehensive methadone treatment that includes prenatal care reduces the risk of obstetrical and fetal complications, in utero growth retardation, and neonatal morbidity and mortality.

## Record Keeping

There are separate record keeping and security requirements for Opioid Treatment Programs. The Code of Federal Regulations requirements for narcotic treatment programs include:

1. Use of DEA Form 222 for all Schedule II narcotic transactions between an Opioid Treatment Program and any registrant, including a manufacturer, distributor, practitioner, or another narcotic treatment program.

2. DEA registration of all Opioid Treatment Programs for the handling of only those narcotic substances applied for on the DEA Form 363 and that are approved for use in maintenance or detoxification (see Figure 14-3).
3. Valid practitioner registration for the administration, dispensing, or storage of controlled substances for treatment of conditions other than narcotic addiction at the treatment program location.

All records associated with a treatment facility must be maintained for 3 years.

## Detoxification: Short Term and Long Term

Short-term detoxification is detoxification with methadone for a period of time less than 30 days. Long-term detoxification is detoxification with methadone for a period of time more than 30 days but less than 180 days. Patients who are unsuccessful for two attempts must consider alternative treatment. Detoxification does not address the social, psychological, or behavioral problems associated with addiction. Short-term detoxification patients are not eligible for take-home medication; however, long-term detoxification patients are eligible.

## Methadone

Methadone is a Schedule II controlled substance approved for severe pain management and opioid treatment addiction. Those practitioners who are not registered to administer narcotics to addicts may *prescribe* methadone for pain management only to patients not enrolled in an Opioid Treatment Program. Those enrolled in an Opioid Treatment Program must receive any narcotic at a registered narcotic treatment program only. An Opioid Treatment Program can administer and dispense narcotics but they cannot prescribe them for enrolled patients.

## Methadone Exceptions to Opioid Treatment

Emergency administration of methadone to an addict:

1. A practitioner who is not part of an Opioid Treatment Program may *administer* methadone to an addicted individual to

relieve that individual's acute withdrawal symptoms while the practitioner makes arrangements to refer the individual to an Opioid Treatment Program. Not more than 1 day's medication may be *administered* at one time. This treatment cannot last more than 3 days and may not be renewed or extended.

2. A hospital that has no narcotic treatment program on the premises may administer narcotics to an addicted individual for either detoxification or maintenance purposes, if the individual is being treated for a medical condition other than narcotic addiction.

## Narcotics for Patients with Terminal Illnesses or Intractable Pain

Narcotic analgesics are used frequently for pain management in patients with a terminal illness or intractable pain. The Code of Federal Regulations requires that all controlled substances have a legitimate medical purpose prescribed by a practitioner acting in the normal course of his or her professional practice. Pain management is a legitimate medical purpose. Pharmacists should not hesitate to dispense or administer narcotics to patients for pain management. When a pharmacist dispenses or administers narcotics in good faith to a patient pursuant to a valid prescription for pain management, the pharmacist need not fear action by the DEA.

Pharmacists need to utilize their professional judgment when dispensing and administering narcotics, recognizing that drug tolerance and physical dependence may develop as a result of long-term use of narcotics for pain management. The DEA is focused on preventing diversion and abuse. The DEA relies on the pharmacist's judgment when they are presented with a questionable prescription. The pharmacist has a responsibility to verify the prescription with the prescriber if there is any doubt as to the legitimacy of the prescription. Together, the pharmacist and the practitioner have a responsibility to monitor the patient receiving the narcotic in an effort to prevent abuse or diversion and to provide effective pain management. The prescriber and the pharmacist each have a corresponding responsibility to ensure the proper prescribing and the proper dispensing of any controlled substance medication to patients.

## SUGGESTED READINGS

United States Department of Health and Human Services. Substance Abuse and Mental Health Services Administration (SAMHSA) Web site. http://www.samhsa.gov. Accessed December 15, 2006.

United States National Library of Medicine (NLM), National Institutes of Health Web site. www.ncbi.nlm.nih.gov/books/bv.fcgi?rid=hstat5. section. 83028. Accessed December 15, 2006.

# 17 Combat Methamphetamine Epidemic Act

## Combat Methamphetamine Epidemic Act (CMEA) of 2005(21 CFR 1300, 1309, 1310, 1314)

This act established new requirements for retail sales of over-the-counter products containing the List I chemicals ephedrine, pseudoephedrine, and phenylpropanolamine. The act amends the Controlled Substance Act. These chemicals can be used to manufacture methamphetamines illegally. The act established daily and 30-day limits on the sales of Schedule I List chemicals to individuals and requires record keeping of most sales.

1. The quantity of each of the chemicals that may be sold to a person in a day is limited to 3.6 g of the chemical without regard to the number of transactions.
2. Nonliquids packaging is limited to blister packs containing no more than two dosage units per blister. If blister packs are not feasible, the product must be packaged in unit dose packets or pouches.
3. Sellers must place the products behind the counter or in a locked cabinet where the public has no access, similar to cabinets used to store cigarettes.
4. Sellers must check the identity of all purchasers. Photo ID is required and it must be state or federal government issued.

*Acceptable forms of identification include*: U.S. passport; Alien Registration Receipt Card; unexpired foreign passport; unexpired

Employment Authorization Document issued by Immigration and Naturalization Service (INS); foreign passport with an Arrival-Departure Record for nonimmigrant alien authorized to work for a specific employer incident to status.

*For those 16 years of age or older:* driver's license or ID card; school ID with photo; voter's registration card; U.S. military card; ID card issued by a governmental agency; military dependent's ID card; Native American tribal documents; Canadian driver's license.

*For those under 18 who cannot produce the above who are 16 or older:* school record or report card; clinic doctor or hospital record; daycare or nursery school record.

5. The seller must record the purchaser's name, address, signature, product sold, quantity sold, date and time of sale in a bound logbook. The logbook must be maintained for at least 2 years from the date of the last entry. If the logbook is maintained electronically, the information must be readily retrievable by the seller and Drug Enforcement Administration (DEA) and others so authorized to inspect.
6. All sellers must train their employees in the new requirements and certify the training.
7. For mobile retail sellers and mail order sales, sellers must limit sales to a person to 7.5 g in a 30-day period. The 30-day limit refers to midnight to midnight not a 24-hour rolling clock.
8. Individuals are limited to the purchase of 9 g in a 30-day period of which not more than 7.5 g may be imported by means of a common carrier or the United States Postal Service.

Phenylpropanolamine was recalled several years ago after being considered unsafe for human consumption. Therefore, there should be no sales for phenylpropanolamine over the counter.

### SUGGESTED READINGS

Combat Methamphetamine Epidemic Act (CMEA) of 2005 (21 CFR 1300, 1309, 1310, 1314).

United States Drug Enforcement Administration Diversion Control Program Web site. www.deadiversion.usdoj.gov. Accessed December 15, 2006.

# 18 United States Postal Service Mailing Requirements for Controlled Substances

## United States Postal Service Mailing Requirements for Controlled Substances

The United States Postal Service (USPS) regulations permit the mailing of any controlled substance, provided that the substances are not outwardly dangerous or of their own force could cause injury to a person's life or health. The following preparation and packaging standards must be met:

1. The inner container of any parcel containing controlled substances is marked and sealed under the provisions of the Controlled Substances Act and its implementing regulations, and placed in a plain outer container or securely wrapped in plain paper.

2. If the controlled substances consist of prescription medicines, the inner container is also labeled to show the name
   and address of the pharmacy, practitioner, or other person
   dispensing the prescription.
3. The outside wrapper or container is free of markings that
   would indicate the nature of the contents.

**SUGGESTED READING**

United States Postal Service Web site. http://www.usps.com/. Accessed
  December 15, 2006.

# 19 Health Insurance Portability and Accountability Act of 1996

## Health Insurance Portability and Accountability Act

The Health Insurance Portability and Accountability Act (HIPAA) (P.L. 104-191) was implemented to save health care costs by reducing administrative inefficiencies, promoting the use of electronic transactions, and exposing and eliminating health care fraud and waste by use of standard codes for data content. The purpose of HIPAA was:

1. To control the dissemination of patient information.
2. To disseminate patient information only with patient authorization.
3. To protect individually identifiable health information transmitted or maintained by electronic or other media.

Protected health information is information used to identify a patient. This information relates to a patient's health status, a patient's health care, or payment for the patient's health care. The use or disclosure of protected health information is limited by HIPAA. The HIPAA privacy rules apply to pharmacies because they provide treatment and/or they submit claims for payment for health care services.

## Patient's Rights

Patient's rights under HIPAA include:

1. Access to health information, including the right to review and copy the information.
2. Control of how the patient information is used and to whom it is disclosed to. Restrictions of the use and disclosure are permissible under certain circumstances.
3. Request amendments to their protected health information.
4. Receive an accounting of disclosures for purposes other than treatment, payment, or health care operations.
5. Receive written notice of information practices from health plans and providers.
6. Recourse if privacy protections are violated.

When protected health information is used for any purpose not generally associated with the treatment, payment, or health care operations of the covered entity, authorizations and acknowledgements from the patient must be obtained. Covered entities include health plans, clearinghouses, and health care providers. Health care providers include pharmacists and pharmacies. The general rule is health care providers must obtain patient consent prior to using or disclosing protected health information to carry out treatment, payment, or health care operations.

## Use of Protected Health Information Without Patient Consent

Health care providers may use protected health information without patient consent under the following conditions:

1. Indirect relationships, that is, radiologist or lab that performs services on or for the patient incident to an order from another provider.
2. Patient is an individual incarcerated in a correctional facility.
3. Patient requests an over-the-counter consultation as long as no record is being kept. In this case, the information is given directly to the patient and not another entity.
4. Third parties picking up prescriptions for the patient.

5. Emergencies.
6. The law requires that a patient be treated.
7. Substantial barriers to communication with the individual, that is, non-English speaking and no one to interpret.

## Consent

Patient consent must:

1. Be written in plain language.
2. Inform the patient that protected health information may be used and disclosed to carry out treatment, payment, or health care operations.
3. Refer the patient to the entity's Notice of Privacy Practice. Each entity must establish a notice of privacy practice that advises the patient how, where, and when his or her protected health information will be used.
4. Advise the patient that the notice of privacy practice may be revised.
5. Inform the patient of the right to request restrictions on the use and disclosure of protected health information.
6. Notify patient that covered entity is not required to agree to requested restrictions.
7. Advise patient of right to revoke consent. A revocation must be in writing.

Consents must be signed and dated by the patient and be kept on file for at least 6 years from the date signed. These may be stored electronically and may be a condition of treatment. Health care providers may condition treatment upon the patient's consent to the use and/or disclosure of protected health information. Health plans may condition enrollment in the plan upon patient's consent to the use and/or disclosure of protected health information. The use of a patient's health information is essential to the appropriate treatment and care of the patient. It is also necessary for the payment for the care and treatment of the patient. There is a limit on the use of psychotherapy notes. The notes can be used only for treatment of the patient by the note taker, in legal action, or for the health and safety of the patient. The consent cannot be combined with the notice of privacy practice but may be combined with other types of legal permissions and research authorizations.

## Authorization for Use of Protected Health Information

If an entity intends to use protected health information for a reason other than treatment, payment, or healthcare operations, the entity must obtain an authorization from the patient.

Authorization requirements:

1. Written in plain language.
2. Contain a specific description of the information to be used or disclosed.
3. Identify the purpose of use.
4. Specifically identify the people/entity authorized to make the request for use or disclosure.
5. Specifically identify the people/entity to whom the disclosure will be made.
6. Statement that the information used or disclosed may be subject to redisclosure by the recipient and may no longer be protected by HIPAA.
7. Statement that the patient has the right to revoke the authorization provided it is done in writing.
8. Definitive end date for the authorization.
9. Patient signature and date of authorization.
10. Statement that covered entity will not condition treatment, payment, enrollment, or eligibility on patient's grant of authorization.
11. Patient's right to inspect or copy the protected health information to be used or disclosed.
12. Patient's right to refuse to sign the authorization.
13. Statement disclosing remuneration if relevant.
14. Research authorization must also contain a description of the extent to which protected health information will be used or disclosed to carry out treatment, payment, or health care operations.
15. No limitation on the right of a covered entity to use or disclose protected health information as required by law or to avert a serious threat to health and safety.

A copy of the signed authorization should be provided to the patient.

Defective authorization:

1. If the expiration date has passed or the expired event has occurred.
2. If the form is not filled out completely or does not include one of the required elements.
3. If the covered entity knows that patient has revoked the authorization.
4. If the covered entity knows that the authorization contains materially false information.

A revocation of the authorization must be in writing. It is only effective to the extent that the covered entity has not taken action in reliance upon it.

# Students

Students are part of the workforce in the pharmacy. Pharmacists and pharmacies are held liable for the behavior of students. Therefore, students should be trained in HIPAA compliance prior to any employment whether for pay or no pay.

# HIPAA Administrative Procedures

Administrative procedures include policies and procedures; employee training; appointing a privacy officer; procedure for handling requests for consumer information from the government, and procedure for handling complaints and violations of HIPAA. A consent obtained by one provider is not valid as to any other provider. Civil penalties can be assessed at $100 per violation, with a cap at $25,000.

Each entity must have a way to deal with patient complaints. There must be a process to receive complaints. The pharmacy must have a contact person. The pharmacy must document the complaint and the resolution. The complaints can be anonymous and pharmacy employees can make complaints.

The entity should have established employee sanctions for violations of HIPAA. There must be a person to whom failure to comply can be reported to. Investigation and discipline must be documented. The entity should do its best to mitigate any harmful effects of a use or disclosure for a violation of policy. Forms of discipline can include informal counseling; verbal warning; written warning; probation; suspension; demotion; termination; or restitution. Employees should be advised of the possible sanctions in advance and the sanctions should be posted in a visible area. Entities should create a policy for informing the patient in the event of an incidental disclosure. The entity should notify its risk manager also.

## Federal Enforcement

Federal enforcement is done through the Office of Civil Rights. The Office of Civil Rights investigates alleged violations; conducts random compliance inspections; and assesses penalties. A complaint must be filed within 6 months after the person knows or should have known that the alleged violation occurred. There can be a waiver of the time limit if a good cause is shown.

*Penalties for civil violations*: $100 per offense with a cap at $25,000 in a calendar year. *Criminal violations*: Up to $50,000 and 1 year prison if person knowingly obtains or discloses protected health information. Up to $100,000 and 5 years prison if person obtains protected health information under false pretenses. Up to $250,000 and 10 years if person obtains or discloses protected health information with intent to sell, transfer, or use information for personal gain or malicious harm.

### SUGGESTED READING

United States Department of Health & Human Services, Office for Civil Rights—HIPAA Web site. www.hhs.gov/ocr/hipaa. Accessed December 15, 2006.

# 20
# USP Chapter <797>

## United States Pharmacopeia Chapter <797>

With a heightened focus on patient safety, *United States Pharmacopeia (USP) Chapter <797> Pharmaceutical Compounding: Sterile Preparations* was developed. It was published in the USP, 27th rev. and the National Formulary, 22nd ext. USP Chapter <797> became effective on January 1, 2004. USP Chapter <797> outlines procedures for compounding sterile preparations. These procedures are applicable to all practice settings that engage in sterile compounding. The force and effect of the standards depend on how state boards of pharmacy chose to enforce them as well as accrediting organizations such as Joint Commission on Accreditation Healthcare Organizations (JCAHO), Accreditation of Health Care, Inc. (ACHC), and Community Health Accreditation Program (CHAP).

USP Chapter <797> is applicable to health care institutions, pharmacies, physician practice facilities, and other facilities where compounded sterile products are prepared, stored, or dispensed.

## Compounded Sterile Products

USP Chapter <797> sets forth the following criteria for compounded sterile products:

1. Preparations prepared according to the manufacturer's labeled instructions where the original contents may be exposed to contamination.
2. Preparations containing nonsterile ingredients or nonsterile components and devices that must be sterilized before administration.

3. Biologics, diagnostics, drugs, nutrients, and radiopharmaceuticals that possess either of the above two characteristics and which may include baths and soaks for live organs or tissue, implants, inhalations, injections, powders for injection, irrigations, metered sprays, and ophthalmic and otic preparations.

## Responsibility of Compounding Personnel

1. Ensure that compounding personnel is adequately educated, skilled, and trained to perform sterile compounding.
2. Ingredients are correctly identified, including quality and amount.
3. Opened or partially used packages for future use are stored properly.
4. Bacterial endotoxins are minimized, with sterilization within 6 hours of after preparation completion.
5. Sterilization methods achieve sterility while maintaining the integrity of the product.
6. Equipment is accurate and clean.
7. Packaging is appropriate for sterility and stability until the beyond use date.
8. Careful evaluation of bioavailability for all substances before dispensing and administration.
9. Maintenance of sterility of compounding area.
10. Accurate labeling and visual confirmation of clarity prior to administration or dispensing.
11. Beyond use dates are utilized based on appropriate scientific criteria.
12. All procedures are followed based on accepted protocols.
13. Deficiencies are quickly identified and corrected.
14. When feasible, compounding procedures are separated from postcompounding quality inspections and review before compounding sterile products is dispensed or administered.

## Microbial Contamination Risk Levels

Risk level classification under USP Chapter <797> is done in general terms except for compounded sterile products prepared from bulk, nonsterile components. These products will always utilize the high-risk level procedure.

**LOW-RISK CONDITIONS**

1. Compounding with aseptic procedures entirely with International Organization of Standardization (ISO) Class 5 environment or better air quality using only sterile ingredients, products, components, and devices.
2. The preparation involves transferring, measuring, and mixing with closed or sealed packages with minimal transfers or manipulations.

In the absence of sterility testing, storage periods cannot exceed 48 hours at room temperature; cannot exceed 14 days at a cold temperature (refrigeration); and not more than 45 days in solid frozen state at -20°C (freezer) or colder. Examples of low-risk compounding include: single transfers of sterile dosage forms from ampuls, bottles, and vials using sterile syringes with sterile needles to transfer sterile drugs from manufacturer original packaging and manually measuring and mixing no more than three manufactured products to compound drug admixtures and nutritional solutions.

**MEDIUM-RISK CONDITIONS**

When compounded sterile products are compounded under low-risk conditions and one or more of the following conditions exists, then there is a medium risk of contamination.

1. Multiple individual or small doses of sterile products combined or pooled to prepare a compounded sterile product for administration to either multiple patients or to one patient on multiple occasions.
2. Compounding process involves complex aseptic compounding.
3. Compounding process is over a very long duration.
4. Sterile compounded products do not contain broad-spectrum bacteriostatic products and the compounded sterile products are administered over several days.
5. Quality assurance includes all steps for low-risk levels.

In the absence of sterility testing, the storage period cannot exceed the following: 30 hours at room temperature; 7 days at cold temperature (refrigeration), and 45 days at solid frozen state at −20°C (freezer) or colder. Examples of medium-risk conditions include:

total parenteral nutrition fluids; filling of reservoirs of injection and infusion devices with multiple sterile drug products and evacuations of air; filling of reservoirs of injection of infusion devices with volumes of sterile drug solutions to be administered over several days at temperatures between 25 and 40°C and transferring from multiple ampuls or vials into a single-final sterile product.

**HIGH-RISK CONDITIONS**

High-risk conditions include:

1. Nonsterile ingredients before terminal sterilization.
2. Sterile ingredients, components, devices, and mixtures are exposed to air quality inferior to ISO Class 5.
3. Nonsterile products exposed to air quality inferior to ISO Class 5 for at least 6 hours before sterilization.
4. Purity of components is assumed but not verified.
5. Quality assurance includes all steps for low-risk levels.

In the absence of sterility testing, storage periods cannot exceed 24 hours at controlled room temperature; 3 days at cold temperature (refrigeration); and 45 days for solid frozen state or −20°C (freezer) or colder. Examples of high-risk conditions include: dissolving nonsterile bulk drug and nutrient powders to make solutions then sterilized; sterile ingredients, components, devices, and mixtures exposed to air quality inferior to ISO Class 5; measuring and mixing sterile ingredients in nonsterile devices before sterilization is performed.

## Personnel Training and Aseptic Skills

Appropriate training of personnel may include: audio/visual; didactic; review; written testing; media fill testing; and fill challenge testing.

## Clean Rooms for Low- and Medium-Risk Conditions

The anteroom should be equipped with air classification or quality that meets ISO Class 8 standards with physical characteristics of smooth walls, floors, ceilings, fixtures, surfaces resistant to sanitizing agents, junctures covered and caulked, wall panel locked together and sealed, floors overlaid with wide sheet vinyl flooring with heat sealed seams and buffer or ante area with no sinks or floor drains.

Gowning of personnel requires the removal of outer coats, makeup, and jewelry. It requires scrubbing hands and arms to the elbow. Gowns should be nonshedding uniforms with hair covers, shoe covers, coveralls or knee length coats, gloves, and facemasks. Upon leaving or reentry, personnel shall remove coveralls, using them for one shift only. High-risk compounding must have a separate ante room.

## Barrier Isolator (Mobile Isolation Chambers [MIC])

An alternative to an ISO Class 5 LAFW (Laminar Airflow Work Area) device in an ISO Class 8 clean room. The physical facility does not need to be located in a Class 8 area. Gowning still includes hair covers, shoe covers, lab coats, and facemasks.

## Quality Assurance Program

The facility needs to establish a quality assurance program. A formal audit program should be in writing, outlining all aspects of preparation and dispensing; a description of the specific monitoring and evaluation activities; specifics on the reporting and evaluation of the results; identification of follow-up mechanisms when action limits have been exceeded and delineation of the individual response for quality assurance program.

### SUGGESTED READING

The United States Pharmacopeia, 27th rev., and the National Formulary. 22nd ed. USP General Information Chapter. Pharmaceutical Compounding—Sterile Preparations. Rockville, MD: The United States Pharmacopeia Convention, 2003. www.usp.org. Accessed December 15, 2006.

# 21   Bar Coding

## Bar Code Rule (21 CFR 201.25)

The Food and Drug Administration (FDA) implemented a final rule in April 2004 requiring bar coding on certain products administered to patient in hospitals in an effort to reduce medication errors. This rule applies to manufacturers, repackers, relablers, and private label distributors of the following products:

1. Prescription drugs, except physician drug samples, allergenic extracts, intrauterine devices, medical gases, radiopharmaceuticals, low density form fill, and seal containers that are not packaged with an over wrap
2. Biological products
3. Over-the-counter products dispensed pursuant to an order and that are *commonly* used in hospitals

At a minimum, the bar code must contain the drug product's National Drug Code (NDC) number in a linear bar code. The bar coding should be used on drugs down to unit-of-use package size. The lot number and expiration date are not required. The manufacturer may include if they so desire.

Before administering a drug product, the bar code on the patient's identification bracelet is scanned and the bar code on the medication is scanned. The computer/personal digital assistant [PDA] checks the medication against the patient's medical record to see if administration of the drug was ordered. If the scan matches, then administration of the drug can follow. If the scan does not match an error warning will alert the practitioner that the medication should not be administered.

## SUGGESTED READING

U. S. Food and Drug Administration Web site. www.fda.gov. Accessed December 15, 2006.

# 22 Regulation of Pharmacy Practice

## Pharmacy Scope of Practice

The practice of pharmacy is defined by the laws, rules, and regulations established by the federal government and each individual state. The practice of pharmacy is referred to as the pharmacist's scope of practice. Federal law has provided the framework for the regulation of pharmacy practice. Most states have used federal law as the basis of their pharmacy practice act, individualizing it as needed to meet the needs of each state. Each state has established its own laws, rules, and regulations on drug products. When there is a conflict between federal law and state law, federal law always prevails under the Supremacy clause of the United States Constitution (the preemption doctrine). However, if state law is more stringent than federal law, the pharmacist will not be in violation of federal law if they comply with state. The best action for the pharmacist to follow is to comply with whichever law is more stringent. By applying the more stringent law, the pharmacist will not be in violation of either federal or state law.

## State Boards of Pharmacy and National Association of Boards of Pharmacy

Most states are regulated by an administrative agency, the state board of pharmacy. The purpose of the board of pharmacy is to protect the public, not advance the pharmacy profession. The National Association of Boards of Pharmacy (NABP) is the national organization of the state boards of pharmacy. NABP is responsible for the North American Pharmacy Licensure Examination (NAPLEX) and the Multistate Pharmacy Jurisprudence Exam (MPJE). Many pharmacy standards are established by NABP. NABP frequently develops model acts and legislation for the states to utilize in implementing the act in their state. Boards of pharmacy are made up of practicing pharmacists in that state with an effort made to represent different practices of pharmacy and different geographic areas in the state. Consumer members are often included on the boards of pharmacy in an effort to bring a consumer perspective to the board. Appointment to the board of pharmacy is usually political whether the appointment is initiated by the governor or another administrative branch of the government.

## License Reciprocation

Many states allow licensed pharmacists to reciprocate their license from one state to another with successful completion of a law examination demonstrating their knowledge of the states law. All candidate qualifications are reviewed by NABP.

## Continuing Pharmaceutical Education

All states require continuing pharmaceutical education for licensure renewal. The Accreditation Council for Pharmacy Education (ACPE) accredits most education that pharmacists receive to maintain their license. Many state boards of pharmacy also accredit continuing pharmaceutical education programs. ACPE is focusing on continuing professional development for evaluating pharmacist competency.

## Pharmacy License

Pharmacy establishments must be licensed also. Licenses for pharmacies are obtained from the state board of pharmacy. Each state has established specific requirements for the operation of a pharmacy, with requirements for equipment, staffing, and counseling.

## Professional Misconduct

State boards of pharmacy have established disciplinary action for those pharmacists who engage in unprofessional conduct. Professional misconduct frequently involves violations that are not related to the practice of pharmacy. There are civil and criminal penalties for violations of laws, rules, and regulations. Many times the repercussions include reprimands, suspensions, censure, and license revocation. If a pharmacist is convicted of a felony such as driving while intoxicated, the state board of pharmacy will probably initiate disciplinary proceedings against the pharmacist for professional misconduct. A pharmacist found guilty of professional misconduct will have his or her license revoked.

Most boards of pharmacy are responsible for licensing pharmacists and pharmacies.

## Pharmacy Applicant Requirements

Each state is responsible for establishing the requirements for each pharmacy applicant to sit for the pharmacy board in that state.

The usual requirements for pharmacist licensure include:

1. Graduation from pharmacy school
2. Internship
3. Age of 21
4. Passing the licensure exam with 75% or better
5. Good moral character

There are a few states that still require citizenship.

Graduation from pharmacy school requires graduation from a pharmacy school accredited by the ACPE. If the applicant sitting for the pharmacy boards is a foreign graduate, the NABP Foreign Pharmacy Graduate Equivalency Examination (FPGEE) is utilized to assess whether the pharmacy school education received by the foreign student is equivalent to the education the applicant would have received in a pharmacy school in the United States.

**SUGGESTED READING**

National Association of Boards of Pharmacy Web site. www.nabp.net. Accessed December 15, 2006.

# 23 Multistate Pharmacy Jurisprudence Exam

## Multistate Pharmacy Jurisprudence Exam (MPJE)

The Multistate Pharmacy Jurisprudence Exam (MPJE) is a computer-adaptive exam. The goal of the exam is to determine the candidate's knowledge in jurisprudence. The adaptive nature of the test selects questions based on the candidate's level of knowledge. As a candidate is successful the exam question becomes more difficult. When a candidate answers a question unsuccessfully, the next exam question is easier. The exam is adapted to the candidate's knowledge level demonstrating the candidate's ability in that specific area. Once a candidate answers a question, a candidate cannot go back and change an answer because of the adaptive nature of the exam. All questions must be answered in order. Therefore, questions cannot be skipped with the intent to return to that question at a later time. ALL QUESITONS MUST BE ANSWERED IN ORDER. DO NOT LEAVE ANSWSERS BLANK.

The MPJE is developed to assess jurisprudence in each state. All exams are approved by state boards of pharmacy through the MPJE Review Committee and item writers that assist in the development of the exam. Exams are state specific. The MPJE is a 2-hour exam consisting of 90 multiple-choice questions. Thirty of the

193

exam questions are tested for use on future exams and are not included in the candidates final score. The MPJE evaluates the candidate's knowledge of federal and state law, rules, and regulations that oversee pharmacy practice. The exam does not make a distinction between federal and state questions. The candidate is expected to apply the laws of the state in which the candidate is seeking licensure.

The MPJE topics covered in the exam include the following:

- Area 1 Pharmacy Practice (approximately 78% of test)
  1. Legal requirements of pharmacist and pharmacy personnel
  2. Requirements for acquisition and distribution of pharmaceuticals
  3. Legal requirements involved in the issuance of a prescription
  4. Dispensing drug products including controlled substance
  5. Counseling patients
  6. Distribution and dispensing of over-the-counter substances including controlled substances
  7. Record keeping
- Area 2 Licensure, Registration, Certification, and Operational Requirements (approximately 17% of test)
  1. Licensure requirements for manufacture, storage, distribution, and dispensing of pharmaceuticals
  2. Registration, licensure, certification related to the practice of pharmacy
  3. Registration, licensure, certification of business entity
- Area 3 Regulatory Structure and Terms (approximately 5% of test)
  1. Laws, rules, and regulations for the manufacture, storage, distribution, and dispensing of pharmaceuticals
  2. Agencies that are responsible for enforcing and regulating the practice of pharmacy

**SUGGESTED READING**

National Association of Boards of Pharmacy (NABP) Web site. www/nabp.net. Accessed December 15, 2006.

# 24 *Medicare Prescription Drug Improvement and Modernization Act of 2003*

## Medicare Prescription Drug Improvement and Modernization Act (MMA) (*Public Law No. 108-173, 117 Stat. 2066*)

The Medicare Prescription Drug Improvement and Modernization Act (MMA) of 2003 produced the largest overhaul of the Medicare program in 38 years. The Centers for Medicare and Medicaid Services (CMS) are responsible for developing and supervising MMA.

There are four programs included in the Medicare act:

1. Medicare Part A which provides hospitalization insurance that covers inpatient hospital, home health, skilled nursing facility, psychiatric hospital, and hospice care services.
2. Medicare Part B which provides medical insurance for physician's services, outpatient services, some mental health services, durable medical equipment, some preventive services, and home health visits not covered under Part A.

3. Medicare Part C which provides enrollees with the opportunity to choose a local managed care option as an alternative to Medicare Part B.
4. Medicare Part D which provides a Medicare prescription drug program. This program is completely voluntary and requires an affirmative action to enroll.

# Medicare Part D

Medicare Part D will:

- Offer assistance for those with limited financial means.
- Offer a choice of at least two drug plans that will cover both brand name and generic drugs.
- Offer convenient access to pharmacies.
- Guarantee that Medicare beneficiaries living in nursing facilities will be able to enroll in the drug plan and take advantage of the new benefit.
- Ensure that beneficiaries who have both full Medicaid and Medicare benefits are automatically be enrolled in a drug plan.

Medicare Part D requirements:

1. Covered Part D drugs are those drugs covered by Medicaid plus insulin, insulin-related supplies, certain vaccines, and smoking cessation agents. Certain drugs may be excluded such as benzodiazepines and barbiturates.
2. There must be sufficient pharmacy access, convenient and available in case of an emergency.
3. Standardized technology in the form of prescription drug benefit cards or other approved identification information.
4. Prescription Drug Plan (PDP) drug formulary must include drugs in every therapeutic category. This does not mean that all drugs in the therapeutic category have to be made available on the formulary.
5. Any plan formulary must be reviewed by a Pharmacy and Therapeutics Committee made up of at least physicians and pharmacists with two independent experts in the form of practicing physician and practicing pharmacist.
6. CMS will rely on United States Pharmacopeia (USP) to develop model guidelines for drug categories and classes. PDP may adopt these model guidelines or develop their

own. Changes may be made at the beginning of each benefit year.

7. PDP must establish procedures to educate health care providers and enrollees.
8. PDP must give notice to CMS, enrollees, physicians, pharmacists, and pharmacies prior to removing a drug from the formulary.
9. PDP must have a cost-effective drug utilization management program, quality assurance measures, medication error reduction systems, and a program to combat and recognize fraud, waste, and abuse.
10. PDP shall have a medication therapy management (MTM) program developed to pay pharmacists for drug therapy management of patients with chronic multiple disease states (diabetes, asthma, anticoagulation, hypertension), high drug costs, and multiple drugs.
11. CMS will promulgate electronic prescribing standards no later than April 1, 2008.
12. PDP shall establish grievance procedures.
13. PDP shall follow Health Insurance Portability and Accountability Act (HIPAA) and confidentiality.
14. PDPs will require pharmacies that dispense covered Part D drugs to advise patients of the availability of generic drugs and their cost savings.

The coverage for the prescription drug benefit is provided through private PDPs that offer drug coverage, or through Medicare Advantage Prescription Drug Plans (MAPD) that offer integrated prescription drug and health care coverage.

## Medication Therapy Management

The law creating the prescription drug benefit requires drug plan sponsors to have an MTM program and offer it to beneficiaries with multiple chronic diseases, such as diabetes, hypertension, hyperlipidemia, and asthma, who use multiple medications covered by Part D and whose expenses on those medications will likely top the cost threshold set by the Department of Health and Human Services. The intent of requiring MTM services for these targeted beneficiaries is to optimize the therapeutic outcomes of Part D covered therapies. Under

423.153(d), a Part D sponsor must have established an MTM program that:

- Ensures optimum therapeutic outcomes for targeted beneficiaries through improved medication use.
- Reduces the risk of adverse events.
- Is developed in cooperation with licensed and practicing pharmacists and physicians.
- Describes the resources and time required to implement the program if using outside personnel and establishes the fees for pharmacists or others.
- May be furnished by pharmacists or other qualified providers.
- May distinguish between services in ambulatory and institutional settings.
- Is coordinated with any care management plan established for a targeted individual under a chronic care improvement program.

Annually, sponsors must submit an MTM program description to CMS for review and approval. A CMS-approved MTM program is one of several required elements in the development of sponsor bids for the upcoming contract year. CMS provides an online link for access to an MTM program template <<http://www.cms.hhs.gov/PrescriptionDrugCovContra/08.asp>>. Pharmacists are recognized as a provider of MTM under the MMA. CMS expects that MTM will enhance patients' understanding of appropriate drug use, increase compliance with medication therapy, result in collaborations between pharmacies and prescribers, and improve detection of adverse drug events. MTM is intended to improve communication between patients and providers, improve communication and collaboration between providers, optimize medication therapy, and improve patient outcomes. All communications will be HIPAA compliant.

### SUGGESTED READING

Centers for Medicare and Medicaid Services Web site. http://www.cms.hhs.gov. Accessed December 15, 2006.

# Review Questions

1. The Food and Drug Administration (FDA) regulates which of the following?
   I. Food, including meat and poultry
   II. Medical devices
   III. Cosmetics
   IV. Drugs

   A. I only
   B. I, III, & IV only
   C. I & IV only
   D. II, III, & IV only
   E. I, II, III, & IV

2. Which of the following Official Compendia does the FDA develop?
   I. National Formulary (NF)
   II. United States Pharmacopeia (USP)
   III. Homeopathic Pharmacopeia

   A. I & II only
   B. II & III only
   C. II only
   D. I, II, & III
   E. None of the above

3. The regulatory agency for the regulation and prevention of diversion of controlled substances is which of the following?

   A. FDA
   B. Drug Enforcement Administration (DEA)
   C. Code of Federal Regulations (CFR)
   D. Homeopathic Pharmacopeia of the United States (HPUS)
   E. Dispensing Information (DI)

4. Which act or amendment was the first to regulate the manufacture or sale of adulterated or misbranded drugs in interstate commerce?

   A. Pure Food and Drug Act
   B. Food, Drug, and Cosmetic Act
   C. Durham-Humphrey
   D. Kefauver-Harris
   E. Fair Packaging and Labeling

5. Which act or amendment was the first to recognize the USP/NF as an official compendium?

   A. Pure Food and Drug Act
   B. Food, Drug, and Cosmetic Act
   C. Durham-Humphrey
   D. Kefauver-Harris
   E. Fair Packaging and Labeling

6. Which act or amendment was the first to require that manufacturers prove that their drug is safe prior to marketing?

    A. Pure Food and Drug Act
    B. Food, Drug, and Cosmetic Act
    C. Durham-Humphrey
    D. Kefauver-Harris
    E. Fair Packaging and Labeling

7. Which act or amendment was the first to regulate medical devices and cosmetics?

    A. Pure Food and Drug Act
    B. Food, Drug, and Cosmetic Act
    C. Durham-Humphrey
    D. Kefauver-Harris
    E. Fair Packaging and Labeling

8. Which act or amendment granted the FDA the authority to inspect factories?

    A. Pure Food and Drug Act
    B. Food, Drug, and Cosmetic Act
    C. Durham-Humphrey
    D. Kefauver-Harris
    E. Fair Packaging and Labeling

9. Which act or amendment required adequate directions for use on the product labeling?

    A. Pure Food and Drug Act
    B. Food, Drug, and Cosmetic Act
    C. Durham-Humphrey
    D. Kefauver-Harris
    E. Fair Packaging and Labeling

10. Which act or amendment established a fast track process of drugs approval for used to treat life-threatening illnesses?

    A. Pure Food and Drug Act
    B. Food, Drug, and Cosmetic Act
    C. Durham-Humphrey
    D. Kefauver-Harris
    E. Fair Packaging and Labeling

11. Which of the following is an example of an adulterated drug product?
    I. Misleading labeling information
    II. Drug product contains an animal body part
    III. Manufacturer does not engage in Good Manufacturing Practices (GMP)

    A. I only
    B. II only
    C. III only
    D. II & III only
    E. I & III only

12. Which of the following are examples of adulteration?
    I. Product does not meet standards of USP.
    II. Product contains an unapproved color additive.
    III. Product is manufactured under unsanitary conditions.

    A. I only
    B. II only
    C. III only
    D. I & II only
    E. I, II, & III

13. Which of the following are examples of misbranding?
    I. Compendial product is combined with a noncompendial product.
    II. Information is not conspicuous.
    III. Product does not contain the product established name.

    A. I only
    B. II & III only
    C. I & III only
    D. II only
    E. III only

14. Which products are regulated by the Combat Methamphetamine Epidemic Act?
    I. Buprenorphine
    II. Pseudoephedrine
    III. Phenylpropranolamine

    A. I only
    B. II only
    C. I & II only
    D. II & III only
    E. I, II, & III

15. Of the drugs referenced in question number 14, which drugs are controlled substances?

    A. I only
    B. II only
    C. III only
    D. I & II only
    E. II & III only

16. Of the drugs referenced in question number 14, which drug(s) was removed from the market?

    A. I only
    B. II only
    C. III only
    D. I & III only
    E. None of the above

17. Which statement accurately reflects the intent of the Combat Methamphetamine Epidemic Act?

    A. The act was intended to regulate the scheduling of over-the-counter (OTC) drugs to controlled substances.
    B. The act was intended to regulate the packaging and labeling of the List 1 Chemicals to alert the consumer to safety issues associated with the drugs.
    C. The act was intended to prevent the illegal manufacture of methamphetamine.
    D. The act was intended to regulate and increase the level of counseling provided when the covered drugs are sold.
    E. None of the above.

18. The drug products regulated by the Combat Methamphetamine Epidemic Act are restricted to sale of what quantity in 1 day?

    A. 1.2 g
    B. 2.4 g
    C. 3.6 g
    D. 4.8 g
    E. 6.0 g

19. Which statement about the packaging of nonliquid drugs regulated by the Combat Methamphetamine Epidemic Act is true?

    A. Blister pack packaging
    B. No more than two dosages/blister
    C. Unit dose packaging
    D. A & B only
    E. A, B, & C

20. Which statement about the display and storage of the drug products regulated by the Combat Methamphetamine Epidemic Act is accurate?

    A. The sale of the drug product must be made by a pharmacist.
    B. The product must be kept behind the pharmacy counter.
    C. The product must be kept behind the counter in the front store with cigarettes.
    D. The product must be kept behind the counter or in a locked cabinet regardless of the location of the counter or the locked cabinet.
    E. The product must contain a security device when placed for OTC sale.

21. What age must a purchaser of the drug products regulated by the Combat Methamphetamine Epidemic Act have attained?

    A. 16 years of age
    B. 18 years of age
    C. 21 years of age
    D. 25 years of age
    E. No age requirement

22. Sale of the drug products covered by the Combat Methamphetamine Epidemic Act must be recorded in what manner?

    A. Prescription record files
    B. Doctor initiated record to the pharmacy
    C. Bound log book
    D. Photocopy of purchasers ID
    E. No record is required

23. What information must the seller record for the sales of those drug products regulated by the Combat Methamphetamine Epidemic Act?
    I. Purchaser name and address
    II. Product name and quantity purchased
    III. Date of sale
    IV. Signature of purchaser

    A. I, II, & III only
    B. I & II only
    C. I, II, & IV only
    D. II & III only
    E. All of the above

24. A record of the sale of the drug products covered by the Combat Methamphetamine Epidemic Act must be maintained for how long a period of time?

    A. 6 months
    B. 1 year
    C. 2 years
    D. 3 years
    E. 5 years

25. For mail order sales what is the maximum quantity that a purchaser may purchase of drug products regulated by the Combat Methamphetamine Epidemic Act?

    A. 1.2 g
    B. 3.6 g
    C. 5.0 g
    D. 6.4 g
    E. 7.5 g

26. The quantity limit for mail order sales referenced in question 25 is applicable for what period of time?

    A. 14 days
    B. 21 days
    C. 28 days
    D. 30 days
    E. 45 days

27. The quantity limit for individual purchase of the drug products regulated by the Combat Methamphetamine Epidemic Act regardless of the source is?

    A. 3.6 g
    B. 7.2 g
    C. 7.5 g
    D. 8.0 g
    E. 9.0 g

28. Methadone is what schedule controlled substance?

    A. I
    B. II
    C. III
    D. IV
    E. V

29. Methadone is approved for use in the treatment of which of the following?
    I. Pain management
    II. Sedation
    III. Narcotic addiction

    A. I only
    B. I & II only
    C. I & III only
    D. III only
    E. II & III only

30. Emergency administration of methadone to an addict is valid for what period of time?

    A. 3 days
    B. 7 days
    C. 21 days
    D. 30 days
    E. Emergency administration is not permissible

31. Which of the following statements about administration of methadone to an addict is correct?

    A. Only a registered narcotic treatment administrator can prescribe methadone to an addict.
    B. All medication must be administered, not prescribed.
    C. No more than a 7 days supply may be dispensed in the event of an emergency.
    D. If the first emergency treatment is not successful, the emergency treatment may be repeated one more time only.
    E. The prescription for emergency treatment written by the prescriber must state on the face of the prescription that it is for emergency treatment.

32. Which of the following was the first drug product(s) approved for the treatment of narcotic addiction?
    I. Buprenorphine
    II. Methamphetamine
    III. Methadone

    A. I only
    B. II only
    C. III only
    D. I & II only
    E. I, II, & III

33. Comprehensive Maintenance Treatment includes which of the following services?
    I. Medical
    II. Psychosocial
    III. Skills training

    A. I only
    B. II & III only
    C. III only
    D. I & III only
    E. I, II, & III

34. What is the recommended period of time of documented addiction required prior to placement in an opioid addiction treatment program?

    A. 3 months
    B. 6 months
    C. 1 year
    D. 2 years
    E. There is no suggested time requirement

35. Which of the following drugs are approved for the treatment of opioid addiction?
    I. Methadone
    II. Buprenorphine
    III. L-$\alpha$-Acetylmethadol (LAAM)
    IV. Naloxone

    A. I only
    B. I & II only
    C. I & III only
    D. I, II, & III only
    E. I, II, III, & IV

36. Which of the following drugs have very limited use in treatment of addiction?
    I. Methadone
    II. Buprenorphine
    III. LAAM
    IV. Naltrexone

A. II only
B. III only
C. IV only
D. III & IV only
E. I, II, III, & IV

37. Patients being treated with naltrexone should abstain from all short-acting opioid drug use for what period of time before starting treatment?

    A. 2 hours
    B. 5 days
    C. 7 days
    D. 10 days
    E. There is no abstinence requirement

38. Patients being treated with naltrexone should abstain from all long-acting opioids for what period of time before beginning opioid addiction treatment?

    A. 1 day
    B. 2 days
    C. 5 days
    D. 7 days
    E. 10 days

39. Which of the following drugs approved for the treatment of opioid addiction are in limited supply?

    A. Methadone
    B. Suboxone
    C. Subutex
    D. LAAM
    E. Naltrexone

40. Which of the following drugs approved for the treatment of opioid addiction are associated with cardiac arrhythmias?

    A. Methadone
    B. Suboxone
    C. Subutex
    D. LAAM
    E. Naltrexone

41. Which statement(s) about opioid treatment programs is correct?
    I. All information is confidential.
    II. Admission to a program is voluntary.
    III. Patient must have demonstrated 2 years of clinical dependence.

    A. I only
    B. II only
    C. I & II only
    D. III only
    E. I, II, & III

42. The initial treatment phase in opioid treatment programs includes which of the following?
    I. Physical examination
    II. Lab work
    III. Psychosocial assessment

    A. I & II only
    B. II & III only
    C. I only
    D. II only
    E. I, II, & III

43. A comprehensive physical assessment for patients in opioid treatment programs includes which of the following?
    I. Evaluation of dependence
    II. Evaluation of suicidal potential
    III. Family member medical history

    A. I only
    B. II only
    C. I & II only
    D. II & III only
    E. I, II, & III

44. What is the goal of medication usage in opioid treatment program?
    I. Prevent onset of withdrawal symptoms for 48 hours or more.
    II. Reduce drug hunger.
    III. Reduce side effects such as euphoria.

    A. I only
    B. II only
    C. II & III only
    D. I & III only
    E. I, II, & III

45. What is the initial recommended dosage of methadone in opioid treatment programs?

    A. 5 mg
    B. 10 mg
    C. 15 mg
    D. 20 mg
    E. 100 mg

46. If the patient in an opioid treatment program does not respond to the initial dosage of methadone, within what period of time will the physician increase the dose of methadone?

    A. 30 minutes
    B. 1 hour
    C. 45 minutes
    D. 2 hours
    E. 5 hours

47. Methadone is used to treat which of the following addictions?
    I. Heroin
    II. Codeine
    III. Diazepam
    IV. Propoxyphene

    A. I only
    B. I & II only
    C. III only
    D. I & IV only
    E. II, III, & IV only

48. Which statement about methadone is correct?

    A. Methadone is used because it does not cause euphoria.
    B. Methadone does not reduce the physiologic cravings of addiction.
    C. Methadone does not have any side effects.
    D. Methadone may cause cardiac arrhythmias.
    E. Methadone is used in combination with LAAM.

49. The Drug Addiction Treatment Act (DATA) utilizes which of the following drugs?
    I. Heroin
    II. Buprenorphine
    III. Buprenorphine
    IV. Methamphetamine

    A. I only
    B. II only
    C. II & III only
    D. IV only
    E. None of the above

50. What is the main reason why naltrexone is not used for addiction treatment?

    A. Naltrexone has no narcotic effect and poor patient compliance.
    B. Naltrexone causes euphoria.
    C. Naltrexone is used in combination with buprenorphine for optimal effect.
    D. Naltrexone does not require abstinence of opioids prior to naltrexone use.
    E. Naltrexone is not available in table formulation.

51. For an 18-year-old to be eligible for maintenance treatment, he or she must have had two documented attempts at detoxification within what period of time?

    A. 3 months
    B. 6 months
    C. 9 months

    D. 12 months
    E. 18 months

52. The acute phase of maintenance treatment in an opioid treatment program focuses on which of the following?

    A. Abrupt withdrawal
    B. Providing patient with skills needed to lead an active productive life
    C. Eliminating the use of illicit opioids for at least 24 hours
    D. Take-home medication for 1 week
    E. Providing counseling

53. The medical maintenance phase of an opioid treatment program requires that the patient be in continuous treatment for how long a period of time?

    A. 6 months
    B. 1 year
    C. 18 months
    D. 2 years
    E. 3 years

54. Which is the most common form of drug testing for patients enrolled in opioid treatment programs?

    A. Urine
    B. Blood
    C. Oral fluid
    D. Fecal
    E. Sweat

55. Why are no clinical decisions made solely on the basis of results of urine testing for patients enrolled in opioid treatment programs?

    A. Too expensive to conduct all the tests necessary
    B. Too inconvenient
    C. Too much paperwork
    D. Too many false positives/ negatives
    E. Clinical decisions are based solely on urine testing

56. Which test is used to detect buprenorphine patient compliance?

    A. Urine
    B. Oral fluid
    C. Blood
    D. Fecal
    E. No test available

57. What is the minimum number of drug tests performed annually on patients enrolled in opioid treatment programs?

    A. 4
    B. 5
    C. 6
    D. 8
    E. 10

58. Patients who are successfully enrolled in an opioid treatment for 90 days of treatment may take home how many unsupervised doses of medication per week?

    A. 1
    B. 2

C. 3
D. 6
E. 14

59. Patients who are successfully enrolled in an opioid treatment program for 4–6 months of treatment may take home how many unsupervised doses of medication per week?

    A. 1
    B. 2
    C. 3
    D. 6
    E. 14

60. Patients who are successfully enrolled in an opioid treatment program for 7–9 months of treatment may take home how many unsupervised doses of medication per week?

    A. 1
    B. 2
    C. 3
    D. 6
    E. 14

61. Patients who are successfully enrolled in an opioid treatment program for 10–12 months of treatment may take home how many unsupervised doses of medication per week?

    A. 1
    B. 2
    C. 3
    D. 6
    E. 14

62. After 1 continuous year of treatment, how many unsupervised doses of medication per week may a patient who has been successfully enrolled in an opioid treatment program take home?

    A. 2
    B. 3
    C. 6
    D. 14
    E. 30

63. The DEA number for a qualified DATA physician begins with what letter?

    A. A
    B. B
    C. C
    D. D
    E. X

64. Which of the following practitioners are qualified to participate in DATA?
    I. Physicians
    II. Nurses
    III. Midlevel practitioners

    A. I only
    B. I & II only
    C. I & III only
    D. III only
    E. I, II, & III

65. Buprenorphine is what schedule controlled substance?

    A. I
    B. II
    C. III

    D. IV
    E. V

66. Which product is used for treatment in the induction phase of DATA?
    I. Methadone
    II. Suboxone
    III. Subutex

    A. I only
    B. II only
    C. III only
    D. II & III only
    E. I, II, & III

67. Which of the following drug product is added to buprenorphine to prevent IV abuse?

    A. Naltrexone
    B. Naloxone
    C. Diazepam
    D. Diphenoxylate
    E. Methadone

68. Which of the following drug products for use to treat narcotic addiction are administered through pharmacies?
    I. LAAM
    II. Methadone
    III. Subutex
    IV. Suboxone

    A. I only
    B. I & II only
    C. III only
    D. IV only
    E. III & IV only

69. Patients enrolled in the DATA for the first 90 days may receive what maximum quantity of take-home medication?

    A. 1 day
    B. 2 days
    C. 3 days
    D. 6 days
    E. 30 days

70. Buprenorphine contains what level of pregnancy warning?

    A. A
    B. B
    C. C
    D. D
    E. X

71. Which type of opioid treatment program is not recommended for pregnant patients?

    A. Methadone
    B. Detoxification
    C. Maintenance
    D. Prenatal care
    E. None of the above

72. Which of the following records must a treatment program maintain?
    I. DEA Form 222
    II. DEA Form 363
    III. Practitioner DEA registration

    A. I only
    B. II only
    C. III only
    D. I & III only
    E. I, II, & III

73. All records for opioid treatment facilities must be kept for how long a period of time?

    A. 1 year
    B. 2 years
    C. 3 years
    D. 5 years
    E. 7 years

74. Short-term detoxification is for what period of time?

    A. Less than 30 days
    B. 30–60 days
    C. 60–90 days
    D. 90–180 days
    E. 30–180 days

75. Long-term detoxification is for what period of time?

    A. Less than 30 days
    B. 30–60 days
    C. 60–90 days
    D. 90–180 days
    E. 30–180 days

76. How many attempts may one patient try at detoxification before he or she must try an alternative treatment?

    A. 1
    B. 2
    C. 3
    D. 4
    E. 5

77. A patient in short-term detoxification may take home how many days of medication?

A. 30
B. 6
C. 2
D. 1
E. 0

78. Which agency is ultimately respon-
    sible for the regulation of controlled
    substances?

    A. SAMSHA (Substance Abuse and
       Mental Health Services Adminis-
       tration)
    B. DEA
    C. OBRA (Omnibus Budget Recon-
       ciliation Act)
    D. BNDD (Bureau of Narcotics and
       Dangerous Drugs)
    E. FDA

79. Marijuana is classified as what
    schedule controlled substance?

    A. I
    B. II
    C. III
    D. IV
    E. V

80. Lysergic acid is classified as what
    schedule controlled substance?

    A. I
    B. II
    C. III
    D. IV
    E. V

81. Amphetamine is classified as what
    schedule controlled substance?

    A. I
    B. II
    C. III
    D. IV
    E. V

82. Morphine is classified as what
    schedule controlled substance?

    A. I
    B. II
    C. III
    D. IV
    E. V

83. Anabolic steroids are classified as
    what schedule controlled substance?

    A. I
    B. II
    C. III
    D. IV
    E. V

84. Products containing 90 mg of codeine
    per dose are classified as what sche-
    dule controlled substance?

    A. I
    B. II
    C. III
    D. IV
    E. V

85. Amobarbital suppositories are classified as what schedule controlled substance?

    A. I
    B. II
    C. III
    D. IV
    E. V

86. Phenobarbital is classified as what schedule controlled substance?

    A. I
    B. II
    C. III
    D. IV
    E. V

87. Benzodiazepines are classified as what schedule controlled substance?

    A. I
    B. II
    C. III
    D. IV
    E. V

88. Opium products containing 100 mg/mL are classified as what schedule controlled substance?

    A. I
    B. II
    C. III
    D. IV
    E. V

89. In what publication are schedule changes published?

    A. *DI*
    B. *Orange Book*
    C. *USP*
    D. *HPUS*
    E. *Federal Register*

90. Exceptions to DEA registration include which of the following?
    I. Manufacturers
    II. Warehouses for storage of controlled substances by registrant
    III. Practitioners office
    IV. Common carriers

    A. I only
    B. I & II only
    C. II, III, & IV only
    D. III only
    E. None of the above

91. Under what circumstances may the DEA suspend or revoke a DEA registration?
    I. Conviction of a felony
    II. Exclusion from Medicare
    III. Falsified DEA application
    IV. Committed an error of omission when dispensing a prescription

    A. I, II, III, & IV
    B. I, II, & III only
    C. II & IV only
    D. III only
    E. I & II only

92. Which form is used to order Schedule I and II controlled substance?

    A. 222
    B. 363
    C. 41
    D. 225
    E. M
    F. None of the above

93. Which form is used to order Schedule IV controlled substances?

    A. 222
    B. 363
    C. 41
    D. 225
    E. None of the above

94. DEA Form 222 is used for which of the following?
    I. Ordering C II, III, & IV
    II. Transferring C IIs
    III. Ordering C Is

    A. I only
    B. II only
    C. III only
    D. II & III only
    E. I, II, & III

95. Copy 1 of DEA Form 222 stays in the custody of which entity?

    A. Supplier
    B. Pharmacy
    C. DEA
    D. FDA
    E. Patient

96. A person who has authority to sign a DEA Form 222 and who is not the DEA registrant must execute what form to make the transaction valid?

    A. DEA Form 41
    B. DEA Form 106
    C. Power of Attorney
    D. DEA Form 363
    E. None of the above

97. An executed DEA Form 222 must be kept on file for how long a period of time from execution?

    A. 1 year
    B. 2 years
    C. 3 years
    D. 5 years
    E. 7 years

98. What action must a pharmacist take when he or she moves to a new pharmacy location if he or she had the authority to execute DEA Form 222?

    A. Complete a Notice of Revocation
    B. Complete a new Power of Attorney for the new pharmacy location
    C. Notify the suppliers of the change in the Power of Attorney for each pharmacy location
    D. All of the above
    E. None of the above

99. Which of the following information is contained on the DEA Form 222?
    I. DEA number of registrant
    II. License number of registrant
    III. Specification of the type of drug activity
    IV. Registrant signature

    A. I, II, III, & IV
    B. I, II, & III only
    C. I, III, & IV only
    D. I & IV only
    E. II, III, & IV only

100. How many numbered lines are there on each DEA Form 222?

    A. 5
    B. 10
    C. 15
    D. 20
    E. 30

101. What action should a registrant take if his or her DEA Form 222 is defective?

    A. Cross out the incorrect information and handwrite the correct information on the form.
    B. Erase the incorrect information and print the correct information.
    C. Draw a line through the incorrect information and type the correct information on the form.
    D. Send the form back to DEA with a request that the DEA correct the form.
    E. Get verbal authorization from the DEA for manual correction of the form.

102. What is the registrant required to complete when filling out the DEA Form for a controlled substance order?

    A. Date of order
    B. Signature of registrant
    C. Total number of lines completed on the order
    D. Name and address of supplier
    E. All of the above

103. How many suppliers may be listed on each DEA Form 222?

    A. 1
    B. 2
    C. 3
    D. 4
    E. 5

104. What information does the supplier record on the DEA Form 222 received from the purchaser?

    A. The purchaser's name
    B. The purchaser's address
    C. The number of bulk containers supplied on each order to the purchaser
    D. Supplier's signature
    E. All of the above

105. The supplier records the above referenced information in question 104 on which copy or copies of the DEA Form 222?

    I. 1
    II. 2
    III. 3

    A. I only
    B. II only
    C. III only
    D. I & II only
    E. II & III only

106. When placing an order, a pharmacy submits which copy or copies of DEA Form 222 to the supplier?

    I. 1
    II. 2
    III. 3

    A. I only
    B. II only

C. III only

D. I & II only

E. I, II, & III

107. The supplier retains which copy of the DEA Form 222 for its records?

A. 1

B. 2

C. 3

D. 1 & 2

E. No copy is retained by the supplier

108. Which copy of the DEA Form 222 is sent to the DEA by the pharmacy?

A. 1

B. 2

C. 3

D. 1 & 2

E. No copy is submitted by the pharmacy

109. Which copy or copies of the DEA Form 222 is sent to the DEA?

A. 1

B. 2

C. 3

D. 1 & 2

E. No copy is sent to the DEA

110. Which entity is responsible for sending a copy of the DEA Form 222 to the DEA?

A. Pharmacy

B. Supplier

C. Patient

D. All of the above

E. None of the above, the DEA does not receive a copy of the form

111. Under what circumstances may a supplier fill a defective order form?

I. Misspelling of the drugs name if there is no question about the identity of the drug.

II. Package size is missing where only one package size exists for the product.

III. Number of lines completed by the purchaser is missing.

A. I only

B. II only

C. I & II only

D. III only

E. I, II, & III

112. Under what circumstances will a suppler reject an order form?

I. Number of lines completed by purchaser is empty.

II. Form is illegible.

III. Placement of ordered items on form is out of order.

A. I only

B. II only

C. II & III only

D. I & II only

E. I, II, & III

113. When the purchaser receives a rejected order form from the supplier, what can the purchaser do to receive the drug products ordered?

    A. Correct the form and send it back to the supplier.
    B. Send the rejected form to the DEA.
    C. Send the rejected form to a difference supplier.
    D. Attach copies of the rejected order to the other portion of DEA Form 222 and maintain with other DEA records, then process a new order and submit to the supplier.
    E. Complete the number of lines section and resubmit.

114. Partial filling of DEA Form 222 must be completed within what period of time?

    A. 30 days
    B. 60 days
    C. 90 days
    D. 180 days
    E. There is no provision for partial filling

115. If the DEA Form 222 order cannot be filled to completion, what happens to the order?

    A. The order becomes invalid if it cannot be filled to completion within the required period of time.
    B. The date can be changed on the original order form to extend the time period.

C. The form does not have an expiration date so it is valid in perpetuity.
    D. Supplier holds onto the form until they can fill the form to completion, inserting a new date for the date that the order is filled to completion.
    E. None of the above, since partial filling is not permissible.

116. Endorsement of an order on a DEA Form 222 form must be done within what period of time?

    A. 30 days
    B. 60 days
    C. 90 days
    D. 180 days
    E. Endorsement is not permissible

117. Which of the following are exceptions to being a DEA registrant and possessing controlled substance?
    I. Practitioners offices
    II. Common carriers
    III. Offices where sales of controlled substances are solicited only

    A. I only
    B. II only
    C. III only
    D. I & II only
    E. I, II, & III

118. DEA registrants must maintain what controlled substance records?
    I. Receipt
    II. Distributed
    III. Destroyed

A. I only
B. II only
C. III only
D. II & III only
E. I, II, & III

119. Which DEA Form must a pharmacist complete to personally register with the DEA?

A. Form 222
B. Form 41
C. Form 224
D. Form 225
E. No registration is required

120. How often does a registrant reregister with the DEA?

A. Every 1 year
B. Every 2 years
C. Every 3 years
D. Every 5 years
E. Every 7 years

121. Under what circumstances may the U.S. federal government suspend revocation of DEA registration?
   I. Registrant is convicted of a felony involving a controlled substance.
   II. Registrant had been excluding from participating in the Medicare program.
   III. Registrant filed a DEA registration with false information.

A. I only
B. II only

C. III only
D. I & III only
E. I, II, & III

122. When issuing a DEA registration, the federal government works with the registrant's state of licensure to review which of the following?
   I. State's disciplinary action involving registrant
   II. Registrant's conviction record in the state
   III. Safety and health issues threatening the safety of the public

A. I only
B. II only
C. III only
D. I & II only
E. I, II, & III

123. Ordering Schedule I controlled substances is done utilizing what form?

A. DEA Form 41
B. DEA Form 222
C. DEA Form 224
D. DEA Form 225
E. DEA Form 363

124. Ordering Schedule II controlled substances is done utilizing which form?

A. DEA Form 41
B. DEA Form 222
C. DEA Form 224
D. DEA Form 225
E. DEA Form 363

125. Ordering Schedule III controlled substances is done utilizing which form?

    A. DEA Form 41
    B. DEA Form 222
    C. DEA Form 224
    D. DEA Form 225
    E. No official DEA form is required

126. Ordering Schedule IV controlled substances is done utilizing which form?

    A. DEA Form 41
    B. DEA Form 222
    C. DEA Form 224
    D. DEA Form 225
    E. No official DEA form is required

127. Ordering Schedule V controlled substances is done utilizing which form?

    A. DEA Form 41
    B. DEA Form 222
    C. DEA Form 224
    D. DEA Form 225
    E. No official DEA form is required

128. The DEA Form 222 is used for which of the following activities?
    I. Ordering
    II. Destroying
    III. Transferring

    A. I only
    B. II only
    C. III only
    D. I & II only
    E. I & III only

129. Which copy of the DEA Form 222 stays with the pharmacy?

    A. 1
    B. 2
    C. 3
    D. 1 & 2
    E. 2 & 3

130. Which copy of the DEA Form 222 stays with the supplier?

    A. 1
    B. 2
    C. 3
    D. 1 & 2
    E. 2 & 3

131. Which copy of the DEA Form 222 is sent back to the pharmacy?

    A. 1
    B. 2
    C. 3
    D. 1 & 2
    E. No copy is sent back to the pharmacy

132. A registrant who wants to grant authority for execution of the DEA Form 222s must complete what form to give authority to someone else?

    A. Power of Attorney
    B. Revocation of Notice
    C. DEA Form 222
    D. All of the above
    E. None of the above

133. How many signatures validate the Power of Attorney form?

    A. 0
    B. 1
    C. 2
    D. 3
    E. 4

134. How long is a Notice of Revocation kept on file?

    A. 6 months from date of execution
    B. 1 year from date of execution
    C. 2 years from date of execution
    D. 3 years from date of execution
    E. 5 years from date of execution

135. When a registrant receives DEA Form 222 from the DEA, which of the following information about the registrant is contained on the form?
    I. Type of activity and type of schedules that registrant can engage in
    II. Registration number of registrant's supplier
    III. Name and address of registrant

    A. I only
    B. II only
    C. I & III only
    D. III only
    E. I, II, & III

136. Practitioners must use what form to obtain Schedule I and II controlled substances?

    A. DEA Form 222
    B. DEA Form 41

C. DEA Form 363
D. Prescription for office use
E. None of the above, practitioners are not permitted to obtain Schedule I and II controlled substances

137. The DEA Form 222 is what type of form?

    A. Single form
    B. Duplicate form
    C. Triplicate form
    D. Quadruple form
    E. None of the above

138. How many items may be ordered on each numbered line on the DEA Form 222?

    A. 1
    B. 2
    C. 3
    D. 5
    E. 7

139. The purchaser completes what section or sections of the DEA Form 222?
    I. Supplier name and address
    II. Purchaser's signature
    III. Number of lines completed by the order on the form

    A. I only
    B. II only
    C. III only
    D. I & II only
    E. I, II, & III

140. How many suppliers may the purchaser order from on each DEA Form 222?

    A. 1
    B. 2
    C. 3
    D. 5
    E. 7

141. When a pharmacy discontinues business and transfers the controlled substances to another pharmacy, what form must the pharmacy use to transfer Schedule I and II controlled substances?

    A. DEA Form 222
    B. DEA Form 41
    C. DEA Form 363
    D. DEA Form 224
    E. Power of Attorney

142. If the purchaser executes a DEA Form 222 and sends it to the supplier for filling and the purchaser does not receive the order from the supplier, what action should the purchaser take?

    A. Purchaser should call the supplier to see if the order was received.
    B. Purchaser should prepare a statement that an order was completed and sent to the supplier and that the supplier did not receive the order and that the order is assumed to be lost or stolen.

    C. Purchaser should complete a new order for transmission to the supplier.
    D. A & C only
    E. A, B, & C

143. What information should the purchaser include in the statement referenced in question 142?

    I. Serial number of the DEA Form 222
    II. Date of order
    III. Statement that order was lost or stolen
    IV. Statement that the DEA was notified by telephone of the potential loss or theft

    A. I & II only
    B. II & III only
    C. III & IV only
    D. I, II, & III only
    E. I, II, III, & IV

144. The purchaser retains the statement referenced in question 143 for how long a period of time?

    A. 6 months
    B. 1 year
    C. 2 years
    D. 3 years
    E. 5 years

145. What controlled substance records must the purchaser maintain?

    I. Copy 2 of all DEA Form 222 executed
    II. Copy 3 of all DEA Form 222 executed

III. All rejected DEA Form 222 received
IV. All statements associated with lost or stolen DEA Form 222

A. I only
B. I & II only
C. II, III, & IV only
D. I, III, & IV only
E. I, II, III, & IV

146. When ordering Schedule I and II controlled substances, which drugs must be ordered on a separate DEA Form 222 from all other Schedule I and II controlled substances?
   I. Marijuana
   II. Etorphine HCl
   III. Carfentanil

A. I, II, & III
B. I & II only
C. II & III only
D. I & III only

147. When a DEA registration is terminated, what should the registrant do with unused DEA Form 222s?

A. Destroy the forms
B. Forward the forms to the location where the drugs are being stored
C. Return the forms to the supplier
D. Return the forms to the DEA
E. Write void across the front of the forms and maintain in a file with all other controlled substance records

148. Under which of the following circumstances would a purchaser return DEA Form 222 to the DEA?
   I. Purchaser address on the form is incorrect.
   II. Purchaser's registration has been revoked.
   III. Purchaser has died.

A. I only
B. II only
C. III only
D. II & III only
E. I, II, & III

149. A supplier receives a DEA Form 222 and is concerned about the validity of the form. What action should the supplier take?

A. Notify the purchaser that the form is rejected.
B. Notify the DEA of the concern.
C. Correct the form if information is missing or incorrect.
D. Fill the order with a notation that there is a concern.
E. Notify the local police department.

150. If a purchaser cancels all or part of an order placed on DEA Form 222, what action must the supplier take when notified of said cancellation?

    A. The supplier is not obligated to take any action after receipt of a valid DEA Form 222.
    B. The supplier must notify the DEA of the cancellation.
    C. The supplier must fill the order as indicated and accept a return of unwanted drug products from the purchaser.
    D. The supplier will make a notation on Copies 1 and 2 of the form by drawing a line through the cancelled items and writing the word "cancelled" in the space provided for the number of items shipped.
    E. The supplier endorses the order over to another suppler.

151. If a supplier voids part or all of an order on a DEA Form 222, what action must the supplier take to affect this?

    A. The supplier must notify the purchaser in writing of the cancellation voiding all or part of the order.
    B. The supplier must indicate void on Copy 1 and 2 of the order.
    C. The supplier must draw a line through the voided items.
    D. The supplier must write "void" in the space provided for the number of items to be shipped.
    E. All of the above.

152. The digital certificate can be used for ordering which schedule controlled substances electronically?

    A. II
    B. III
    C. IV
    D. V
    E. I, II, III, IV, & V

153. Which statement about the use of e222 is correct?

    A. Use of e222 is mandatory.
    B. Use of e222 is limited to the ordering of Schedule I and II controlled substances.
    C. A purchaser using the e222 does not need to be a DEA registrant.
    D. Digital certificates for pharmacy registrants are renewed every year.
    E. Digital certificates for manufacturers are valid for 1 year.

154. How often does the supplier report to the DEA, when an e222 is filled for a purchaser?

    A. Every business day
    B. Every other business day
    C. Every third business day
    D. Every Friday
    E. Every other week

155. What information does the supplier report to the DEA for orders filled using e222?
    I. Purchaser's name, address, and DEA number
    II. Date order was sent to purchaser

III. Date order was signed by purchaser
IV. Name of controlled substance, National Drug Code (NDC) number
V. Quantity of items shipped

A. I, II, III, IV, & V
B. I, II, IV, & V only
C. I, III, & IV only
D. I, III, IV, & V only
E. II, IV, & V only

156. The digital certificate that is used for e222 requires which of the following information?
I. Unique number for tracking purposes
II. Name of supplier
III. Name of controlled substances
IV. Quantity in a single package

A. I, II, III, & IV
B. I, III, & IV only
C. II, III, & IV only
D. III & IV only
E. III only

157. Which statement about endorsement of e222 is correct?

A. Endorsement is not permissible because of the problem with linking of files.
B. The DEA must be notified prior to an endorsement.
C. Endorsement must be done within 15 days.

D. Due to ease of generating a new order, endorsement may not be used often.
E. None of the above.

158. Revocation of digital certificates may occur under which of the following circumstances?
I. Registrant has changed his or her business address.
II. A Notice of Revocation has been signed and is on file.
III. Password has been forgotten.

A. I only
B. II only
C. III only
D. I & III only
E. I, II, & III

159. What action must a DEA registrant take when the pharmacy terminates its DEA registration?
I. Send any used DEA Form 222 to the DEA
II. Write "VOID" across the face of the unused DEA Form 222
III. Send all opened containers of Schedule II controlled substances to the DEA for destruction

A. I only
B. I & II only
C. III only
D. I & III only
E. I, II, & III

160. How long must the terminating pharmacy maintain the records of the controlled substances upon termination?

    A. 6 months
    B. 1 year
    C. 2 years
    D. 3 years
    E. No records are required to be maintained upon termination

161. When a pharmacy terminates its business operation, what must the pharmacy do with the controlled substances remaining in the pharmacy upon close of business?

    A. Controlled substances may be transferred to another pharmacy.
    B. Controlled substances may be returned to the supplier where purchased.
    C. Controlled substances may be destroyed.
    D. Controlled substances must be sent to the DEA for further disposition.
    E. A, B, & C

162. When transferring Schedule I and II controlled substances, what form must the receiving pharmacy registrant use?

    A. DEA Form 41
    B. DEA Form 363
    C. DEA Form 222
    D. DEA Form 224
    E. DEA Form 225

163. What form must be used when transferring Schedule III–V controlled substances?

    A. DEA Form 222
    B. DEA Form 224
    C. DEA Form 225
    D. DEA Form 363
    E. The transfer must be in writing; however, there is not a particular form that must be used

164. Within what period of time must the DEA be notified if one registrant is transferring his or her business to another DEA registrant?

    A. 5 days
    B. 7 days
    C. 10 days
    D. 14 days
    E. 30 days

165. What information must the DEA receive about the proposed transfer of business?

    A. Name, address, and registration number of discontinuing business.
    B. Name, address, and registration number of acquiring business.
    C. Date when controlled substances will be actually transferred.
    D. Whether the business will continue at the new location.
    E. All of the above.

166. On the date of business transfer, who is responsible for conducting a controlled substance inventory?

A. DEA
B. Pharmacy discontinuing the business
C. Pharmacy acquiring the business
D. B & C
E. No inventory is required by either party

167. Which entity referenced in question 166 maintains the controlled substance inventory?

A. DEA
B. Pharmacy discontinuing business
C. Pharmacy acquiring business
D. B & C
E. Since no inventory is required no entity needs to maintain a copy

168. For how long a period of time must the controlled substance inventory be maintained by the discontinuing business?

A. 1 year
B. 2 years
C. 3 years
D. 5 years
E. No time requirement since there is no requirement that an inventory be conducted and maintained

169. For how long a period of time must the controlled substance inventory be maintained by the acquiring business?

A. 1 year
B. 2 years

C. 3 years
D. 5 years
E. No time requirement since there is no requirement that an inventory be conducted and maintained

170. When is the acquiring business required to send a copy of the controlled substance inventory to the DEA?

A. Within 7 days of the controlled substance transfer
B. Within 14 days of the controlled substance transfer
C. Within 30 days of the controlled substance transfer
D. Within 60 days of the controlled substance transfer
E. A copy is not sent to the DEA

171. When is the discontinuing business required to send a copy of the controlled substance inventory to the DEA?

A. Within 7 days of the controlled substance transfer
B. Within 14 days of the controlled substance transfer
C. Within 30 days of the controlled substance transfer
D. Within 60 days of the controlled substance transfer
E. A copy is not sent to the DEA

172. When the transfer of controlled substances is from a pharmacy to a supplier or manufacturer, the pharmacy must maintain a record of the transfer that contains which of the following information?
    I. Date of transaction
    II. Name, strength, quantity of controlled substance
    III. Suppliers or manufacturer's name, address, and registration number
    IV. Inventory of all controlled substances received from the supplier or manufacturer

    A. I only
    B. II only
    C. I, II, & III only
    D. I, II, & IV only
    E. I, II, III, & IV

173. All records for the disposal or destruction of controlled substances must be kept by the pharmacy for what period of time from the date of disposal or destruction?

    A. 1 year
    B. 2 years
    C. 3 years
    D. 5 years
    E. No record is necessary

174. When a pharmacy uses a reverse distributor for the destruction of controlled substances, what steps must the pharmacy take to be compliant with the law?

    A. Contact the nearest DEA Field Office for disposal instructions.
    B. Determine if the reverse distributor is registered with the DEA.
    C. Follow the laws of the state where the pharmacy is registered.
    D. Request authorization from the DEA for disposal through the reverse distributor.
    E. All of the above.

175. What form must pharmacies complete for the once-a-year DEA authorization for destruction of controlled substances?

    A. DEA Form 222
    B. DEA Form 41
    C. DEA Form 363
    D. DEA Form 224
    E. DEA Form 225

176. In addition to the form referenced in question 175, what information must the pharmacy provide to the DEA before approval will be granted?

    A. List of drugs to be destroyed
    B. Letter requesting permission
    C. Method of destruction to be used
    D. Proposed date of destruction
    E. All of the above

177. For the once-a-year destruction of controlled substances, how many witnesses must be present for the destruction?

    A. 0
    B. 1

C. 2

D. 3

E. 5

178. Which of the following are qualified to witness the destruction of controlled substances?
    I. Pharmacy technician
    II. Pharmacist
    III. Nurse practitioner
    IV. Local police officer

    A. I, II, III, & IV
    B. I & II only
    C. II & IV only
    D. II, III, & IV only
    E. I, II, & IV only

179. The required documents for the once-a-year destruction of controlled substances must be received by the DEA within what time frame?

    A. 5 days before the date of destruction
    B. 10 days before the date of destruction
    C. 2 weeks before the date of destruction
    D. 1 week after destruction
    E. 2 weeks after destruction

180. What type of notification does the registrant receive that the DEA has been granted authority for once-a-year destruction of controlled substances?

A. DEA telephones the registrant with an authorization code.

B. Authority is granted by DEA via telephone through the local state regulatory agency.

C. DEA notifies the registrant in writing.

D. DEA posts a notice on its web site with an authorization code that the registrants must include on the paperwork that accompanies the destruction.

E. There is no notification from the DEA.

181. What form is the registrant required to send to the DEA once the controlled substances are destroyed?

    A. DEA Form 222
    B. DEA Form 41
    C. DEA Form 224
    D. DEA Form 225
    E. DEA Form 363

182. With regard to the form referenced in question 181, how long must the registrant maintain a copy of the form sent to the DEA?

    A. 1 year
    B. 2 years
    C. 3 years
    D. 5 years
    E. There is no requirement that the record be maintained

183. Prior authorization from the DEA to destroy controlled substances is not necessary if which of the following occurs?

    A. The local environmental authority is present during the destruction.
    B. If the DEA has previously advised the registrant that prior authorization is not necessary.
    C. If state law enforcement is present during destruction.
    D. A, B, & C
    E. There is no waiver of the prior authorization allowed.

184. When a pharmacy transfers Schedule I and II controlled substances to a registered reverse distributor, what form must the distributor issue to the pharmacy?

    A. DEA Form 41
    B. DEA Form 363
    C. DEA Form 224
    D. DEA Form 225
    E. DEA Form 222

185. Under the circumstances stated in question 184, which party is responsible for submitting the DEA form to the DEA?

    A. Reverse distributor
    B. Pharmacy
    C. Local regulatory agency
    D. Local environmental agency
    E. Form 41 is not submitted to the DEA

186. What registrants are issued blanket authorization for destruction of controlled substances on a limited basis by the DEA?
    I. Retail pharmacies
    II. Hospitals
    III. Clinics

    A. I only
    B. I & II only
    C. I & III only
    D. II & III only
    E. I, II, & III

187. Which of the following criteria is reviewed by the DEA prior to authorizing a blanket authorization for the destruction of controlled substances?
    I. Frequency of destruction
    II. Method of destruction
    III. Security and storage of controlled substances
    IV. Registrant's past history with controlled substances

    A. I & II only
    B. III & IV only
    C. I, II, & III only
    D. I, II, & IV only
    E. I, II, III, & IV

188. When a registrant is granted a blanket authorization, what form does the registrant complete upon destruction of the drug products?

    A. DEA Form 41
    B. DEA Form 222
    C. DEA Form 224

D. DEA Form 225

E. DEA Form 363

189. If a pharmacy suspects a theft of controlled substances, what action should the pharmacy take?

A. Notify the DEA

B. Notify corporate headquarters for the pharmacy, if a chain

C. Notify local law enforcement

D. All of the above

E. None of the above

190. Within what period of time should a pharmacy notify the DEA of a suspected theft?

A. Immediately upon discovery of the suspected theft or loss

B. Within 2 hours of the suspected theft or loss

C. Within 5 hours of the suspected theft or loss

D. Within 12 hours of the suspected theft or loss

E. Within 24 hours of the suspected theft or loss

191. If the pharmacy is unsure if a theft or loss of a controlled substance has occurred, what action should the pharmacy take?

A. Notify DEA immediately if unsure

B. Wait 24 hours to determine if the drug products appear

C. Perform an internal investigation and notify DEA in 48 hours

D. Hire a private investigator to conduct an investigation with notification to DEA if it was determined that a theft occurred

E. Notify DEA prior to biennial inventory

192. Any documentation that the pharmacy maintains with regard to a suspected theft or loss should be maintained for how long a period of time from the documentation?

A. 6 months

B. 1 year

C. 2 years

D. 5 years

E. 7 years

193. What form is used to report the theft or loss of controlled substances to the DEA?

A. DEA Form 41

B. DEA Form 106

C. DEA Form 222

D. DEA Form 224

E. DEA Form 363

194. With reference to question 193, how many copies of the form should the pharmacy make?

A. 1

B. 2

C. 3

D. 4

E. 0

195. With reference to question 194, how are the copies distributed?

    A. Original to the DEA, 1 copy to local law enforcement, 1 copy stays with the pharmacy
    B. Original and 1 copy to DEA, 1 copy stays with the pharmacy
    C. Original to the DEA, 1 copy stays with the pharmacy
    D. Original and 2 copies to the DEA
    E. Original and 1 copy stays with the pharmacy. The DEA does not require a copy

196. What form does the pharmacy file if the investigation does not discover a theft or loss?

    A. DEA Form 41
    B. DEA Form 106
    C. DEA Form 222
    D. DEA Form 224
    E. No form need be filed

197. All records associated with a theft or loss of controlled substance should be kept on file in the pharmacy for how long a period of time?

    A. 6 months
    B. 1 year
    C. 2 years
    D. 3 years
    E. 5 years

198. Under what circumstances may the federal government get involved in an investigation of a theft of a controlled substance?

    I. If the replacement cost of the drug products is less than $250.
    II. A registrant suffers bodily harm during the commission of the robbery.
    III. A person is killed during the commission of the robbery.

    A. I, II, & III
    B. I & III only
    C. II & III only
    D. I & II only
    E. II only

199. Penalties for a conviction for a theft of a controlled substance as mentioned in question 198 may include which of the following?

    I. Maximum fine of $35,000 when a weapon was used in the commission of the crime.
    II. Twenty-five years imprisonment when a weapon was used in the commission of the crime.
    III. Life imprisonment if death results from the crime.

    A. I & II only
    B. III only
    C. II & III only
    D. I & III only
    E. I, II, & III

200. If an order for controlled substances is filled by a supplier and the order does not ultimately reach the pharmacy, which party is responsible for advising the DEA of the suspected theft or loss?

    A. Supplier
    B. Pharmacy

C. Transit carrier
D. Local police department
E. State regulatory authority

201. If a pharmacy has breakage or spillage of controlled substances, what form does the pharmacy complete and send to the DEA?

A. DEA Form 41
B. DEA Form 106
C. DEA Form 222
D. DEA Form 224
E. DEA does not consider breakage or spillage, a theft or loss but a minor inventory adjustment

202. If some product is recovered from a spill, what should the pharmacy do with the recovered product?

A. Discard the portion recovered
B. Salvage what is recoverable and use for dispensing
C. Return to the DEA
D. Return to a reverse distributor
E. Turn over to the local environmental agency

203. If a chain pharmacy requests that all controlled substance records be maintained at a central location, notification will be received in what format from the DEA?

A. Written permission from the DEA
B. Posting of notice on DEA web site with authorization number
C. Telephone notification with authorization number

D. No response from the DEA is acquiescence
E. No permission is required

204. With reference to question 203, what period of time does the pharmacy need to wait before it can store the records centrally?

A. 5 days
B. 7 days
C. 14 days
D. 21 days
E. There is no time requirement

205. Controlled substance prescription records may be stored in what manner?

A. One file for all Schedule II controlled substances, one file for Schedule III–V controlled substances, and one file for all noncontrolled drug products dispense.
B. One file for all Schedule II controlled substances dispensed and one file for all other drugs (noncontrolled and Schedule III–V provided Schedule III–V are readily retrievable).
C. One file for all Schedules II–V dispensed provided all controlled substance prescriptions are readily retrievable and one file for all noncontrolled prescriptions.
D. A, B, & C
E. A & B only

206. What information must be retrievable when accessing original online records of controlled substance records?
    I. Original prescription number
    II. Date of dispensing
    III. Prescriber's name, address, and DEA number
    IV. Drug name prescribed

    A. I only
    B. I, II, & III only
    C. I, III, & IV only
    D. II & III only
    E. I, II, III, & IV

207. Computer retrieval of refill controlled substance information must access which of the following?
    I. Original date of prescription
    II. Name of controlled substance
    III. Total number of refills dispensed

    A. I, II, & III
    B. II & III only
    C. II only
    D. III only
    E. I & III only

208. Controlled substance prescription records should be printed out how often?

    A. Daily
    B. Weekly
    C. Every 2 weeks
    D. Every 3 weeks
    E. Monthly

209. Who is responsible for verifying the accuracy of the controlled substances dispensed?

    A. The pharmacy supervisor for the pharmacy
    B. The pharmacist who filled each prescription is responsible for verifying all prescriptions they filled
    C. DEA
    D. State regulatory authority
    E. All of the above

210. The controlled substance record that the pharmacy prints out must be maintained for how long a period of time?

    A. 6 months
    B. 1 year
    C. 2 years
    D. 3 years
    E. 5 years

211. What does a pharmacy do with the controlled substance inventory?

    A. Send it to the DEA upon completion.
    B. Send it to the local regulatory authority upon completion.
    C. Post it on the pharmacy's web site.
    D. Maintain in the pharmacy readily retrievable for inspection and copying.
    E. Send to the local law enforcement.

212. When a new pharmacy opens for business and the pharmacy obtains a DEA registration, an initial inventory of controlled substances must include which of the following?
    I. Inventory date
    II. Drug name and strength

III. Estimate of all controlled substances packaged in quantities of 100 or less

IV. Number of units/volume

A. I, II, III, & IV
B. I, II, & IV only
C. I, II, & III only
D. II, III, & IV only
E. II & IV only

213. When a new pharmacy opens for business and the pharmacy has no controlled substances in stock, the pharmacy records an inventory of what number?

A. 0
B. Estimate of 10
C. Estimate of 25
D. Estimate of 50
E. Estimate of 100
F. No record is made

214. How often does a pharmacy conduct a controlled substance inventory?

A. Every day, a perpetual inventory must be kept
B. Once a year
C. Every 2 years
D. Every 3 years
E. Every 5 years

215. The controlled substance inventory must be maintained for what period of time from the date of the inventory?

A. 6 months
B. 1 year

C. 2 years
D. 3 years
E. 5 years

216. For quantities of 100 or less, the controlled substance inventory requires an exact count of which of the following?

I. Schedule II
II. Schedule III
III. Schedule IV
IV. Schedule V

A. I only
B. I & II only
C. I & IV only
D. III only
E. I, II, III, & IV

217. Estimates of controlled substances may be done for which of the following?

I. Schedule II
II. Opened containers of Schedule III in quantities more than 1000 dosage units
III. Schedule V in quantities less than 240 mL

A. I, II, & III
B. II only
C. III only
D. I & III only
E. I & III only

218. What is the main distinction between a prescription and a medication order?

    A. A medication order is intended for self-administration.
    B. A prescription is intended to be administered to the patient by a health care professional.
    C. A prescription is intended for dispensing to an ultimate user.
    D. A medication order is intended to be administered to the patient by a health care professional.
    E. C & D

219. What information must a controlled substance prescription contain?
    I. Patient name and address
    II. Practitioner's name, address, and DEA number
    III. Drug's, name, strength, and dosage form
    IV. Directions for use
    V. Date of issue

    A. I, II, III, IV, & V
    B. I & II only
    C. I, II, & IV only
    D. I, II, & V only
    E. I, II, IV, & V only

220. Which health care professionals may be authorized to use a hospital's DEA number?
    I. Pharmacist
    II. Intern
    III. Resident

    A. I only
    B. II only
    C. III only

    D. II & III only
    E. I, II, & III

221. Exempt practitioners must include what identification on controlled substance prescriptions?

    A. DEA number
    B. Social security number
    C. Agency and service identification number
    D. All of the above
    E. No number is required since the practitioner is exempt

222. Midlevel practitioners' DEA number begins with what letter?

    A. A
    B. B
    C. C
    D. M
    E. X

223. A practitioner who requires Schedule II controlled substances for interoffice use must execute which of the following?

    A. DEA Form 222
    B. A prescription for the drug product that states on the face of the prescription for office use
    C. Execution of an order with the local pharmacy
    D. C & D
    E. DEA Form 41

224. Schedule II controlled substance prescriptions must be filled within how many days of the date of issue?

A. 15 days
B. 20 days
C. 30 days
D. 60 days
E. There is no time limit

225. What is the maximum days supply that a practitioner may prescribe a Schedule II controlled substance for a patient?

A. 15
B. 30
C. 45
D. 60
E. There is no maximum days supply

226. Emergency refers to which of the following situations?
   I. Immediate administration of the drug is necessary for proper treatment of the patient.
   II. No alternative treatment is available.
   III. Patient cannot pick up the written prescription within a reasonable period of time.

A. I, II, & III
B. I only
C. II only
D. III only
E. I & II only

227. In a true emergency, how may the practitioner transmit a prescription for a Schedule II controlled substance to the pharmacy?

A. Electronically
B. Facsimile
C. Telephone
D. B & C
E. A, B, & C

228. What quantity of Schedule II controlled substance may the practitioner authorize in an emergency?

A. 3 days supply
B. 5 days supply
C. 7 days supply
D. 30 days supply
E. Quantity necessary to treat the patient during the emergency period

229. The pharmacist receiving the emergency Schedule II controlled substance prescription must do which of the following?
   I. Confirm the identity of the prescriber
   II. Reduce the prescription to writing
   III. Confirm the identity of the patient

A. I, II, & III
B. I & III only
C. II only
D. I only
E. II & III only

230. What action must the practitioner take after an emergency prescription for a Schedule II controlled substance has been transmitted to the pharmacy?

    A. Practitioner may provide the patient with the prescription for delivery to the pharmacy provided the patient delivers it within 30 days.
    B. Practitioner must provide the pharmacy with a signed prescription within 7 days of the emergency authorization.
    C. Practitioner must write the words "Authorization for Emergency Dispensing" on the face of the prescription.
    D. B & C
    E. A, B, & C

231. If the pharmacy does not receive the prescription referenced in question 230, what action must the pharmacy take?

    A. Pharmacy must call the practitioner to remind the practitioner to send the written follow-up prescription.
    B. Pharmacy must notify the patient that it is his or her responsibility to obtain the written follow-up prescription from the practitioner.
    C. Pharmacy stamps the back of the prescription with a statement that states that the follow-up prescription was not received within the required period of time.

    D. Pharmacy must notify the nearest DEA Diversion Field Office that the required follow-up prescription was not received.
    E. No action on the part of the pharmacy is required.

232. How many refills may a practitioner authorize on a Schedule II controlled substance prescription?

    A. 0
    B. 1
    C. 2
    D. 5
    E. 12

233. Partial dispensing of Schedule II controlled substance prescriptions is permissible under which of the following circumstances?
    I. Patient requests a quantity lesser than that prescribed.
    II. Pharmacy is unable to fill the entire quantity prescribed.
    III. Patient is a resident of a Long-Term Care Facility.

    A. I only
    B. II only
    C. III only
    D. II & III only
    E. I & II only

234. When a Schedule II controlled substance prescription is partially dispensed, the pharmacist must note the following information?
    I. Date of partial filling
    II. Quantity partially filled on that date

III. Quantity remaining on that particular fill

IV. Initials or signature of the dispensing pharmacist

A. I, II, III, & IV
B. I & IV only
C. II & III only
D. I, III, & IV
E. II, III, & IV only

235. Partially filled Schedule II controlled substance prescriptions are valid for what period of time from the date of issue?

A. 10 days
B. 30 days
C. 60 days
D. 180 days
E. There is no time limit

236. If a practitioner transmits a fax to the pharmacy for a Schedule II controlled substance prescription for an emergency, the practitioner must send a follow-up prescription within what period of time?

A. 3 days of date of emergency
B. 5 days of date of emergency
C. 7 days of date of emergency
D. 10 days of date of emergency
E. Fax is treated as an original and follow up is not required

237. Fax prescriptions for Schedule II controlled substances are treated as the original prescriptions under which of the following circumstances?

I. Patients in hospice care certified under Medicare
II. At the patient's request
III. Patients receiving home infusion/intravenous (IV) pain therapy

A. I only
B. III only
C. I & II only
D. II & III only
E. I & III only

238. Schedule III, IV, and V controlled substance prescriptions may be transmitted to the pharmacy by which of the following means?
I. Written
II. Oral
III. Fax
IV. Electronic

A. I, II, III, & IV
B. I, II, & III only
C. I & II only
D. I, III, & IV only
E. I only

239. How many times may the practitioner authorize refills for prescriptions for Schedule III, IV, and V controlled substance prescriptions?

A. 0
B. 1
C. 3
D. 5
E. 7

240. Within what period of time must a prescription for a Schedule III, IV, or V controlled substance be filled?

   A. 10 days from the date of issue
   B. 20 days from the date of issue
   C. 30 days from the date of issue
   D. 60 days from the date of issue
   E. 6 months from the date of issue

241. Refills on a Schedule III, IV, or V controlled substance prescription expire within what period of time from the date of issue?

   A. 1 month
   B. 2 months
   C. 3 months
   D. 6 months
   E. 1 year

242. What information must the pharmacist record when refilling a Schedule III, IV, or V controlled substance prescription?
   I.   Dispensing pharmacist initials
   II.  Date of refill
   III. Refills remaining
   IV.  Amount of drug dispensed

   A. I, II, III, & IV
   B. I & II only
   C. I, II, & III only
   D. I, II, & IV only
   E. II only

243. Which schedule of controlled substances may be transferred between pharmacies?

   I.   II
   II.  III
   III. IV

   A. I only
   B. II only
   C. III only
   D. II & III only
   E. I, II, & III

244. Which statement about refill transfers is correct?

   A. Transfers may be done on a one-time basis.
   B. All refills may be transferred electronically if the pharmacies share a real time online database.
   C. Schedule II prescriptions cannot be transferred.
   D. Transfer must occur between two pharmacists.
   E. All of the above.

245. What quantity of a Schedule III, IV, or V controlled prescription may a practitioner prescribe in an emergency?

   A. 3 days
   B. 5 days
   C. 7 days
   D. 30 days
   E. Amount necessary to treat the patient during the emergency

246. A follow-up prescription referenced in question 245 must be received by the pharmacy within what period of time?

    A. 3 days from date of emergency
    B. 5 days from date of emergency
    C. 7 days from the date of emergency
    D. 30 days from date of emergency
    E. No follow-up is required for Schedule III, IV, or V.

247. What action must the pharmacy take if the follow-up is not received within the required time period?

    A. No action is necessary because no follow-up is necessary.
    B. Pharmacy must call the practitioner to obtain the follow up.
    C. Pharmacy must notify the DEA if the follow-up is not received.
    D. Pharmacy makes a notation on the prescription that the follow up has not been received.
    E. Pharmacy must notify patient that they must deliver the prescription to the pharmacy.

248. Partial filling of Schedule III, IV, or V controlled substance prescriptions must be completed within what period of time?

    A. 30 days of date of issue
    B. 60 days of date of issue
    C. 3 months of date of issue
    D. 6 months of date of issue
    E. 1 year of date of issue

249. A purchaser of OTC controlled substances must be how old?

    A. 16
    B. 18
    C. 20
    D. 21
    E. There is no age requirement

250. Who is authorized to dispense the OTC controlled substances to the purchaser?

    A. Pharmacy cashier
    B. Pharmacy technician
    C. Pharmacist
    D. A & B
    E. A, B, & C

251. What quantity of opium-containing product may the pharmacy sell to a purchaser over the counter?

    A. Not more than 48 dosage units
    B. 360 mL
    C. 460 mL
    D. 52 dosage units
    E. None of the above

252. How often may the purchaser purchase OTC controlled substances?

    A. 12 hour period of time
    B. 24 hour period of time
    C. 36 hour period of time
    D. 48 hour period of time
    E. 60 hour period of time

253. The Schedule V bound book must be maintained by the pharmacy for what period of time?

    A. 6 months
    B. 1 year
    C. 2 years
    D. 3 years
    E. 5 years

254. A prescription label for a controlled substance prescription must contain which of the following information?
    I. Patient name
    II. Pharmacy name and address
    III. Prescription number
    IV. Drug name

    A. I, II, III, & IV
    B. I, II, & III only
    C. I, III, & IV only
    D. II, III, & IV only
    E. I & IV only

255. Internet pharmacies that dispense controlled substance prescriptions must have a legitimate doctor–patient relationship. What four elements demonstrate the existence of this relationship?
    I. Medical complaint
    II. Medical history
    III. Physical examination
    IV. Complaint, history, and examination demonstrate the need for a controlled substance

    A. I only
    B. II only
    C. III only

    D. I, II, & III only
    E. I, II, III, & IV

256. Which schedule controlled substance may be transmitted electronically?

    A. II
    B. III
    C. IV
    D. V
    E. None of the above

257. Which act or amendment established five schedules of control substances?

    A. Drug Abuse Control Amendments
    B. FDA Modernization Act
    C. Orphan Drug Act
    D. Comprehensive Drug Abuse Prevention and Control Act
    E. Food, Drug, and Cosmetic Act

258. Which act or amendment established that any new drug marketed in the United States had to be safe?

    A. Food, Drug, and Cosmetic
    B. Durham-Humphrey
    C. Kefauver-Harris
    D. Pure Food and Drug
    E. Orphan Drug

259. Which act or amendment established strict reporting requirements for sample drug products?

    A. Food, Drug, and Cosmetic
    B. FDA Modernization Act
    C. Medical Device Amendments
    D. Kefauver-Harris
    E. Prescription Drug Marketing Act

260. For what period of time does the Post Market Surveillance, Phase IV last?

    A. 2 weeks
    B. 1 month
    C. 1 year
    D. 5 years
    E. The life of the drug product

261. When a manufacturer has changed the formulation of an approved drug product, the manufacturer submits what type of drug application to the FDA?

    A. Investigational New Drug (IND) Application
    B. Abbreviated New Drug Application (ANDA)
    C. Supplemental New Drug Application (SNDA)
    D. New Drug Application (NDA)
    E. Non Formulary New Drug Application (NFNDA)

262. Class I, General Controls, applies to which of the following devices?
    I. Elastic bandages
    II. Surgical drapes
    III. Powered wheel chairs
    IV. Replacement heart valves

    A. I only
    B. I & III only
    C. I, II, & III only
    D. II & IV only
    E. I, II, III, & IV

263. Which statement about cosmetics is accurate?

    A. Cosmetic products list all ingredients in ascending order based on predominance.
    B. Cosmetic manufacturers are not required to register with the FDA.
    C. Cosmetic manufacturers must adhere to GMP.
    D. Cosmetic products cannot be combined with drug products.
    E. Manufacturers of cosmetics are required to submit safety data to the FDA.

264. A drug recall where use or exposure to a drug product may cause temporary or medically reversible adverse health consequences or where probability of serious harm is remote is classified as what class recall?

    A. I
    B. II
    C. III
    D. IV
    E. V

265. Which statement about homeopathic drugs is correct?

    A. Homeopathic drugs must go through the NDA process.
    B. Under the Food, Drug, and Cosmetic Act , homeopathic drugs are subject to safety review.
    C. Homeopathic drugs are exempt from expiration dating.
    D. Homeopathic drugs are not subject to OTC review.
    E. Homeopathic drugs are assumed to be safe and effective.

266. Dietary supplements may contain which of the following?
   I. Vitamin
   II. Amino acid
   III. Analgesic

   A. I only
   B. I & II only
   C. III only
   D. I & III only
   E. I, II, & III

267. Which of the following actions can the FDA take with regard to drug products?
   I. Request that the manufacturer initiate a drug product recall
   II. Injunction
   III. Seize the drug product

   A. I only
   B. II only
   C. III only
   D. II & III only
   E. I, II, & III

268. Which of the following drug products are exempt from poison prevention packaging?
   I. Throat lozenges
   II. Aerosols
   III. Oral contraceptives
   IV. Prescription products dispensed by a pharmacist

   A. I only
   B. I & II only
   C. III only
   D. II & III only
   E. I, II, III, & IV

269. Which letter(s) designates that a drug product is pharmaceutically equivalent?

   A. A
   B. B
   C. BC
   D. RLD
   E. X

270. Which category of pregnancy warning is represented by the following statement, "Indicates that there have been adequate, well-controlled studies in pregnant women that demonstrate no risk to the fetus during the 1st trimester or during the last two trimester"?

   A. A
   B. B
   C. C
   D. D
   E. X

271. DEA registrations are valid for how long a period of time?

   A. 1 year
   B. 2 years
   C. 3 years
   D. 4 years
   E. 5 years

272. Straight opiates of codeine and morphine are classified as what schedule controlled substance?

   A. I
   B. II

C. III
D. IV
E. V

273. If a pharmacist has to partially fill a prescription for a narcotic because he or she does not have a sufficient quantity to fill the prescription, the remainder of the prescription must be filled within how many days or hours of dispensing?

    A. 24 hours
    B. 36 hours
    C. 72 hours
    D. 30 days
    E. 60 days

274. Which of the following information must be included on the label of a prescription for methadone?
    I. Date of issue
    II. Patient name
    III. Pharmacist name
    IV. Drug name

    A. I, II, III, & IV
    B. I, II, & IV only
    C. II & IV only
    D. II only
    E. I & II only

275. Health Insurance Portability and Accountability Act (HIPAA) acknowledgements must be kept on file for how long a period of time?

    A. 6 months
    B. 1 year
    C. 5 years

D. 6 years
E. 7 years

276. The FDA Bar Coding Rule applies to which of the following?
    I. Prescription drug samples
    II. Biological products
    III. OTCs used commonly in hospitals

    A. I only
    B. I & II only
    C. III only
    D. II & III only
    E. I, II, & III

277. USP Chapter <797> is applicable to which of the following facilities?
    I. Health care institutions
    II. Physician compounding facilities
    III. Sterile compounding pharmacies

    A. I only
    B. II only
    C. III only
    D. II & III only
    E. I, II, & III

278. The DEA Form 222 is used to order which of the following?
    I. Marijuana
    II. Demerol
    III. Amobarbital suppositories

    A. I only
    B. II only
    C. III only
    D. I & II only
    E. I, II, & III

279. Drug manufacturers are inspected by the federal government how often?

    A. Once a year
    B. Every 2 years
    C. Every 3 years
    D. Every 5 years
    E. They are exempt from inspection

280. This statement describes which pregnancy warning, "Should be considered to be contraindicated in pregnant women, or in most instances, for any woman of childbearing age unless appropriate contraceptive methods are being used"?

    A. A
    B. B
    C. C
    D. D
    E. X

281. When determining whether a drug product is equivalent for substitution purposes, what letter indicates that the product is not equivalent?

    A. A
    B. B
    C. C
    D. D
    E. X

282. Which of the following entities have the authority to initiate a recall?
    I. Pharmacies
    II. Manufacturer
    III. FDA

    A. I only
    B. II only

C. I & III only
D. I & II only
E. I, II, & III

283. What is the maximum period of time that can be restored to a drug patent?

    A. 1 year
    B. 2 years
    C. 3 years
    D. 5 years
    E. 17 years

284. The term "grandfathered" drugs refers to what time period?

    A. Drugs marketed prior to 1938
    B. Drugs marketed prior to 1951
    C. Drugs marketed between 1906 and 1938
    D. Drugs marketed between 1938 and 1962
    E. Drugs marketed after 1962

285. The Orphan Drug Act established which of the following?

    A. Two classes of drugs: OTC and legend
    B. Special packaging to protect children from poisoning
    C. Tax and licensing incentives for manufacturers to develop and market products for rare disease
    D. Reporting requirements for manufacturers and importers of medical devices that malfunctioned
    E. More stringent controls on the distribution of prescription drug samples

286. Which statement about the *USP* is *incorrect*?

   A. The *USP* is recognized by the Food, Drug, and Cosmetic Act.
   B. The *USP* is published every 5 years.
   C. The FDA is responsible for the publication of the *USP*.
   D. The *USP DI* is not a publication of the FDA.
   E. A product for which there is a *USP* monograph must meet *USP* compendial standards whether the product bears the *USP* symbols after the name or not.

287. Which act or amendment established two classes of drugs?

   A. Food, Drug, and Cosmetic
   B. Durham-Humphrey
   C. Kefauver-Harris
   D. Pure Food and Drug
   E. Orphan Drug

288. Which statement about the 1906 Pure Food and Drug Act is correct?

   A. Any new drug had to be proven safe.
   B. Act established two classes of drugs: OTC and legend.
   C. Act established GMP.
   D. Act established requirements for informed consent for individuals in clinical research.
   E. Act prohibited the distribution of drugs through interstate commerce that were misbranded or adulterated.

289. Which was the first act or amendment that applied to the regulation of cosmetics and medical devices in addition to drug products?

   A. Pure Food and Drug
   B. Food, Drug, and Cosmetic
   C. Medical Device
   D. Drug Efficacy
   E. Durham-Humphrey

290. Which of the following act or amendment recognized the USP and NF as acceptable sources of drug product standards?

   A. Harrison Narcotic Act
   B. Heroin Act
   C. Pure Food and Drug Act
   D. Kefauver-Harris
   E. Orphan Drug

291. Which act or amendment was the first to require adequate directions for use?

   A. Pure Food and Drug
   B. Food, Drug, and Cosmetic
   C. Color Additive
   D. Fair Packaging and Labeling
   E. Drug Price Competition and Patent Term Restoration

292. What term is generally used for drug products marketed prior to 1938?

   A. Misbranded
   B. Adulterated
   C. Counterfeit
   D. Grandfathered
   E. DESI (Drug Efficacy Study Implementation Program)

293. Which of the following is an example of an adulterated drug product?
    I. GMP were not followed by the manufacturer.
    II. Labeling of the product is false.
    III. Drug product contains metal shavings.

    A. I only
    B. III only
    C. I & II only
    D. II & III only
    E. I & III only

294. Which act or amendment defines misbranding and adulteration?

    A. Pure Food and Drug Act
    B. Durham-Humphrey
    C. Kefauver-Harris
    D. Orphan Drug
    E. Food, Drug, and Cosmetic

295. The Legend: Caution: Federal law prohibits dispensing without a prescription was established by which act or amendment?

    A. Food, Drug, and Cosmetic
    B. Durham-Humphrey
    C. Kefauver-Harris
    D. Comprehensive Drug Abuse Prevention and Control
    E. Comprehensive Methamphetamine Control Act

296. The term "sodium free" refers to which of the following?

    A. Maximum daily dose is 5 mg or less.
    B. Maximum daily dose is 75 mg or less.
    C. Maximum daily dose is 140 mg or less.
    D. Maximum daily dose is 200 mg or less.
    E. Maximum daily dose is 250 mg or less.

297. The term "very low sodium" refers to which of the following?

    A. Maximum daily dose is 5 mg or less.
    B. Maximum daily dose is 35 mg or less.
    C. Maximum daily dose is 140 mg or less.
    D. Maximum daily dose is 200 mg or less.
    E. Maximum daily dose is 250 mg or less.

298. The labeling of OTC products for oral ingestion shall contain calcium content per dosage unit if the calcium content of a single maximum recommended dose is what amount or more?

    A. 1 mg
    B. 5 mg
    C. 10 mg
    D. 15 mg
    E. 20 mg

299. The labeling of OTC products for oral ingestion shall contain magnesium content per dosage unit if the magnesium content of a single maximum recommended dose is what amount or more?

A. 1 g
B. 2 g
C. 5 g
D. 7 g
E. 8 g

300. The labeling of OTC products for oral ingestion shall contain potassium content per dosage unit if the potassium content of a single maximum recommended dose is what amount or more?

    A. 1 g
    B. 2 g
    C. 3 g
    D. 4 g
    E. 5 g

301. When there is a conflict between state and federal law, which law prevails?

    A. Federal law
    B. State law
    C. More stringent law
    D. Federal law when dealing with controlled substances
    E. None of the above

302. A pharmacy that wants to be VIPPS (Verified Internet Pharmacy Practice Sites) accredited must meet which of the following requirements?
    I. Must meet all state requirements for every state that the pharmacy does business in.
    II. Must be HIPAA compliant.
    III. Must demonstrate quality assurance policy and procedure.

A. I only
B. II only
C. III only
D. I & III only
E. I, II, & III

303. Which federal program monitors the use of the drug isotretinoin?

    A. MEDMARX
    B. iPLEDGE
    C. STEPS
    D. MEDWATCH
    E. SMART

304. Which federal program monitors the use of thalidomide?

    A. MEDMARX
    B. iPLEDGE
    C. STEPS
    D. MEDWATCH
    E. SMART

305. How many negative pregnancy tests must women have before they can be prescribed isotretinoin?

    A. 0
    B. 1
    C. 2
    D. 3
    E. 4

306. How many forms of contraception must the patient use while taking the medication referenced in question 305?

    A. 0
    B. 1
    C. 2
    D. 3
    E. 4

307. All pregnancies associated with the use of isotretinoin must be reported to which of the agency?
    I. MEDMARX
    II. STEPS
    III. iPLEDGE
    IV. MEDWATCH

    A. I, II, III, & IV
    B. I & III only
    C. II & IV only
    D. III & IV only
    E. III only

308. Homeopathic product labeling must include which of the following?
    I. Name and address of manufacturer
    II. Expiration dating
    III. Adequate directions for use
    IV. Quantity of ingredients

    A. I, II, III, & IV
    B. I, III, & IV only
    C. I & IV only
    D. I & III only
    E. II, III, & IV only

309. If the homeopathic product contains a legend drug, what additional labeling must accompany the product?
    I. Caution: Federal law prohibits dispensing without a prescription
    II. Expiration and stability information
    III. Instructions for self-administration

    A. I only
    B. I & II only
    C. I & III only
    D. II only
    E. I, II, & III

310. Which of the following drugs are exempt from poison prevention packaging?
    I. Oral contraceptives
    II. Sublingual nitroglycerine
    III. Cough syrups

    A. I only
    B. II only
    C. III only
    D. I & II only
    E. I, II, & III

311. Which drugs are exempt from anti-tampering packaging?
    I. Dermatologics
    II. Throat lozenges
    III. Cough syrups

    A. I only
    B. I & II only
    C. I & III only
    D. II & III only
    E. I, II, & III

312. The most important aspect of OBRA to pharmacy practice is which of the following?

    A. Compounding
    B. Counseling
    C. Medication error reduction
    D. Prescription labeling
    E. Record keeping

313. Which drug is used to treat narcotic addiction in the retail pharmacy setting?

    A. Methadone
    B. LAAM
    C. Buprenorphine
    D. All of the above
    E. None of the above

314. Opioid treatment program records must be maintained for what period of time?

    A. 2 weeks
    B. 1 month
    C. 2 years
    D. 3 years
    E. 5 years

**Directions:** For questions 315 through 324, utilize the following prescription. Assume that the prescription meets all legal requirements.

Joe Smith          12/15/2007
2 River Road       Male
Paris, NY          DOB 5/5/35
Morphine 10 mg

#120
Sig: 1 qid
MDD 4
Refills 2          Dr. Smythe

315. Morphine is classified as what schedule controlled substance?

    A. II
    B. III
    C. IV
    D. V
    E. Not classified as a controlled substance

316. If the prescription is filled on 12/15/2007, when may Mr. Smith obtain the first refill?

    A. 12/30/2007
    B. 1/1/2008
    C. 1/14/2008
    D. 1/15/2008
    E. Prescription cannot be refilled

317. On what date may Mr. Smith obtain the second refill?

    A. 1/31/2008
    B. 2/1/2008
    C. 2/14/2008
    D. 2/15/2008
    E. Prescription cannot be refilled

318. Mr. Smith can only afford 10 tablets, within what period of time must Mr. Smith fill the prescription to completion?

    A. 72 hours
    B. 5 days
    C. 7 days
    D. 30 days
    E. Mr. Smith forfeits the balance of the prescription

319. If the pharmacy only has 15 tablets, within what period of time does the pharmacy have to fill the prescription for the full amount?

    A. 24 hours
    B. 36 hours
    C. 72 hours
    D. 5 days
    E. 30 days

320. If Mr. Smith is a patient of a Long-Term Care Facility, how many tablets may Mr. Smith receive on 12/15/07?

    A. Partial filling of the prescription is permissible as long as it is documented that Mr. Smith is a resident of a Long-Term Care Facility.
    B. If Mr. Smith requests a quantity less than 30, he will forfeit the remaining quantity.
    C. Mr. Smith may receive 10 tablets on 12/15/07.
    D. Mr. Smith may receive 30 tablets only.
    E. None of the above.

321. If partial filling is permissible by federal law, within what period of time must the prescription be filled to completion?

    A. 10 days
    B. 30 days
    C. 60 days
    D. 90 days
    E. Partial filling is not permissible

322. Is the prescription transferable to another pharmacy?

    A. Yes
    B. No

323. If Dr. Smythe calls the prescription in as an emergency prescription, what quantity may Dr. Smythe call into the pharmacy?

    A. 3 day supply
    B. 5 day supply
    C. 15 day supply
    D. 30 day supply
    E. Quantity necessary to treat the emergency

324. What action must Dr. Smythe take after he calls in the emergency prescription to the pharmacy?

    A. No action is necessary.
    B. Dr. Smythe must send a follow-up prescription to the patient for transmittal to the pharmacy.
    C. Dr. Smythe must send a follow-up prescription to the pharmacy within 3 days of the date the

emergency prescription was called in to the pharmacy.

D. Dr. Smythe must send a follow-up prescription to the pharmacy within 7 days of the date the emergency prescription was called in to the pharmacy.

E. Dr. Smythe must notify the DEA that he has called an emergency prescription into a pharmacy for John Smith.

**Directions:** For questions 325 through 335, please use the following prescription. Assume prescription meets all legal requirements for the issuing of a prescription.

```
Jane Doe              1/1/08
187 Main Street       Female
Nurenberg, NY         DOB 6/21/58
Phenobarbital 60 mg
#120
Sig: 1 qid
MDD 4
Refills 5             Dr. Lee R.
                      Tompkins
```

325. What schedule controlled substance is the above prescription?

   A. II
   B. III
   C. IV
   D. V
   E. Not a controlled substance

326. How many refills are permissible?

   A. 0
   B. 1

C. 2
D. 3
E. 5

327. May the prescription be partially filled at the patient's request?

   A. Yes
   B. No

328. May the prescription be faxed?

   A. Yes
   B. No

329. May the prescription be transferred?

   A. Yes
   B. No

330. May the prescription be partially filled if the patient is terminally ill?

   A. Yes
   B. No

331. If partial filling is permissible, within what period of time must the prescription be filled to completion?

   A. Partial filling is not permissible
   B. 72 hours
   C. 5 days
   D. 30 days
   E. 60 days

332. Partial fillings for each refill may not exceed what quantity of medication?

    A. 0
    B. 10
    C. 30
    D. 60
    E. 120

333. How many partial refills are permissible?

    A. Partial filling is not permissible
    B. 1
    C. 5
    D. 30
    E. There is no limit on the number of partial fillings

334. The prescription must be filled by what date?

    A. Date of issue
    B. Within 30 days of the date of issue
    C. Within 30 days of the date filled
    D. Within 6 months of the date filled
    E. Within 12 months of the date filled

335. If the prescription is filled on 1/1/08, when will the prescription expire?

    A. Date of issue
    B. 30 days from the date of issue
    C. 30 days from the date of filling by the patient
    D. 6 months from the date of issue
    E. 6 months from the date of filling by the patient

336. What form is used to order the medication?

    A. DEA 41
    B. DEA 222
    C. DEA 331
    D. DEA 224
    E. No form is used

337. If a Schedule III controlled substance is partially filled, when must all of the partial fillings be completed by?

    A. Partial filling of Schedule III controlled substances is not permissible
    B. 30 days from the date of issue
    C. 60 days from the date of issue
    D. 6 months from the date of issue
    E. 12 months from the date of issue

338. Within how many days does Dr. Tompkins have to deliver a written cover to the pharmacy for an emergency prescription for phenobarbital?

    A. 1
    B. 5
    C. 7
    D. 30
    E. No written cover is required

339. What quantity of phenobarbital may Dr. Tompkins phone in as an emergency supply for the patient?

    A. 3 days supply
    B. 5 days supply
    C. 30 days supply
    D. 6 months supply
    E. Amount necessary to treat the emergency

340. If the originating pharmacy does not share a real time online database, how many of the five refills in the above-mentioned phenobarbital prescription may be transferred to another pharmacy.

    A. Refill transfers are not permissible
    B. One at a time
    C. Two at a time
    D. Three at a time
    E. All five

341. Within what period of time does Dr. Tompkins need to send a cover for a faxed phenobarbital prescription?

    A. 3 days of the date of the fax
    B. 5 days of the date of the fax
    C. 7 days of the date of the fax
    D. 30 days of the date of the fax
    E. No cover is necessary

342. Under what circumstances is the prescriber exempt from sending a follow up to a faxed Schedule II controlled substance prescription?
    I. Patient has an emergency and cannot pick up the prescription and bring it to the pharmacy.
    II. Patient is a resident of a Long-Term Care Facility.
    III. Patient is receiving home infusion/IV pain therapy.

    A. I only
    B. II only
    C. II & III only
    D. I & III only
    E. I, II, & III

343. Which clinical phase utilizes healthy people who do not have the disease state that the drug is intended to treat?

    A. I
    B. II
    C. III
    D. IV
    E. V

344. Which clinical phase is used to determine if the drug is safe and effective for study in appoximately 100–200 patients with the disease state that the drug is intended to treat?

    A. I
    B. II
    C. III
    D. IV
    E. V

345. Which clinical phase uses thousands of patients and a variable geographic area for the patients involved in the study?

    A. I
    B. II
    C. III
    D. IV
    E. V

346. Which clinical phase(s) utilizes subjects that have the disease state that the drug is intended to treat?
    I. I
    II. II
    III. III
    IV. IV

    A. I only
    B. III only
    C. II & III only
    D. II, III, & IV only
    E. I, II, III, & IV

347. Institutional Review Boards assist in the clinical study process in which of the following ways?
    I. Protect the rights and welfare of the patients enrolled in the study
    II. Approve research
    III. Make modifications to research

    A. I only
    B. II only
    C. I & III only
    D. I & II only
    E. I, II, & III

348. The manufacturer wants to change the product literature format on an approved product. What type of application will the manufacturer file with the FDA?

    A. No application is necessary because the product is already approved
    B. IND
    C. NDA

D. SNDA
E. ABNA

349. A manufacturer wants to change an approved drug product from a caplet to a tablet. What application will the manufacturer file with the FDA?

    A. No application is necessary because the product is already approved
    B. IND
    C. NDA
    D. SNDA
    E. ABNA

350. A generic manufacturer has a generic product of a drug product that just recently came off patent. What application will the manufacturer file with the FDA?

    A. No application is necessary because the product is already approved
    B. IND
    C. NDA
    D. SNDA
    E. ABNA

351. The Drug Price Competition and Patent Term Restoration Act of 1984 (P.L. 98-417) provides manufacturers with an opportunity to extend the life of the patent for how many additional years?

    A. 0
    B. 1
    C. 5

D. 10

E. 17

352. With the extension mentioned in question 351 above, the total patent life of the drug product cannot exceed how many years from the approval date of the drug product?

    A. 0

    B. 5

    C. 14

    D. 17

    E. 20

353. Which of the following safety programs are implemented by the FDA?
    I. MEDMARX
    II. MEDWATCH
    III. iPLEDGE
    IV. STEPS

    A. I only

    B. III & IV only

    C. II, III, & IV only

    D. I, II, & IV only

    E. I, II, III, & IV

354. Which of the FDA safety programs address safety labeling changes, Class I recalls, and withdrawals?

    A. MEDMARX

    B. MEDWATCH

    C. iPLEDGE

    D. STEPS

    E. SMART

355. If the FDA wants to initiate a Public Health Advisory, which program would it utilize?

    A. MEDMARX

    B. MEDWATCH

    C. iPLEDGE

    D. SMART

    E. STEPS

356. Which program collects data from health systems and hospitals on medication errors and adverse events?

    A. MEDMARX

    B. MEDWATCH

    C. iPLEDGE

    D. SMART

    E. STEPS

357. Which of the following programs receive their data voluntarily?
    I. MEDMARX
    II. MEDWATCH
    III. iPLEDGE
    IV. STEPS

    A. I only

    B. II only

    C. I & II only

    D. II, III, & IV only

    E. I, II, III, & IV

358. The iPLEDGE program replaces which of the following programs?

    A. STEPS

    B. SMART

    C. MEDWATCH

    D. MEDMARX

    E. It does not replace any program

359. Conditions under which OTC ingredients are generally recognized as safe and effective and are not misbranded are classified as which category by the OTC Review Process?

    A. I
    B. II
    C. III
    D. IV
    E. X

360. Conditions under which OTC ingredients are not generally recognized as safe and effective or are misbranded are classified as which category by the OTC Review Process?

    A. I
    B. II
    C. III
    D. IV
    E. X

361. Conditions under which the available data are insufficient to permit final classification at this time as Category I or II are classified as which category by the OTC Review Process?

    A. I
    B. II
    C. III
    D. IV
    E. X

362. How can drug products be switched from prescription status to OTC status?

    I. Manufacturer submits an SNDA.
    II. A petition for reclassification is filed.
    III. The OTC Review Process may initiate review through the Nonprescription Drug Review Committee.

    A. I only
    B. II only
    C. III only
    D. II & III only
    E. I, II, & III

363. The Orange Book's official name is which of the following?

    A. *Approved Drug Products with Therapeutic Equivalence and Evaluations*
    B. *Approved Generic Drug Products*
    C. *Drug Information for the Health Care Professional*
    D. *Approved Drug Products and Legal Requirements*
    E. *Therapeutic Equivalence Guide for the Practitioner*

364. The Orange Book does not contain which of the following drug products?

    A. Topical drug products
    B. Homeopathic drug products
    C. Grandfathered drug products
    D. Injectible drug products
    E. Aerosol drug products

365. When using the Orange Book, the term *reference listed drug* (RLD) refers to which of the following?

A. The standard against which all generic drug products are compared.
B. Drug products that are manufactured by several manufacturers.
C. Drug products with the same active ingredients, same dosage form, same route of administration, and identical in strength or concentration.
D. The rate that the active ingredient of the drug product is absorbed from the product and made available to the site of action.
E. Drug products that contain the same therapeutic moiety, but are different salts, esters, or complexes of that moiety, or are different dosage forms or strengths.

366. When using the Orange Book, the term *multisource drug products* refer to which of the following?

A. The standard against which all generic drug products are compared.
B. Drug products that are manufactured by several manufacturers.
C. Drug products with the same active ingredients, same dosage form, same route of administration, and identical in strength or concentration.

D. The rate that the active ingredient of the drug product is absorbed from the product and made available to the site of action.
E. Drug products that contain the same therapeutic moiety, but are different salts, esters, or complexes of that moiety, or are different dosage forms or strengths.

367. When using the Orange Book, the term *pharmaceutical alternative* refers to which of the following?

A. The standard against which all generic drug products are compared.
B. Drug products that are manufactured by several manufacturers.
C. Drug products with the same active ingredients, same dosage form, same route of administration, and identical in strength or concentration.
D. The rate that the active ingredient of the drug product is absorbed from the product and made available to the site of action.
E. Drug products that contain the same therapeutic moiety, but are different salts, esters, or complexes of that moiety, or are different dosage forms or strengths.

368. When using the Orange Book, the term *pharmaceutical equivalence* refers to which of the following?

    A. The standard against which all generic drug products are compared.
    B. Drug products that are manufactured by several manufacturers.
    C. Drug products with the same active ingredients, same dosage form, same route of administration, and identical in strength or concentration.
    D. The rate that the active ingredient of the drug product is absorbed from the product and made available to the site of action.
    E. Drug products that contain the same therapeutic moiety, but are different salts, esters, or complexes of that moiety, or are different dosage forms or strengths.

369. When using the Orange Book, the term *bioavailability* refers to which of the following?

    A. The standard against which all generic drug products are compared.
    B. Drug products that are manufactured by several manufacturers.
    C. Drug products with the same active ingredients, same dosage form, same route of administration, and identical in strength or concentration.
    D. The rate that the active ingredient of the drug product is absorbed from the product and made available to the site of action.
    E. Drug products that contain the same therapeutic moiety, but are different salts, esters, or complexes of that moiety, or are different dosage forms or strengths.

370. When using the Orange Book, the term *bioequivalent drug products* refer to which of the following?

    A. Products that are pharmaceutically equivalent that provides the same results of drug delivery with the same pharmacokinetic properties.
    B. Drug products that are manufactured by several manufacturers.
    C. Drug products with the same active ingredients, same dosage form, same route of administration, and identical in strength or concentration.
    D. The rate that the active ingredient of the drug product is absorbed from the product and made available to the site of action.
    E. Drug products that contain the same therapeutic moiety, but are different salts, esters, or complexes of that moiety, or are different dosage forms or strengths.

371. When using the Orange Book, the term *therapeutic equivalence* refers to which of the following?

    A. Those products that are pharmaceutical equivalents and bioequivalent.
    B. Drug products that are manufactured by several manufacturers.
    C. Drug products with the same active ingredients, same dosage form, same route of administration, and identical in strength or concentration.
    D. The rate that the active ingredient of the drug product is absorbed from the product and made available to the site of action.
    E. Drug products that contain the same therapeutic moiety, but are different salts, esters, or complexes of that moiety, or are different dosage forms or strengths.

372. When using the Orange Book, the term *narrow therapeutic index* refers to which of the following?

    A. Those products that are pharmaceutical equivalents and bioequivalent.
    B. Drug products that may require close patient monitoring to achieve the maximum effectiveness of the medication.
    C. Drug products with the same active ingredients, same dosage form, same route of administration, and identical in strength or concentration.

    D. The rate that the active ingredient of the drug product is absorbed from the product and made available to the site of action.
    E. Drug products that contain the same therapeutic moiety, but are different salts, esters, or complexes of that moiety, or are different dosage forms or strengths.

373. Drugs that are considered to have a narrow therapeutic index have a ratio less than or equal to what number?

    A. 0
    B. 1
    C. 2
    D. 3
    E. 5

374. Are narrow therapeutic drugs officially recognized in the Orange Book?

    A. Yes
    B. No

375. Medical devices that are very simple by design and have a very low potential to cause harm are classified as what Class Medical Device?

    A. I
    B. II
    C. III
    D. IV
    E. V

376. Class I refers to what level of medical device classification?

    A. Performance Standards
    B. General Controls
    C. Premarket Approval
    D. Restricted Devices
    E. Pharmacist Only Devices

377. Which of the following devices require premarket approval?
    I. Toothbrushes
    II. Electric heating pads
    III. Heart pacemakers

    A. I only
    B. II only
    C. III only
    D. II & III only
    E. I, II, & III

378. Which of the following devices are considered restricted devices?
    I. Breast implants
    II. Diaphragms
    III. TENS (**T**ranscutaneous **E**lectrical **N**erve **S**timulation) unit

    A. I only
    B. II only
    C. III only
    D. II & III only
    E. I, II, & III

379. How often are cosmetic manufacturers inspected by the FDA?

    A. Every 1 year
    B. Every 2 years
    C. Every 3 years

    D. Every 5 years
    E. The FDA does not inspect cosmetic manufacturers

380. What type of packaging is required on all liquid oral hygiene products and all cosmetic vaginal products if sold over the counter?

    A. Tamper proof
    B. Tamper resistant
    C. There are no special packaging requirements for these products

381. Cosmetics that are intended to treat or prevent disease or alter a body function are considered drug products. Which of the following are considered cosmetic drug products?

    A. Suntan lotion
    B. Moisturizing cream
    C. Antiperspirants
    D. A & B only
    E. A, B, & C

382. A cosmetic that contains an animal body part in it would be considered which of the following?

    A. Misbranded
    B. Adulterated
    C. Tampered
    D. Pure
    E. Drug product

383. Who has the authority to initiate a drug recall?

    A. USP
    B. DEA

C. FDA
D. Manufacturer
E. None of the above

384. Which level of drug recall can affect the patient or the physician depending on the extent of the distribution of the product?

 A. Consumer
 B. Retail
 C. Wholesaler
 D. All of the above
 E. None of the above

385. Which level of drug recall affects the pharmacy, dispensing physicians, clinics, hospitals, and long-term care facilities?

 A. Consumer
 B. Retail
 C. Wholesaler
 D. All of the above
 E. None of the above

386. Which level of drug recall affects retailers and wholesalers?

 A. Consumer
 B. Retail
 C. Wholesaler
 D. All of the above
 E. None of the above

387. Which class recall has a reasonable probability that the use of the product or exposure to the product will cause serious, adverse health consequences or death?

 A. I
 B. II
 C. III
 D. IV
 E. V

388. Which class recall involves products that the use of the product or exposure to the product may cause temporary or medically reversible health consequences or where probability of serious harm is remote?

 A. I
 B. II
 C. III
 D. IV
 E. V

389. Which class recall involves the use of or exposure to a product that is not likely to cause adverse health consequences?

 A. I
 B. II
 C. III
 D. IV
 E. V

390. Inclusion of material not intended for inclusion in the product such as dirt, plastic, animal parts is an example of which class drug recall?

 A. I
 B. II
 C. III
 D. IV
 E. V

391. A subpotent drug product is an example of which class drug recall?

    A. I
    B. II
    C. III
    D. IV
    E. V

392. A label mix-up of two potent drugs or a defective replacement heart valve is an example of which class drug recall?

    A. I
    B. II
    C. III
    D. IV
    E. V

393. Of the five categories of pregnancy warning which warning is described by the following, "adequate, well-controlled studies in pregnant women have not shown an increased risk of fetal abnormalities?"

    A. A
    B. B
    C. C
    D. D
    E. X

394. Of the five categories of pregnancy warning which warning is described by the following, "animal studies have shown an adverse effect to the fetus and there are no adequate and well-controlled studies in pregnant women?"

    A. A
    B. B
    C. C
    D. D
    E. X

395. Of the five categories of pregnancy warning which warning is described by the following, "animal studies have shown an adverse effect, but adequate and well-controlled studies in pregnant women have failed to demonstrate a risk to the fetus?"

    A. A
    B. B
    C. C
    D. D
    E. X

396. Of the five categories of pregnancy warning which warning is described by the following, "Studies, adequate well-controlled or observational, in animals or pregnant women have demonstrated positive evidence of fetal abnormalities. The use of the product is contraindicated in women who are or may become pregnant?"

    A. A
    B. B
    C. C
    D. D
    E. X

397. Of the five categories of pregnancy warning which warning is described by the following, "Studies, adequate well-controlled or observational, in pregnant women have demonstrated a risk to the fetus. However, the

benefits of therapy may outweigh the potential risk?"

A. A
B. B
C. C
D. D
E. X

398. Package inserts are intended for which of the following?

A. Professional
B. Patient
C. Consumer

399. Additional information necessary for the appropriate use of the medication is usually contained in which of the following pieces of literature?

A. Package insert
B. Patient package insert
C. Medication guides
D. Power of Attorney

400. Homeopathic drugs are exempt from which of the following?
 I. Expiration dating
 II. Tamper-resistant packaging
 III. From including adequate directions for use in labeling

A. I only
B. II only
C. I & II only
D. III only
E. I, II, & III

401. Official homeopathic drugs that have been monographed and accepted are included in what official publication?

A. *USP/NF*
B. *HPUS*
C. *Approved Drug Products with Therapeutic Equivalence and Evaluations*
D. *Approved Drug Products and Legal Requirements*
E. *Drug Information for the Health Care Professional*

402. Which act or amendment recognizes homeopathic drugs?

A. Pure Food and Drug Act
B. Food, Drug, and Cosmetic Act
C. Durham-Humphrey
D. Orphan Drug Act
E. Kefauver-Harris

403. Which of the following structure or function claims are permissible for use with dietary supplements?
 I. Description of the role of the dietary supplement in affecting the structure or function of the body.
 II. Description of the benefit from consumption of the supplement.
 III. Description of how the dietary supplement will cure a particular disease.

A. I only
B. II only
C. III only
D. I & II only
E. I, II, & III

404. If a manufacturer of a dietary supplement makes a claim of a benefit of a classic nutrient deficiency disease, what additional information must the manufacturer include in the labeling of the dietary supplement?

   A. The prevalence of the disease in the United States must be stated in the claim.
   B. The role of the dietary supplement in affecting the structure or function of the body.
   C. Identification of the mechanism utilized by the dietary supplement to maintain structure and function.
   D. A statement that the supplement helps the body to adapt and to promote physical performance.
   E. A description of the benefit from consumption of the supplement.

405. Dietary supplement must contain additional statement on the labeling if they make a claim. What statement must be included?

   A. Caution: Federal Law prohibits dispensing without a prescription.
   B. Caution: Federal Law prohibits the transfer of the medication to another person.
   C. Warning: The safety of this product has not been determined.
   D. This statement has not been evaluated by the FDA. This product is not intended to diagnose, treat, cure, or prevent any disease.
   E. This product is not intended for pediatric use.

406. Which drug product was involved in tampering that precipitated the Anti-tampering Laws?

   A. Valium
   B. Suboxone
   C. Tylenol
   D. Methamphetamine
   E. Morphine

407. Tamper-resistant packaging refers to which of the following?

   A. Packaging that contains an indicator or barrier that if missing can reasonably be expected to alert the consumer to the possibility that tampering has occurred.
   B. A permanent barrier to the product that only the consumer can remove after purchase.
   C. A permanent barrier that the store removes before the consumer purchases.
   D. An alarm that notifies the retailer that a product has been tampered with.
   E. A statement on the outside of the package that alerts the consumer to the possibility of tampering.

408. Which of the following products must be packaged with tamper-resistant packaging?
   I. Prescriptions dispensed by a pharmacist
   II. Vaginal products
   III. All OTC human drug products

A. I only
B. II only
C. III only
D. II & III only
E. I, II, & III

409. Which of the following products are exempt from tamper-resistant packaging?
   I. Cosmetic liquid oral hygiene products
   II. Contact lens
   III. Prescriptions dispensed by a pharmacist
   IV. Throat lozenges

   A. I & II only
   B. II & III only
   C. III & IV only
   D. I, III, & IV only
   E. I, II, III, & IV

410. OTC products that consist of two-piece hard gelatin capsules must have how many forms of tamper-resistant mechanisms in the packaging?
   A. 1
   B. 2
   C. 3
   D. 4
   E. 0

411. Which of the following products must be packaged in child-resistant packaging?
   I. Hazardous household substances
   II. Prescription drugs
   III. All food products

   A. I only
   B. II only

C. I & II only
D. II & III only
E. I, II, & III

412. Who has the authority to issue a blanket waiver of the child protection requirement?

   A. Physician
   B. Midlevel practitioner
   C. Pharmacy
   D. Patient
   E. Hospital

413. If a prescriber initiates a waiver for a patient, how long is the waiver valid for?

   A. Valid until revoked by the prescriber
   B. Valid for the duration of a specific prescription for which the prescriber initiated the waiver
   C. Valid until revoked by the patient
   D. Valid until revoked by the pharmacy
   E. Valid until revoked by the FDA

414. How long must a blanket waiver of the child protection requirement be kept on file?

   A. Until revoked by the patient
   B. Until revoked by the prescriber
   C. Until revoked by the pharmacy
   D. Until revoked by the midlevel practitioner
   E. Until revoked by the FDA

415. A product that violates the Poison Prevention Act is classified as what?

    A. Adulterated
    B. Misbranded
    C. Counterfeit

416. Which of the following products are exempt from poison prevention packaging?
    I. Hormone replacement therapy
    II. Oral contraceptives
    III. Sublingual nitroglycerin

    A. I only
    B. II only
    C. III only
    D. I & II only
    E. I, II, & III

417. The term "unit-of-use" packaging when referring to poison prevention packaging describes which of the following?

    A. Packaging in a blister pack.
    B. Refers to repackaging in a hospital setting.
    C. A product that is packaged with information necessary for the safe administration of the product to the patient requiring that the product remain in the original packaging.
    D. Refers to repackaging in a long-term care setting.
    E. Refers to packaging for product over the counter.

418. What are examples of unit-of-use products?

    I. Urocit
    II. Isosorbide dinitrate
    III. Cytotec

    A. I only
    B. I & III only
    C. II only
    D. II & III only
    E. I, II, & III

419. What term is used to describe minimum standards used in the manufacturing process that assure that the product meets requirements of safety, identity and strength, quality, and purity?

    A. *USP/NF*
    B. *HPUS*
    C. GMP
    D. FDA approved
    E. DEA approved

420. Manufacturers are inspected by the FDA how often?

    A. Every 6 months
    B. Every 1 year
    C. Every 2 years
    D. Every 5 years
    E. They are not inspected by the FDA

421. Expiration dating refers to which of the following?

    A. The date after which the product's stability is not guaranteed.
    B. The date by which the product must be purchased by.

C. The date that the pharmacy affixes to the product after determining the pharmacy's storage conditions.

D. The date that the pharmacy affixes to the dispensed product as required by law.

E. The date the product must be returned to the wholesaler by.

422. Which of the following drug products are exempt from expiration dating?

I. Homeopathic drugs

II. Allergenic abstracts labeled, "No U.S. Standard of Potency"

III. New drug products

A. I only

B. II only

C. I & II only

D. III only

E. I, II, & III

423. Beyond use dating is used for which of the following products?

A. Suspensions that water is added to.

B. Compounds where two products are mixed together.

C. Sterile products compounded in USP Chapter <797> units.

D. A, B, & C.

E. None of the above.

424. What expiration date must the pharmacist include on dispensed medication?

A. The manufacturer's expiration date for the product.

B. The USP expiration date listed for the product.

C. One year from the date of dispensing.

D. The pharmacists must use their professional judgment to determine the date.

E. There is no requirement that the pharmacist include an expiration date on the dispensed product.

425. What type of facilities does the FDA require the use of beyond use dating in?

A. Retail pharmacies

B. Long-term care facilities

C. Acute care hospitals

D. Group homes

426. Drug Utilization Review under OBRA 90 requires review of which of the following?

I. Underutilization of drugs

II. Prescribing errors

III. Adverse drug effects

IV. Generic substitution

A. I & II only

B. II, III, & IV only

C. I, II, & IV only

D. I & IV only

E. I, II, III, & IV

427. The Drug Utilization Review required by OBRA 90 examines what type of drug use?

   A. Retrospective
   B. Prospective
   C. Prescriber mandated review for certain disease states
   D. A & B
   E. A, B, & C

428. What entity established the VIPPS in response to public safety concerns about Internet pharmacies?

   A. FDA
   B. DEA
   C. NABP (National Association of Boards of Pharmacy)
   D. USP
   E. MEDWATCH

429. A practitioner treating a patient for narcotic addiction who is not enrolled in an opioid treatment program may administer how many days of methadone to the patient?

   A. 1
   B. 2
   C. 3
   D. 5
   E. 30

430. In reference to question 429 above, how many days may the practitioner administer to the patient at once?

   A. 1
   B. 2
   C. 3

   D. 5
   E. 30

431. Which statement about mailing controlled substances via the United States Postal Service (USPS) is correct?

   A. Mailing of controlled substances via the USPS is prohibited.
   B. The outside wrapper or container containing the controlled substance is free of markings that would indicate the nature of the contents.
   C. Only Schedule V controlled substances may be mailed via the USPS.
   D. Only Schedule III, IV, and V controlled substances may be mailed via the USPS.
   E. Controlled substances may be mailed only within the same state.

432. What was the purpose of HIPAA?

   I. To protect individually identifiable health information transmitted or maintained by electronic or other media.
   II. To disseminate patient information only without patient authorization.
   III. To control the dissemination of patient information.

   A. I only
   B. I & II only
   C. III only
   D. I & III only
   E. I, II, & III

433. Patient's rights under HIPAA include which of the following?
  I. Restrictions of the use and disclosure are permissible under all circumstances.
  II. Access to health information, including the right to review and copy the information.
  III. Receive written notice of information practices from health plans and providers.

  A. I only
  B. II only
  C. II & III only
  D. I & III only
  E. I, II, & III

434. Which entities are considered covered entities under HIPAA?
  I. Health plans
  II. Clearing houses
  III. Health care providers

  A. I only
  B. II only
  C. III only
  D. I & II only
  E. I, II, & III

435. Are pharmacies considered covered entities under HIPAA?

  A. Yes
  B. No

436. Under HIPAA, what must covered entities obtain prior to using or disclosing protected health information to carry out treatment, payment, or health care operations?

  A. Medical records of the patient
  B. Billing information for the patient
  C. Patient consent
  D. Patient's insurance information
  E. List of all of the patient's health care providers

437. Under what circumstances may health care providers use protected health information without patient consent?
  I. Emergencies
  II. Substantial barriers to communication with the individual
  III. Patient is an individual incarcerated in a correctional facility

  A. I only
  B. II only
  C. II & III only
  D. I & II only
  E. I, II, & III

438. How often must a health care provider revise the patient consent acknowledgement form under HIPAA?

  A. There is no requirement that the form be revised
  B. Every 1 year
  C. Every 2 years
  D. Every 5 years
  E. Every 10 years

439. What type of penalties may be assessed for HIPAA violations?
    I. $100 per offense with a cap at $25,000 in a calendar year
    II. Up to $250,000 and 10 years of imprisonment if person obtains or discloses protected health information with intent to sell, transfer, or use information for personal gain or malicious harm
    III. Life imprisonment

    A. I only
    B. II only
    C. I & II only
    D. II & III only
    E. I, II, & III

440. USP Chapter <797> applies to which of the following settings?
    I. Health care institutions where compounded sterile products are prepared, stored, or dispensed.
    II. Pharmacies where compounded sterile products are prepared, stored, or dispensed.
    III. Physician practice facilities where compounded sterile products are prepared, stored, or dispensed.

    A. I only
    B. II only
    C. III only
    D. I & III only
    E. I, II, & III

441. The Bar Code Rule applies to which of the following entities?
    I. Manufacturers
    II. Repackers
    III. Exporters

    A. I only
    B. II only
    C. III only
    D. I & II only
    E. I, II, & III

442. Which of the following products must comply with the Bar Code Rule?
    I. Prescription drugs
    II. Allergenic extracts
    III. Intrauterine devices
    IV. OTC products dispensed pursuant to an order and that are commonly used in hospitals

    A. I only
    B. II, III, & IV only
    C. I, III, & IV only
    D. II & IV only
    E. I, II, III, & IV

443. With reference to question 442, what drug products are exempted?

    A. Medical gases
    B. Radiopharmaceuticals
    C. Low density form fill and seal containers that are not packaged with an over wrap
    D. Biologicals
    E. Physician drug samples

444. What information does the Bar Code Rule require?
    I. Drug product's NDC number in a linear bar code
    II. Lot number
    III. Expiration date

    A. I only
    B. II & III only

C. I & III only

D. I & II only

E. I, II, & III

445. Reciprocation refers to what process in pharmacy practice?

A. Endorsement of a valid license by another state

B. Dispensing prescriptions in another state

C. Transferring prescriptions to another location

D. Validating prescription information across state lines

E. Finding another supplier for ordering Schedule II controlled substances

446. The national organization that accredits continuing pharmacy education programs is known as which of the following?

A. American Pharmaceutical Association (APhA)

B. American Society of Health-System Pharmacists (ASHP)

C. American Council for Pharmaceutical Education (ACPE)

D. American College of Clinical Pharmacy (ACCP)

E. NABP

447. Continuing pharmacy education is mandatory for pharmacy license maintenance?

A. True

B. False

448. Pharmacy schools in the United States are accredited by which of the following organizations?

A. APhA

B. ASHP

C. ACPE

D. ACCP

E. NABP

449. Which exam does a foreign pharmacy graduate complete prior to sitting for the pharmacy boards?

A. Pharmacy Technician Certification (PTCB)

B. NABP Pharmacy Boards

C. NABP Foreign Pharmacy Graduate Examination

D. ASHP Residency Exam

450. For professional misconducts claims brought against a pharmacist, what actions may be taken against the pharmacist.

I. Reprimands

II. Suspensions

III. Censure

IV. License revocation

A. I & II only

B. II & III only

C. III & IV only

D. I, II, & IV only

E. I, II, III, & IV

# Answers

| | | | | | | | | | |
|---|---|---|---|---|---|---|---|---|---|
| 1. | D | 19. | E | 37. | C | 55. | D | 73. | C |
| 2. | E | 20. | D | 38. | E | 56. | E | 74. | A |
| 3. | B | 21. | E | 39. | D | 57. | D | 75. | E |
| 4. | A | 22. | C | 40. | D | 58. | A | 76. | B |
| 5. | A | 23. | E | 41. | C | 59. | B | 77. | E |
| 6. | B | 24. | C | 42. | E | 60. | C | 78. | B |
| 7. | B | 25. | E | 43. | E | 61. | D | 79. | A |
| 8. | B | 26. | D | 44. | C | 62. | D | 80. | A |
| 9. | B | 27. | E | 45. | D | 63. | E | 81. | B |
| 10. | B | 28. | B | 46. | D | 64. | A | 82. | B |
| 11. | D | 29. | C | 47. | B | 65. | C | 83. | C |
| 12. | E | 30. | A | 48. | A | 66. | C | 84. | C |
| 13. | B | 31. | B | 49. | B | 67. | B | 85. | C |
| 14. | D | 32. | C | 50. | A | 68. | E | 86. | D |
| 15. | A | 33. | E | 51. | D | 69. | E | 87. | D |
| 16. | C | 34. | C | 52. | C | 70. | C | 88. | E |
| 17. | C | 35. | D | 53. | D | 71. | B | 89. | E |
| 18. | C | 36. | D | 54. | A | 72. | E | 90. | C |

| | | | |
|---|---|---|---|
| 91. | B | | |
| 92. | A | | |
| 93. | E | | |
| 94. | D | | |
| 95. | A | | |
| 96. | C | | |
| 97. | B | | |
| 98. | D | | |
| 99. | C | | |
| 100. | B | | |
| 101. | D | | |
| 102. | E | | |
| 103. | A | | |
| 104. | C | | |
| 105. | D | | |
| 106. | D | | |
| 107. | A | | |
| 108. | E | | |

| 109. B | 134. C | 159. B | 184. E | 209. B | 234. A |
|--------|--------|--------|--------|--------|--------|
| 110. B | 135. C | 160. C | 185. A | 210. C | 235. C |
| 111. C | 136. A | 161. E | 186. D | 211. D | 236. C |
| 112. E | 137. C | 162. C | 187. E | 212. B | 237. E |
| 113. D | 138. A | 163. E | 188. A | 213. A | 238. B |
| 114. B | 139. E | 164. D | 189. D | 214. C | 239. D |
| 115. A | 140. A | 165. E | 190. A | 215. C | 240. E |
| 116. B | 141. A | 166. D | 191. A | 216. A | 241. D |
| 117. E | 142. E | 167. D | 192. C | 217. C | 242. D |
| 118. E | 143. E | 168. B | 193. B | 218. E | 243. D |
| 119. E | 144. C | 169. B | 194. C | 219. A | 244. E |
| 120. C | 145. C | 170. E | 195. B | 220. D | 245. E |
| 121. E | 146. C | 171. E | 196. E | 221. C | 246. C |
| 122. D | 147. D | 172. E | 197. C | 222. D | 247. D |
| 123. B | 148. E | 173. B | 198. C | 223. A | 248. D |
| 124. B | 149. A | 174. E | 199. E | 224. E | 249. B |
| 125. E | 150. D | 175. B | 200. A | 225. E | 250. C |
| 126. E | 151. E | 176. E | 201. E | 226. A | 251. A |
| 127. E | 152. E | 177. C | 202. D | 227. D | 252. D |
| 128. E | 153. E | 178. D | 203. D | 228. E | 253. C |
| 129. C | 154. B | 179. C | 204. C | 229. A | 254. B |
| 130. A | 155. A | 180. C | 205. D | 230. D | 255. E |
| 131. E | 156. A | 181. B | 206. C | 231. D | 256. E |
| 132. A | 157. D | 182. B | 207. B | 232. A | 257. D |
| 133. C | 158. E | 183. C | 208. A | 233. D | 258. A |

| | | | | |
|---|---|---|---|---|
| 259. E | 284. A | 309. A | 334. D | 359. A | 384. A |
| 260. E | 285. C | 310. D | 335. D | 360. B | 385. B |
| 261. C | 286. C | 311. B | 336. E | 361. C | 386. C |
| 262. E | 287. B | 312. B | 337. D | 362. D | 387. A |
| 263. B | 288. E | 313. C | 338. C | 363. A | 388 B |
| 264. B | 289. B | 314. D | 339. E | 364. C | 389. C |
| 265. C | 290. C | 315. A | 340. B | 365. A | 390. C |
| 266. B | 291. B | 316. E | 341. E | 366. B | 391. B |
| 267. E | 292. D | 317. E | 342. C | 367. E | 392. A |
| 268. E | 293. E | 318. E | 343. A | 368. C | 393. A |
| 269. A | 294. E | 319. C | 344. B | 369. D | 394. C |
| 270. A | 295. B | 320. A | 345. C | 370. A | 395. B |
| 271. C | 296. A | 321. C | 346. D | 371. A | 396. E |
| 272. A | 297. B | 322. B | 347. E | 372. B | 397. D |
| 273. C | 298. E | 323. E | 348. D | 373. C | 398. A |
| 274. E | 299. E | 324. D | 349. D | 374. B | 399. B |
| 275. D | 300. E | 325. C | 350. E | 375. A | 400. A |
| 276. E | 301. A | 326. E | 351. C | 376. B | 401. B |
| 277. E | 302. E | 327. A | 352. C | 377. C | 402. B |
| 278. D | 303. B | 328. A | 353. C | 378. E | 403. D |
| 279. B | 304. C | 329. A | 354. B | 379. E | 404. A |
| 280. E | 305. C | 330. A | 355. B | 380. B | 405. D |
| 281. B | 306. C | 331. E | 356. A | 381. D | 406. C |
| 282. B | 307. D | 332. E | 357. C | 382. B | 407. A |
| 283. D | 308. B | 333. E | 358. B | 383. D | 408. D |

| | | | | | |
|---|---|---|---|---|---|
| 409. C | 416. E | 423. D | 430. A | 437. E | 444. A |
| 410. B | 417. C | 424. E | 431. B | 438. A | 445. A |
| 411. C | 418. B | 425. B | 432. D | 439. C | 446. C |
| 412. D | 419. C | 426. E | 433. C | 440. E | 447. A |
| 413. B | 420. C | 427. D | 434. E | 441. D | 448. C |
| 414. A | 421. A | 428. C | 435. A | 442. E | 449. C |
| 415. B | 422. C | 429. C | 436. C | 443. E | 450. E |

# Index

Page numbers followed by *f* refer to figures; page numbers followed by *t* refer to tables.

narrow therapeutic index drugs,
41, 43
National Association of
Boards of Pharmacy
(NABP), 156
FPGEE and, 191
pharmacies and, 189–190
pharmacists and, 190
National Drug Code (NDC), 111
bar coding and, 187
*National Formulary* (NF), 2
Federal Pure Food and Drugs
Act and, 6
National Institute on Drug
Abuse (NIDA), 157
NDA. *See* New Drug
Applications
NDC. *See* National Drug Code
New Drug Applications (NDA),
24*f*, 26–27
abbreviated, 26–27
patent protections for, 27
supplemental, 26
NF. *See National Formulary*
NIDA. *See* National Institute on
Drug Abuse
North American Pharmacy
Licensure Examination
(NAPLEX), 189–190
Nutrition Labeling and
Education Act (1990), 17

**O**
Office of National Drug Control
Policy, U.S., 17
Omnibus Budget Reconciliation
Act (1990), 79–81
DUR under, 80
Medicaid review under,
79–80

"most-favored customer"
status under, 79
pharmacist counseling under,
80–81
opioid addiction, treatments
for, 157–168. *See also* L-α-
acetylmethadol; methadone
buprenorphine use in, 159,
161, 164–165
buprenorphine-naloxone use
in, 159, 161, 165
under Children's Health Act,
165
under Comprehensive Drug
Abuse Prevention and
Control Act, 157
DEA oversight for, 165
under Drug Addiction
Treatment Act, 165
drug testing during, 163
history of, 157–159
LAAM and, 159, 161
maintenance treatment
phases for, 162–163
methadone use in, 157, 161
Naloxone use in, 165
naltrexone use in, 159, 162
for patients with terminal
illnesses, 168
pharmacotherapy for, 159
physical assessments for,
160–162
plans for, 160
take-home medication as part
of, 164
Opioid Treatment Programs,
157–159
detoxification in, 167
discharge/withdrawal from,
165–166